To all my friends and family and the men and women of the British forces.

MAN DOWN

Mark Ormrod

Royal Marine

CORGI BOOKS

TRANSWORLD PUBLISHERS
61–63 Uxbridge Road, London W5 5SA
A Random House Group Company
www.randomhouse.co.uk

MAN DOWN
A CORGI BOOK: 9780552159494

First published in Great Britain
in 2009 by Bantam Press
an imprint of Transworld Publishers
Corgi edition published 2010

Addresses for Random House Group Ltd companies outside the UK
can be found at: www.randomhouse.co.uk
The Random House Group Ltd Reg. No. 954009

Penguin Random House is committed to a sustainable future for
our business, our readers and our planet. This book is made from
Forest Stewardship Council® certified paper.

MIX
Paper from
responsible sources
FSC® C018179

Typeset in 11.5/15pt Palatino by Falcon Oast Graphic Art Ltd.
Printed in the UK by Clays Ltd, Elcograf S.p.A

Acknowledgements

I would like to thank the following people as I wouldn't be here without them: the lads of 40 Commando RM on the ground with me in Afghanistan; Warrant Officer Bob Toomey RM and the medic known to me only as 'Dave' who kept me alive; the Chinook pilots and crew who got me to Camp Bastion; the Medical Emergency Response Team in the Chinook who resuscitated me and the surgeons, doctors, nurses and support staff at Camp Bastion JMTF who treated me with such skill and dedication.

My thanks also to all the staff at Selly Oak Hospital, Birmingham, who worked through Christmas to ensure my initial recovery.

To everyone at Headley Court DMRC who worked so hard on my rehabilitation.

To my wife, Becky, and my daughter, Kezia, who immediately saw past the injuries and gave me the motivation to get to where I am today.

To all my friends and family who didn't let what happened change the way they felt about me.

To the Royal Marines for their support since my return from Afghanistan – they could not have done more. In particular, thanks to our family liaison Warrant Officer Jel Jenner RM.

For help with this book, I would like to thank: Captain Mike Davis-Marks RN, Lieutenant Commander Phil Rosindale RNR and Lieutenant Colonel Woody Page RM for their support and guidance.

To Robert Kellaway for helping me to write it and to Rebecca, Millie and Joseph for helping him get it done. Thanks to Barbara Levy, my literary agent, for *Man Down*, and to my editor Brenda Kimber and all at Bantam Press for their hard work. Good effort guys.

Photo Acknowledgements

Photographs not credited below have been kindly supplied by the author. The publishers have made every effort to contact the copyright holders where known. Copyright holders who have not been credited are invited to get in touch with the publishers.

Picture section page 5 top: SWNS; page 6 top: Getty Images; middle: Barry Batchelor/PA Archive/Press Association Images; bottom: Steve Parsons/PA Archive/Press Association Images; page 7 top: SWNS; bottom: The Black Knights, Royal Artillery Parachute Display Team; page 8 all: courtesy of Ross Matthews, Dartmoor Studios Photography Ltd.

How to Speak Bootneck

Biff – useless
Bollocky buff – naked
Bootneck or Bootie – Royal Marine
Browners – dead
Bug out – retreat from combat
Cam – camouflage (net/cream), or camera
Catch it up – get hit in combat
Chad/uber-chad – naff/*really* naff
Crabs – RAF personnel
Dhoby – laundry
Dicker – enemy observer
Digging out blind – giving maximum effort
Dit – story
Drip – moan
Endex – end of exercise
Eyebrows – I'm not lying
Gash – garbage
Gash bag – bin liner
Gen dit – true story
Go firm – adopt a prone position, weapon ready
Gopping – horrible/bad

Grav / gravel belly – infantryman
Grot – sleeping accommodation
Growler – moustache
Hanging – very tired
Hanging out of my hoop – exhausted
Honking – dirty/bad
Hoofin' – excellent
Loadie – loadmaster
Naafi – a canteen, bar or shop run by the Navy, Army and Air Force Institutes
Pax – persons
Phot – photograph/photographer
Phys – fitness training
Ping – assign to a duty
Pit – bed
Pongos – Army personnel
Redders – hot
Scran – food
Scuffers – Military Police
Slug – bed roll
Spinning dits – telling stories
Terp – interpreter
Terry – Terry Taliban
Threaders – angry
Troop Stripey – Troop Sergeant
Toppers – full
Wet – tea, coffee or beer
Wrap – give up

Abbreviations

ANA – Afghan National Army
C-CAST – Critical Care Air Support Team
CSM – Company Sergeant Major
CTC RM – Commando Training Centre, Royal
  Marines (Lympstone, Devon)
ECM – electronic counter measure
ERT – Emergency Response Team
FOB – forward operating base
GMLRS – guided multiple launch rocket system
GPMG – general-purpose machine gun
HLS – helicopter landing site
HMG – heavy machine gun
IDF – indirect fire
IED – improvised explosive device
JMTF – Joint Medical Treatment Facility
KAF – Kandahar Airfield
LSW – light support weapon
M/T – Motor Transport Troop
MRE – meals ready to eat
MSR – Main Supply Route

NCO – non-commissioned officer
OSM – Operational Service Medal
PRR – personal role radio
PX – Post Exchange, a shop in a base (US military
   shorthand)
REMF – rear echelon mother fucker (personnel
   working in the rear)
REMFed up – equipped to luxurious standards
RPG – rocket-propelled grenade
RSM – Regimental Sergeant Major
SOPHIE – product name of a night vision aid
SSAFA – Soldiers, Sailors, Airmen and Families
   Association
SUSAT – sight unit, small arms, trilux
UGL – underslung grenade launcher
WMIK – weapons mounted installation kit
   (an open-topped Land Rover with mounted
   weapons)

1

There was a massive bang. I don't know if I was thrown up in the air or what. I just remember seeing a big black cloud of smoke to my left and sand and stone and gravel to the right. I seemed to be looking down on the ground from above and thought to myself, 'What the fuck am I doing up here?'

The next thing the smoke was gone and I was on the deck again. On my back. The sky was blue crystal.

My brain was rattling around in my head. It took a few seconds to remember what I was supposed to be doing. We were on patrol. We were on the top of a hill in a shallow dip shaped like a bowl near a rock landmark the lads called North Fort. I was in charge of half of our section, me and three men. Each of us had an arc to cover. There were no Taliban around but there could be any second. We had to protect ourselves and cover another patrol that was due to cross the ground below us about 200 metres to our front.

A shitload was going on in my head. I didn't have a clue what had happened. I was just thinking quick time, 'What to do now, what do I do now?'

Initially I thought I'd been hit by a rocket or mortar, that it had impacted on the wall of the bowl behind me and knocked me on my arse. That meant the Taliban were close after all. I tried to turn around and get into the firing position I'd chosen and realized I couldn't move. 'Why can't I move, what's happened to me?' I looked down to where my legs should be. They'd gone.

The sight made me think of a ragged Christmas present with the wrapping paper torn off and ripped to pieces. Bits were hanging out everywhere. My trousers were shredded. There did not seem to be that much blood. My Osprey body armour, a heavy Kevlar vest with ceramic plates covering my chest and upper back, had been ripped clean off. My SA80A2 rifle was nowhere to be seen. My helmet had been knocked on to the back of my head and the chin strap, still fastened, was wedged up under my nose covering my mouth, making it difficult to breathe.

I had been loaded with multiple weaponry and various types of ammunition. My rifle was equipped with an underslung grenade launcher. I had a 51mm light mortar tube in a daysack on my back. I also had a drop bag with about twelve grenades and one high-explosive round for the mortar. All of this was torn away in the blast. I was lucky none of it had detonated. They found the mortar tube later. It is made of tempered steel about 3mm thick; the force of the explosion had peeled it open like a banana. As for the drop bag and the day-sack I have no idea. I guess they got incinerated with my trousers.

What had happened to my legs began to sink in. The injury was horrific. I could see it was a catastrophic wound and that I was a T1 casualty – the most seriously injured you can be without being dead.

It was mega-weird, because it didn't hurt. All I could feel was intense pins and needles in both stumps. They were buzzing away but I could cope with it. I was obviously in a state of massive shock but I was able to think things through logically and seemed to have time enough to work out what had happened. How messed up is that?

My first feeling wasn't fear or pain, it was anger at myself. I just felt stupid and embarrassed. 'You're a Marine,' I thought. 'You're supposed to be one of the most professionally trained soldiers on the planet. What a prick! What a fucking idiot! How could you do something so stupid?'

The state I was in really started to come home to me. It was unreal. My left leg was gone below the knee. I could see loose, sand-covered flesh hanging where my right calf muscles once were. The stumps that were left were beginning to throb like crazy now, and I realized I had the same feeling in my right arm.

I stared at it. It had been flayed open from the fold of the elbow down through the muscles on the inside of my forearm, exposing the ulna and radius bones along their full length. The palm of my hand was cleaved in two. It made me think of that scene in *The Terminator* when Arnold Schwarzenegger has to prove he is a robot and takes a knife, cuts into his forearm and rips off the flesh and skin of his lower arm and hand like a glove. Then he holds up his bloody metal skeleton for Miles Dyson to see. That's what my arm looked like.

'Hoofin',' I thought sarcastically.

Suddenly, more thoughts started flashing through my head: of home, my little girl Kezia, my girlfriend Becky. I loved them both to bits. Kezia was going to be three years old in exactly a month's time. I had no doubt that I would see her turn three. These injuries were just not hurting enough to kill me. I knew it. I could survive this. I could get back to her. I just didn't know what state I would be in when I got there.

'Do I want to go back and live like this?'

The thought stopped me dead. A massive feeling of guilt welled up inside me. How would it be for my daughter when I turned up to pick her up from school? Would she get picked on by the other kids because her daddy was a freak? Would Becky stay with me if I looked like this?

'Great, I'm fucked,' I thought. 'My whole life is fucked. Even if Becky does decide to stay with me, it'll never be the same.'

I was threaders. Pissed off to the max. With my left hand I unclipped my helmet and threw it over to where my body armour lay. Would it be better for me to lie here and die or was my life worth fighting for? My mind was racing with questions I couldn't answer.

Throwing the helmet was a bit stupid in retrospect because it might have set off other landmines nearby, but I still didn't have a clue what was really going on at that stage. The explosion had torn into the patrol and most of us thought we were under mortar or rocket attack. Everyone was shaken up and struggling to make sense of what had happened and where the threat was.

All the lads in my half section were blasted across or out of the bowl by a few metres. They were covered in a layer of dirt, their faces and desert rig uniforms the exact same shade of grey. They were bashed about, but none of them was seriously hurt.

The other half of our patrol was hit by the blast as well. Three Marines with the section leader, Corporal Sean Helsby, had taken a separate fire position about five metres from us a few seconds before the explosion. The force of the detonation lifted all four of them off the deck and threw a couple of them down the hill.

One of them, a Marine named Stu, caught up a

nasty piece of shrapnel that smashed into his arm, knocked him unconscious and hurled him into a trench on his belly. He was bleeding quite badly from the wound. My mate, Marine Ryan Wordsworth, picked himself up and charged into the trench to help Stu. As far as Ryan was concerned we were under mortar attack and could be in very big trouble. Any mortar crew in the world that gets a round down on target follows it up immediately with a rapid 'fire for effect' pattern on to the exact same spot to cause maximum damage. If we were under mortar attack, all we could hope was that they were a 'shoot and scoot' team and didn't have any more ammunition, or were too scared of catching it up on the counter-attack to hang around.

Ryan concentrated on dragging Stu out of the trench as fast as possible to get him out of the killing zone before more mortars started coming in. He got him into the best cover available, injected him with morphine, pulled the first field dressing pack from Stu's webbing and applied it to his arm.

Ryan was the section signaller, so next he was straight on the battlefield radio to Zero, our HQ, rattling out our patrol callsign and precious little else: 'Zero. Romeo One Zero. Contact. Explosion. Wait out.'

'No shit,' I thought. 'Get me a medic.'

The short message did an important job: it told everyone on the net to shut the fuck up and pay close attention to his next signal while he worked out how much trouble we were in.

Ryan headed back up the hill towards me and looked into the trench. What he saw made his blood freeze. The explosion had shaken the ground up. Exposed in the walls were the unmistakable signs of landmines, or improvised explosive devices, wedged into the side of the trench. Chinese 107mm rocket warheads attached to pressure-plate detonators had been buried in the ground all around us. Ryan had dragged Stu about ten feet along the bottom of this trench, and to this day he has no idea how he bustled past them with Stu in tow quick time and failed to detonate a thing.

Luck of the draw.

At least the section now knew what the threat was. We were in the middle of an anti-personnel minefield. Live explosives were all around us. The Taliban had buried at least five IEDs in the position knowing that sooner or later a patrol would take cover there. The devices had been dug in weeks earlier and heavy rain had washed a thick layer of mud over them since. There were no warning signs or disturbance on the ground to give us any clues that they were there. In fact, I must have walked over that landmine two or three times before I detonated it, there was that much mud on top of it.

The 107mm warhead that blew me up is quite a beast. It carries more than a kilogram of high explosive and has enough power to demolish a small building. You can imagine what that does to a bit of flesh and bone.

Ryan took one look at me and knew I was T1. He got on to the radio again transmitting a 'Nine-Liner' message back to Zero. This gave our ZAP numbers, which are short coded versions of name and service numbers for Stu and me, our condition (T2 and T1 respectively), blood groups and other info.

HQ relayed the message back to Camp Bastion and an Emergency Response Team scrambled on to a Chinook helicopter equipped with as much medical equipment as they could make fit to fly.

The other lads in the patrol were all screaming and shouting now. 'Rammers, are you OK? Are you all right, Rammers?' I think they were just trying to keep me talking and conscious so they knew I was still alive.

'Yeah, great,' I thought. 'Thanks for asking.' I was trying to keep myself together and deal with what had happened as best I could.

The lad closest to me was one of the newest in the section, a kid just out of training. He was flapping a bit, but you can't really blame him. He was badly shaken up. I must have been a real sight. Apart from the horrific nature of my injuries, my face was white as a sheet apparently. He was like, 'Shit, I can't do this.'

I was able to tell him what he had to do. 'Clear a path towards me. Start your mine clearance drills. Be careful but hurry up. Don't look at me if it helps.

Just do what you have to do. Remember the training. Do it now.'

A few weeks earlier some of these lads were still at the Royal Marines' training centre at Lympstone in Devon and had just passed out as Commandos. Now they were in the middle of a war zone witnessing this shit so soon out of the box. I was embarrassed to have put them in that position. We were an irregular company, pulled together from troops with different specializations. It was the first time we had patrolled together since they arrived.

As hard as it was, they couldn't just come running to me with first aid because we now knew we were in a minefield. The first thing they did was correct: freeze. Otherwise they risked setting off devices with every move they made.

The Marine nearest me got over his shock pretty quick and responded brilliantly. He started his mine clearance drills and got to me in good time. His professionalism and pure balls contributed massively to keeping me alive.

For mine clearance you use a steel probe or a bayonet and push it into the ground at a 45-degree angle in front of you. The aim is to detect mines by touching them without setting them off, then dig away the dirt to expose them. You sweep across in a semi-circle in front of you, then you push stakes into the ground either side and attach white marker tape to show where the cleared path lies. It is a mega-slow, methodical process. Mistakes are very bad news.

'Hurry up,' I groaned.

It was about midday on Christmas Eve. The sun was blazing but it was the middle of the Afghan winter. The day was cold and clear and the air was clean – no dust and no flies – but I felt absolutely redders, much hotter than I've ever felt during summer at home.

Still propped up against the edge of the bowl, I let my head slump back. Reality was kicking in.

'Oh great. This is shit. I've just been blown up.'

It felt like a bad dream. The stumps of my legs and my mashed-up arm were jangling like crazy, like an extreme version of when your foot goes to sleep and you try to move: you can feel it's still there but it's all numb and weird. I shut my eyes and just pretended I was on holiday in some hot country, lying next to the pool, just chilling out.

Then I realized someone was talking to me. Cpl Sean Helsby had come up from his position and I could hear his voice. He was determined to keep me conscious and make sure I didn't wrap. 'I'm coming, Rammers, hang in there. Hold tight, we'll get you out of there.' Everyone was talking and shouting to me to make sure I was still conscious. As long as I was talking they knew I was breathing and hadn't started choking on my own blood or vomit.

We were only about 200 metres from our camp, Forward Operating Base Robinson, or FOB ROB as we called it. Ryan's message had got through and the base commanders got a medic out to me. I could hear a vehicle come screaming out of the camp and stop at the bottom of the hill. Then I heard people scrambling up the loose rocks of the hillside towards me, and one of them was the medic. The lads cleared a path to me and out of the minefield mega-quick, and he was alongside me about ten minutes after the explosion.

He was a South African called Dave. The first thing he did was to start applying tourniquets to my legs and arm. My stumps were oozing blood and he got as many field dressings on to them as he could. Blood wasn't spurting out of me like in a horror movie, but I'd lost a shedload of it in the last ten minutes. All the medic could do was try to stop the flow, get me to a proper field hospital as fast as possible and hope I didn't end up browners.

He asked me to help him. 'Hold this a minute. Pull this tight. Do that one up.' It was a way of keeping me talking, keeping me conscious. I managed to tighten the tourniquet on my shattered right arm. Dave jabbed a needle into my left arm and hooked up a bag of fluids and morphine, squeezing the bag to get the liquids into me.

The lads brought up a canvas stretcher. It was quite difficult to get me on because of the bowl and the angle I was at. As they dragged me on to it I felt a fresh burst of pain rip up my right leg and looked down to see a huge muscle strand still connecting my thigh to my boot, which I think still had my foot in it. It was dragging over the ground as they shifted me and I roared out in pain. I grabbed the boot, pulled it off the deck and cradled it over my lower belly. I couldn't believe what I had just done: picked up my own foot and rested it on my stomach.

The lads stretchered me down the hill while I hugged my boot. I just kept my eyes shut, drifting away and imagining I was somewhere else. The lads continued shouting and talking just to get some sort of response out of me.

They put me in the back of a Supacat, a six-wheeled all-terrain vehicle that looked to me like a sort of moon buggy. It is open-topped and has seats for a driver and passenger up front with a big roll cage to protect them if it goes over. It's got fat tyres about two feet tall and there's room for three blokes down each side in the back. It was mainly used for lugging kit around the base.

Company Sergeant Major Bob Toomey was driving. The job of a CSM is to be responsible for casualty evacuation. They have to account for every one of the lads in the company, dead or alive. The CSMs are fanatical about the role. Most of them would prefer to catch it up themselves than leave a man behind. It means a lot to know that the CSM will bust his bollocks to come and get you no matter where you are or what state you are in.

Bob had already got Stu into the front seat of the Supacat and was waiting for me to get on. As the stretcher bearers loaded me on to the back of the vehicle, the medic Dave climbed in after me and turned to formally give me the good news: 'Rammers, you have sustained a serious injury to both legs.'

It was too much for me. I'd been lying up there for half an hour coming to terms with the state I was in. 'No shit,' I replied. 'I guess my dancing days are over?'

I hardly remember saying it, but apparently that one sentence spread across southern Afghanistan in a couple of hours and the lads were pissing themselves laughing about it.

Sgt Major Toomey was trying to drive twice as fast as the Supacat could go. I was getting thrown about all over the place in the back. 'Whoever's driving this vehicle tell him he's a dickhead because he's going too fast!' I yelled. Normally I would have crossed the road to avoid a Sergeant Major, now I was calling him every name under the sun, and all because he was trying to get me to the field hospital as fast as he could.

The morphine was kicking in and I was in and out of consciousness but I could tell from the terrain where I was. I felt us get on to the main road at the bottom of the hill and the diesel engine hammering as Bob Toomey floored it. Then we were off on to the rough again so I knew we were getting close to the base.

The Supacat roared through the front gate of FOB ROB and past Sangar Four, the watchtower I'd fought the Taliban from. The guys manning the sangars had seen me get blown up and knew that a helicopter was already on its way. Bob drove straight to the helicopter landing site within the perimeter on the southern side of the camp.

My condition was worsening. I'd lost a massive amount of blood and my heart was struggling to pump enough up to my brain. That and the morphine were making me talk garbage. Apparently I was making stupid jokes about what had happened, attempting to take the piss out of my injuries and then passing out. The medic could see I was getting worse and that the next stages were unconsciousness and death. The boys were very concerned but there was little more they could do. We just stayed there in the Supacat parked out on the HLS in the sun.

I have snatches of memory of my last seconds at the FOB. One was hearing the Chinook coming. It is a beast of a helicopter with two gigantic main rotors, one at the front above the cockpit, another at the back above the tail-ramp, the whole thing powered by twin jet engines. The inside of the helo is about the size of a shipping container, except not as tall. In the middle of the ramp there's a tail gunner with a belt-fed M60 machine gun on a special mount. Directly behind the cockpit on the right-hand side is a door gunner with either another M60 or a Gatling-type M134 six-barrelled minigun. The rotors smashed the air with such a *whop-whop-whop* it sounded like heavy machine-gun fire as it came hammering across the desert. The sandstorm they kick up is horrendous. Kneeling in the rotor wash after getting off you just get pelted with rocks and gravel.

On board were four aircrew and a group of four medics – the Emergency Response Team. They are a medical unit based at Camp Bastion on standby 24/7 with a fully kitted-up Chinook to bring as much medical aid as close to the front line as possible.

Bob Toomey walked the other injured Marine, Stu, who was now fully conscious, up the tail-ramp on to the Chinook and sat him down with his weapon. I came next, on the stretcher. I felt a blast of wind hit us from the rotors and the hot turbine exhaust with the smell of burned jet fuel washed over me as they carried me up the ramp into the dark interior.

As soon as we were in, the helo just went, tipping hard forward and banking out over the perimeter wall across the desert in a storm of dust. The pilots up front had both engines throttled up to the max. They say they want to fly at 1,000mph when they've got a casualty like me on board but the Chinook only does about 160 knots.

I was in the air sixty minutes after the explosion but I was in a ridiculously shit state. I don't remember a thing after feeling the hot exhaust fumes beating down on me. I've found out since what went on.

The ERT crews are brave men and women. They have to attend to horrendous injuries, flying in and out of front-line positions while the Taliban try to kill them and blow up their helos with mortars. They've been strafed with machine guns and had as many close shaves as any individual soldier in Afghanistan. They picked me up from a well-defended camp and we were not under fire at the time, but the pilots still spent as little time on the ground as possible. They know they are the number one dream target for Taliban mortar crews and that FOB ROB had been getting attacked by indirect fire regularly up until a couple of days earlier.

Inside the helo, Lieutenant Colonel Jeremy Field, the leader of the team and a consultant anaesthetist, and his medics were on me like a Formula One pit-stop crew. They've had a lot of experience dealing with catastrophic injury and have worked out medical priorities that are different from civilian accident and emergency procedure. The first thing they go for is to stop the bleeding at all costs.

They've got some amazing kit. They use a bandage called a HemCon which contains an extract made from prawn shells. It sounds weird but the shells contain chitosan, a substance with an ability to stick itself to wounds, sealing them from germs, and making the blood clot. The medics call it a haemostatic agent. The bandages smell like mouldy prawn crackers.

But in my case there wasn't a lot more blood to

come out. I was really in the shit at this point. I'd lost about five pints, more than half the blood in my body. My brain, heart and lungs were right on the limit, about to shut down for good.

Lt Col Field couldn't find my pulse. The medics needed to dump fluids into what was left of my bloodstream quick time or I was going to die right there on my stretcher. Their best guess was that I was about three minutes from death at this point. In a civvy hospital they would have put intravenous drips into major blood vessels and pumped fluids in from there. In the back of a Chinook flying its bollocks off, banking hard over to 80 degrees to avoid ground fire, it's impossible to find a vein and insert a needle. In my case, the anaesthetist didn't have that many veins left to choose from in the first place.

Lt Col Field knew exactly what to do. He grabbed a battery-operated drill like a mini Black and Decker called an EZ-IO. He drilled straight into the bone marrow inside my hip at the top right front of my pelvis. The drill bit is a hollow needle with a tap on the outside end of it. They pumped fluids through this into the marrow and it all went straight into my bloodstream from there.

They got me on oxygen from a portable cylinder and continued ramming liquids into me. There wasn't much point hooking me up to the life-signs monitor. Either they'd got enough fluids into me in time, or I was dead.

The helo hammered back to Bastion and the pilots radioed ahead to warn of our arrival. The Chinook set down at the heliport and the medics ran me down the ramp on my stretcher into the back of an ambulance waiting on the flight line. The vehicle took us the few hundred metres to the field hospital, where the ERT handed me over to the Joint Medical Treatment Facility.

The JMTF was still a collection of tents when I was treated there, but even so it was world class. It had room for twenty-five wounded with eight intensive care beds, two operating theatres, a CT scanner and two X-ray machines. More importantly for me, some of the best military surgeons in the world worked there.

The team on the helo had done a hoofin' job. They had carried out exactly the right procedure at record speed with textbook precision. The result was incredible. Within a few minutes of coming off the helo I was gobbing off about something, talking garbage but definitely back in the land of the living.

While I was waiting to go into the operating theatre, I cried out suddenly. One of the doctors, a professor of orthopaedics, came hurrying over to see what was wrong. Apparently I complained about the fact that I'd spent £120 on a pair of trainers a few days before deployment. I was threaders at this waste of hard-earned cash. The doctor was taken aback. He wasn't expecting a T1 casualty in my state to start dripping and cracking bad jokes. I don't remember this conversation and only learned about it months afterwards.

The surgical team pumped a total of twenty-four pints of blood into me while they amputated what was left of my right arm and right leg. They closed up the shredded major blood vessels and cauterized hundreds of minor ones with an electric zapper designed for the job. All the while they cleaned out major debris, shrapnel fragments and gravel that had got into the wounds; they knew I would need further operations to remove smaller shrapnel pieces and fragments of shattered bone. They cut away the dead, burned and dying tissue until they got back to healthy muscle and bone, then packed gauze bandages over the flesh before sedating me heavily. The skin would only be closed over the stumps at a later stage. For now they had saved my life. Job done. Get me out of there.

I was transferred by Hercules from Bastion to Kandahar Airfield, which takes about an hour, with the RAF's Critical Care Air Support Team looking after me during the transit back to the UK. The C-CAST guys are the best in the world at what they do. Instead of managing the decline of a casualty during transport as most of their oppos do, they actually look on the transit as an opportunity to enhance the recovery. They have the kit and the skills to do it and get upset if they don't hand over a casualty in better nick than when they received him.

Kandahar Airfield is a massive US-run base and the food is awesome. Every Thursday the Yanks fly in around five thousand T-bone steaks and lobster tails and anyone who wants it can get steak and lobster for their dinner. The dining halls seat about three hundred. The Yanks have a rule that all military personnel on the camp must carry a loaded weapon at all times, including dinner. It's weird seeing three hundred heavily armed men and women, loaded rifles piled up beside them, stuffing their faces with luxury food looking like they are about to invade Cuba. The base also has some cool coffee shops and a great PX where you can buy any-thing from TVs to sunglasses at very good prices. You pay in US dollars and get change in US Army and Air Force Exchange Service cardboard coins. The brightly coloured discs can be used at any shop in a US military camp but are useless anywhere else. The place gets rocketed every now and then but the food and facilities are a class above.

Unfortunately I'd had no chance to enjoy the KAF on the way in and no chance now either.

The base was the main air hub for UK forces because the runway was long enough for the RAF's Tristar jets to get in. I was loaded on board that night's Tristar flight back to RAF Brize Norton in Oxfordshire. At this point I was still heavily sedated. They stretchered me on to the aircraft and transferred me to an aeromedical bed. There are three of these in the equivalent of the first-class cabin in a commercial airliner. Only officers and casualties qualify for business class on these RAF flights. The beds are equipped with oxygen bottles and electronic equipment to monitor your vital signs.

It can't have been great for the morale of passengers sitting in seats a few inches away to see me all smashed up and comatose like that. Prince Harry found it hard when he flew home from Afghanistan in March 2008. He was on the same flight as another critically wounded Marine, Ben McBean, who lost an arm and a leg when he stepped on a landmine in the desert. He flew home like me, out cold. When Harry got off the plane it was obvious he had been humbled by Ben's condition. He told the press waiting at Brize that he was 'no hero' and that people should think of the wounded like Ben. Fair play to Prince Harry.

My flight was ten weeks prior to Prince Harry's and Ben's and I was deeply unconscious throughout. The Tristar diverted to Birmingham Airport to drop me off before going on to Brize. I arrived at the Selly Oak Hospital in Birmingham on Christmas Day. Becky had been informed and came straight up to see me. She was there with my family by the time I arrived, in the early afternoon, a little more than twenty-four hours after the explosion.

Happy Christmas, Becky. Nice one.

She had been told exactly what my injuries were and had prepared herself for the very worst. When she came in, I was tucked up in bed with just my chest and face showing and looked almost whole. I had the feeding tube and oxygen mask on, an IV drip and wires stuck to my chest monitoring my vital signs. Apart from looking like something out of *The Six Million Dollar Man* she said it seemed as if I was just getting my head down. She told me that her first thought was that my face was unmarked and that I was still the bloke she had fallen in love with. She also said I looked gorgeous, which would have given me some useful encouragement if I'd known about it.

I started to come round on the 28th. I remember feeling very confused and weak. Then I began to choke. I could hardly lift my bandaged left hand to my face, but I started scrabbling at the feeding tube with it, trying as hard as I could to pull it out. I couldn't breathe and was getting distressed.

I heard Becky's voice nearby. I recognized it instantly.

The oxygen mask was getting in the way. She could see I was trying to pull out the tube and mumble something to her. She bent down and put her ear close to hear what I was saying.

'What is it, Mark? What did you say to me?'

I had been writing a letter in Afghanistan to Becky's parents and was planning to post it the day I got blown up. It was a rough copy, covered in crossings-out and asterisks and needed writing out fair. It was old school, asking their permission first, which in an ideal world is the way I would have wanted it. As it was, I thought I'd better just go for it.

'Will you marry me?' I asked.

2

Getting hurt was the last thing on my mind when we arrived in Afghanistan. I was excited and looking forward to the tour of my life. I wasn't going to be the one getting smashed up. If it came to it, I was going to be the one doing the smashing.

I was revved up for it because I was getting what I wanted, front-line infantry. After six years with the Marines I was deploying as a gravel belly at last. My background had been with Motor Transport Troop (M/T), driving and maintaining tracked vehicles and trucks. I wanted action, not to spend six months in the rear around Camp Bastion fixing up trucks and working on my tan. I had already requested a transfer to specialize as a grav in the UK but thought there was no way it would be processed in time for deployment to the Afghan. As it turned out my unit, 40 Commando Royal Marines, was short of gravs because there was so much to do and they were pinging blokes from all sorts of troops to tour as infantry whether they requested it or not. That suited me fine. I just saw it as a shortcut that did away with the formal transfer.

I had toured the world with M/T and had a brilliant time with them but in my mind nothing could match this tour. It was going to be proper warfighting. The tales coming back from the Afghan were electrifying. Bootnecks were going into battle with fixed bayonets in company strength. Mortar teams and artillery were putting down more live rounds in a month than some had fired in their whole careers.

This was the real thing. The Taliban were ferocious and fanatical. Unlike the Iraqi insurgents, they loved a scrap and were prepared to stand and fight like a proper enemy. They weren't idiots either. Some of our blokes had been well impressed watching them fire and manoeuvre during contacts. The enemy had received decent infantry training and wasn't afraid to put it to use. You had to respect the fact that they were prepared to go toe to toe with us and I couldn't wait to have a crack at them.

It was going to be the ultimate test. We had trained for it all our professional lives and I wanted to find out what was bullshit and what was real. Would I be any good at it? I was a pretty good Marine on exercise but no man can predict how he or his mates will behave under fire. I wanted to know the answers.

We knew that people could get hurt or even

killed. There were enough reminders that something could happen at any moment before we even got off the plane.

When the Tristar started its approach to Kandahar Airfield a buzz went around the aircraft. The new lads were all excited and couldn't wait to get stuck in. Some of the older blokes, or young ones on their second tours, were quieter. They were thinking about the realities, I suppose, whereas to me it was just a big adventure. I didn't give it a second thought when we were ordered to dig out our body armour and helmets from the overhead lockers and put them on for the landing, in case the Taliban had a crack at the aircraft during the final approach or as it taxied in after landing. The Tristars have a suite of defensive counter-measures including flares to decoy heat-seeking missiles while in the air; the threat on the ground is from mortars or rocket attacks into the base. If rounds or shrapnel started coming through the aircraft you would just have to trust in luck and body armour. It hadn't happened yet and no one really believed it would. Or at least not while they were on the plane it wouldn't. If you started thinking like that you would never get out of bed, and anyway, it's never going to happen to you, is it? You're strapped into your seat and there's no action you can take to improve your chances, so there's no point worrying about it.

The plane bumped down on to the tarmac and taxied over to its hard standing with no dramas. As the three big turbines wound down there was another reminder about coming under attack. 'This is the air movements officer,' said one of the RAF cabin crew over the speaker system. He was wearing the sandy-pink all-in-one jumpsuit the Crabs dress up in. 'Your "Actions On" in the event of a rocket or mortar attack on leaving the aircraft are as follows . . .' and he told us what to do if indirect fire started coming in as we walked away from the jet. On another flight the officer came out with this: 'Please follow the directions of the air movements staff, and bear in mind that due to the lack of hardened accommodation this may simply involve lying down.' That got a few wry laughs.

'Welcome to Afghanistan,' I thought to myself.

We gathered up the rest of the gear from the battered overhead lockers. These planes were ten years old when the RAF bought them in about 1980 and it showed. The interiors have been flogged around the world for almost forty years. Some of those lockers will do you an injury if you don't watch it.

We walked down the steps of the plane. It was 8 October 2007, my first day of a six-month tour in country. I was twenty-four years and two months old and had no idea what to expect. I just hoped it would be exciting.

We walked across the tarmac and were loaded into a shitty little bus. It was honking, covered in dust inside and out. The seats were like sandpits. The bus growled off the runway and on to a dirt track. Clouds of mega-fine clay powder came billowing in the windows and stuck to our skin and clothing. We were doing about ten miles an hour. We thought we were going to choke before we even got to arrivals.

The windows were caked with dust but I could just about see on one side of the track a chain-link fence. Beyond it were a load of stunted trees rooted in hardened clay throwing ghostly shadows in the moonlight. The ground was potholed and un-cultivated. What a shithole.

The other side of the track was walled in with Hesco, galvanized steel mesh formed into a cube about four feet square containing a big polymer bag that is packed with sand and gravel. The Engineers line them up in grids and fill them two at a time with a bulldozer shovel then some poor sprog has to level them off with a spade by hand. You stack them in pyramids two or three high and top them off with razor wire to make a bomb-proof perimeter wall. They can be used to make bunkers or to give blast protection to anything that needs it. They come flat-packed from a company in America for the Engineers to set up. There are thousands and thousands of them in Afghanistan and Iraq sitting on hundreds of miles of NATO perimeter. We would see them everywhere we turned, unless we were out on a patrol.

The bus bumped off the track on to a graded hard-core surface and dropped us at the arrivals area.

There were about forty lads from my unit and we were being scattered across southern Afghanistan to plug gaps as needed.

The boss was calling himself the chalk commander until we got to Bastion. 'Chalk' is a term for about thirty blokes assigned to an aircraft. It dates from World War Two when a platoon of Paras would write its number in chalk on the side of the aircraft to help keep themselves and their kit together. In my mind, being in a 'chalk' meant you might be jumping or fast-roping out of an aircraft at some point. In reality we were a troop of Bootnecks and only a couple of us were parachute trained; I certainly wasn't. The Sgt was a great bloke named Harry and he could call himself whatever he liked, but chalk was for blackboards. He was the Troop Stripey to me.

Harry was from 40 Commando and knew me well. We had worked together in Air Defence Troop a few years earlier when we were looking after twelve BV amphibious vehicles, go-anywhere personnel carriers designed for the Arctic. They were weird things, like two mini-tanks held together by a hydraulic ram to articulate them. It was developed into the Viking, a bigger and better version that arrived in the Afghan in 2006. Viking did such a hoofin' job the vehicles hadn't been allowed to return to the UK and were still there when I arrived. The lads were beginning to discover there was only one flaw: they were vulnerable to rolling under certain conditions. You didn't want to be the top gunner when that happened.

Harry was a Corporal when I worked with him and a keen sportsman. He played football for the Marines and loved it. He got more time off than Rambo's safety catch to play football for the Corps. I didn't mind as I was allowed to run the shop while he was away.

At Kandahar, Harry pinged me to help him deal with the chalk's bergens and weapons which the RAF ground crew had dumped in a pile outside the arrivals tent. As we sorted through, a light breeze blew and brought with it a cloud of air smelling of chemically treated, slowly rotting shit.

'Aaargh, Harry, have you dropped your guts, mate?'

'Not me, Rammers, that is the great smell of KAF. It's the sewage treatment plant. When the wind's in the wrong direction there ain't nothing you can do about it. The food here is so good everyone stuffs their faces while they've got the chance. What goes in must come out.'

'What a gopping stench.' The place really was a shithole.

We identified 40 Commando's kit and shifted it, getting the rifles secured to a pallet for the Hercules flight from Kandahar to Camp Bastion. The only weapons we had in transit were our personal rifles and attached SUSAT optical sights. They were packed five at a time into valises, soft containers that rolled up like a bed roll. Each valise was marked with the rifle serial numbers and the names of the Marines they belonged to.

The SA80 was introduced in the early 1980s, but these were very different weapons from that old gun. After years of problems, in 2000 the military handed the rifle to Heckler and Koch and said 'sort it out'. It is now an excellent weapon with a thirty-round magazine and can fire single-shot or fully automatic. The addition of a 40mm grenade launcher turns a good rifle into a hoofin' weapon.

We also brought a light support weapon for each section, basically an SA80 with a longer barrel and a bipod to steady it. It was meant to give a section of eight blokes a load more punch, but the designers had forgotten some of the basics of infantry fighting. It has a thirty-round mag when what you really need is belt-fed firepower. You don't want to be mucking about changing magazines every few bursts when you are trying to keep a load of Taliban heads down. We used the LSW as a marksman's weapon out to about 600 metres, halfway between a standard and a sniper rifle.

In the role the LSW was meant to fill we used a hoofin' Belgian gun called the Minimi. It was the same 5.56mm calibre as our rifles but was belt-fed, fully automatic and could put down hundreds of rounds of suppressing fire in a few tens of seconds. My kind of weapon.

There was no need to pack ammunition. All

you could ever use was in the Afghan already.

My bergen contained all my field kit and was packed and ready to go. All up it weighed about 40kg. I had also packed a laptop and a grip bag with my phys kit and a few luxuries including a photo album with pictures of me and my daughter Kezia, Becky, a few of my civvy mates and my mum, dad and sister.

Whenever you put any piece of kit on the floor, it picked up a coating of clay dust so fine it was like talcum powder. Keeping kit clean and functional was going to be a nightmare.

Harry and me bundled the bergens into a pile for the lads to collect and went to check in at RAF arrivals – a white fabric tent on a galvanized steel framework on a concrete slab put down by the Engineers. Hundreds of Marines and soldiers of all ranks in desert camouflage and civilians with blue body armour and helmets were crammed into this permanent marquee about the size of a tennis court. Inside there were trestle tables, strip lights, fizzy drink machines, stacks of water bottles piled up in cardboard boxes and a set of check-in desks knocked together from spare pallet timber. There were UK powerpoints attached to the beams at floor level so you could charge up your phone, laptop or whatever. The formalities of British military personnel arriving in the Afghan theatre were dealt with here. Slowly.

I made myself a wet from an urn of hot water and

looked at the bleary-eyed, pissed-off collection of men and women around me. It was the middle of the night. The smokers on the flight stood outside puffing away. Someone had rigged up a powerpoint projector and was playing *Pirates of the Caribbean* from their laptop. I was happy just to chill out and watch the movie while the RAF movers got their act together and processed us through. Everything was pretty chilled; it didn't feel like a war zone at all. The chances of getting hurt seemed about as real as Johnny Depp's ridiculous sword fight with Orlando Bloom in the movie.

After about two hours they had checked our passports and recorded our arrival in theatre. They processed us through and it was back on the shitty bus to the Hercules heading for Camp Bastion.

The four massive six-bladed propellers of the C130 were already tearing at the air as we marched into the cargo area from the back of the aircraft, walking up the tail-ramp against a prop wash strong enough to blast you off your feet. It was mega-noisy inside and the loadie pointed us towards nylon webbing seats slung between aluminium poles down both sides of the aircraft. More seats were set up back to back along the centre line forward, and we all piled in, clipping into the seat belts, as the loadies heaved the massive pallet of guns and bergens into the cargo space at the rear and chained it down. They then passed round a cardboard bucket full of yellow-foam earplugs, which were welcome as the engines sounded like a hundred giant hammer drills screaming at once. You could barely make out someone shouting at full volume an inch from your ear.

The pilots taxied us out as the loadies closed up the tail-ramp. It was pitch black outside and we couldn't see a thing. The aircraft interior glowed red with lighting to protect our night vision. We all tipped sideways as the pilot lined up on the runway and hit the brakes before piling on full power. The turbo-props screamed as they ripped the air at full whack, and we were away.

The pilots performed a tactical landing at Bastion dropping out of the sky at the steepest angle possible, and we got down about a minute ahead of our guts. The loadies hate clearing up vomit and get upset if any grav fails to puke into his own helmet. They don't exactly make their own lives easy, though. Their favourite trick on anyone looking a bit airsick is to pass round a sick bag containing the cold contents of a tin of vegetable soup. Nice. The Herc taxied to a collection of shipping containers at the end of the gravel runway at Camp Bastion. These and a couple of thunderbox toilets out in the desert were what passed for the arrivals hall. It took me a while to realize the whole airstrip and welcoming thunderboxes were inside the perimeter. The base was massive. It was not so much a camp as a tent-pod town with fortifications like something out of *Mad Max*, but on an enormous scale. Its Hesco perimeter was more than 20 miles long.

We climbed into the back of a four-ton truck which ground its way along a compacted sand road. The camp contained everything a warfighting soldier in Afghanistan could need and it felt safer than Plymouth on a Saturday night. Massive rubberized bladders 20 and 40 feet square containing aviation fuel, diesel, petrol and water were everywhere. The Engineers had sunk seven borehole wells to feed water to the camp. There was a firing range inside the perimeter, air-conditioned tented gyms, a replica Taliban compound for incoming troops to practise assaulting, hundreds of hot showers and comfy toilets, a field hospital, dining halls and beds for about 2,500 troops, vehicle workshops, a fixed wing runway and a separate heliport with maintenance hangars for the Apache attack helos and the fleet of Chinooks. An HQ compound directed the tactical fight against the Taliban and resupply of front-line callsigns across Helmand Province, an area about three times the size of Wales. The camp even had its own sewage farm, just like Kandahar. It didn't smell quite as gopping, but then the food wasn't quite as good. Dotted along the perimeter were watchtowers made from shipping containers the Engineers had stacked up like giant Lego bricks. You could see all the way to the horizon and there was no scrap of cover, not a bush or dip in the ground as far as you could see. It was so flat and barren that it was a bit like looking out to sea.

The location was chosen by the Afghans whose tactical use of terrain was awesome. Bastion's location miles from anywhere in a flat desert made it a very tough target to attack. Taliban mortar teams just couldn't get close. It felt mega-safe, and it must have been. Gordon Brown has visited the camp, and *Top Gear* filmed an episode there.

The flight from Kandahar had only taken an hour or so but it was about two a.m. when we got to the transit accommodation. The excitement at arriving in country had worn right off by the time we walked into a giant hangar filled with hundreds of empty bunk beds. We piled the kit on to the lower bunks, unrolled our slugs on to bare mattresses, used our body armour as pillows and were asleep in seconds.

The rifles crackled as we zeroed the sights on the range. We were shooting at targets 100 metres away in a ten-lane range marked out in the desert just inside the Bastion perimeter. I drew ten rounds in a clip from two Pongos in the back of a Land Rover and bombed up the magazine. I attached the speed loader to the top and inserted the clip, pressing my thumb on top of the rounds until they zipped neatly into the magazine. When we were fighting, every fifth round would be tracer, for now it was plain 5.56mm standard NATO ball ammunition.

I lay prone on the bund line, propped up on my elbows, and levelled the rifle at the target. I flicked the fire selector lever on the left-hand side of the butt to semi-automatic for single shot and pushed the safety catch cross-bolt above the trigger from safe to off. Pressing my cheek to the nylon pad on the stock, I looked through the SUSAT. The sight has a single crosshair running from the six o'clock position terminating in a needle point at the centre. I looked at the target, a black and brown image of a soldier from the waist up, helmet and rifle visible, magnified four times in the SUSAT. I consciously relaxed as I placed the tip of the point over a box on the target that indicated the centre of mass, then lowered the point on to the bottom centre of the box, breathed out and squeezed the trigger.

Bam.

A tenth of a second later, sand splashed behind the target as the lead slug passed through it at 2,000mph and buried itself into the berm directly behind. The scalding hot spent brass cartridge ejected to my right and hit the deck a fraction of a second later. If you want to see how hot the cartridge is on ejection there's a hoofin' video posted on the internet of some Army lads in the middle of a big contact, fighting from the back of a Bulldog armoured vehicle in Iraq. Two of them are standing side by side putting down the rounds and the bloke on the left's cartridge ejects straight down the back of his buddy's body armour. The bloke yelps like he's been shot and jiggles around because it's near red-hot and it's stuck between his skin and the ceramic plate. Any infantryman looking at that cannot help but laugh.

I could see I had hit the target but I wasn't sure where. I repeated the process, taking four more shots. Rounds complete, all ten of us walked up to the targets to see how we had done. My shots were nicely grouped about eight inches to the right and two inches high of the aiming point.

The instructor took a look. 'Try three clicks left and one down,' he said. I took my combi-tool and adjusted the SUSAT as instructed.

Five more rounds, all on target. Tighten up the sight to lock the adjustment. Each shot had hit the centre of the target within a space about the size of a man's fist. Not Olympic standard, but good enough.

One individual weapon ready for anything. One individual ready to put his feet up in the Naafi with a copy of *FHM*.

We spent most of that first day in the bunk hangar taking lectures and briefings from various Army officers to bring us up to speed. We got an intelligence briefing setting out the latest tactics being used by the Taliban and covering recent activity around Helmand Province, the area under British control in southern Afghanistan. It was the Taliban's heartland.

Many of the people lived in isolated rural communities that apart from tatty little motorbikes and

AK47s hadn't changed for a thousand years. They rested up in homes made from mud bricks held together with mud mortar and finished with mud render. Electricity, when there was any, was used mainly for irrigating the opium poppies.

The Helmand River flows down through the mountains around Sangin and out on to the desert plain at Gereshk. It passes through the capital Lashkar Gah and on to Garmsir towards Pakistan in the south before taking a sharp right turn towards Iran in the west. The green zone of farmland around the Helmand River was some of the most fertile in the Afghan. Almost all of it was being used to grow opium poppy. It was tragic. In the sixties, apparently, it was all wheat, barley, fruit trees and almonds.

The intelligence officers told us that it was fairly quiet around the province at that time because the population was busy planting that year's opium crop. We didn't know it then, but it was going to be a record harvest. The numbers made you think. About 200,000 farming families in Helmand would plant 103,500 hectares of poppy – an area about the size of Bedfordshire. This produced about five tonnes of raw opium and put half a billion US dollars in hard cash into the hands of the farmers. Each poppy farmer earned about $6,000 a year from his crops, around twice the average wage in Helmand Province. You try telling them to grow wheat. The same farmer would have earned about $1,800. To the farmers, it was a no-brainer.

The first planting was going in as we took the briefing. A second, fast-growing type would go into the ground in late February or March the following year, to avoid the coldest part of winter. Both types would be ready for harvest about a month after the end of our tour in May.

Nearly two thirds of the heroin on the streets of Britain came from Helmand, we were told. The opium was refined in factories on the border with Pakistan and trafficked to the West. The crop is blatantly paying for the insurgency. Opium goes out of Helmand and back come newly recruited foreign fighters, weapons and US dollars. Each harvest earns the Taliban around £200 million.

I wanted to know why we didn't just torch the whole lot of it. The Taliban would be skinters and screwed overnight. It turned out to be a shitload more complicated than that, but that's why I'm a Bootneck not a diplomat. If the Brits eradicated the crop they would put hundreds of docile Afghan farmers out of work and take $500 million out of the pockets of the locals. Those people were just trying to earn a living. If you burned down the crops they busted their arse to put in, then they were going to get mad.

And the Afghans believe in vengeance. It is unmanly and shames your whole family to leave a blow unavenged. Fighting was the Afghan national sport, and they were hosting the World Cup of war.

Trashing the opium would be the best recruiting sergeant the Taliban ever had.

That was the theory, anyway, so we were going to leave the poppy alone. Some sections on patrol left kilos of unrefined opium worth hundreds of thousands of pounds in rural Afghan compounds untouched so as not to upset the locals. The strategy was to target the big boys and take down the factories where possible.

For new Taliban arrivals, just off the bus from Pakistan, Chechnya, Bradford, Birmingham or wherever, Garmsir district down south was the first chance to test themselves against British forces. Our lads down there at FOB Delhi were manning a front line along the high street of Garmsir's main market town Darvisham like a scene from World War One. A string of checkpoints along the street controlled a no-man's land stretching about 1,000 metres to the south. From here the lads could call down 105mm artillery, 81mm mortars and airstrikes on to Taliban positions. The area was riddled with Taliban trench systems and bunkers.

The town is a major crossing point on the Helmand River and stop-off point on the route from Lashkar Gah to Pakistan. Any Taliban who survived the fight down south came on to Sangin to have a crack at us at the other mountain strongholds, Musa Qala, Nowzad and Kajaki. At Kajaki, the job was to keep the hydroelectric dam producing electricity for the people of Helmand. The

Taliban were determined to turn out the lights.

To be honest, I didn't think much about the Taliban or what motivated them. I knew they killed teachers on sight because they didn't want anybody to know anything about the modern world. They will teach their blokes to strip an AK blindfold, ride a motorbike and fight, but that's it. They particularly hated girls being educated and would even come after families who sent their daughters to school.

Before British forces arrived, teachers got warnings called 'night letters'. A notice from the local Taliban commander would be pinned to their door in the middle of the night warning that if they continued teaching they were under a death sentence. One teacher in Lashkar Gah told a Pongo Colonel the story about a brave friend of his who ignored the night letters. The Afghan teacher was at his dad's funeral when the Taliban came for him. As he lowered his dad's coffin into its grave, they shot him in the back of the head and threw him in on top. The teacher who told that story was a fully qualified headmaster. After seeing that done to his mate he gave up and started to grow opium poppy for a living like everyone else.

In a village down near Darvisham, a troop from 45 Commando were patrolling through and chatting to the locals when a teacher popped out of the woods looking like Ben Gunn. He was wearing a loincloth and flip-flops and had a beard down to his bollocks. He must have weighed all of six stone sopping wet. The bloke had been living rough in the treeline because if the Taliban saw him they would kill him. He'd seen the Commando patrol go in and knew it would be safe for him to enter the village to see a couple of his mates. He was jabbering away to people like he'd had no one to talk to for months. The village was a moderate one by local standards and used to hide little bowls of food for him out in the fields, even though by doing so they were risking the lives of every member of their community. That was how badly the Taliban wanted teachers dead.

During my tour, there was only one girls' school in Helmand, in Lashkar Gah. It had more than 7,000 pupils. That's how badly the local Afghans wanted their daughters to go to school. If British forces left the school would have shut down the same day and the teachers gone into hiding. I've got a little girl. Imagine a place where people want to kill you for sending your daughter to school. It's messed up.

The officers were clear enough as to why we were in Afghanistan. Helmand Province was the Taliban's backyard and cradle of the 9/11 attacks. Our job was to deny a safe haven to terrorists who posed a threat to the people of the United Kingdom.

Personally, I was there to do a job and test myself to the limit. If I did any fighting it would be for myself and the lads who stood next to me and to stop any bastard having a crack at us. Taking on the terrorists was fine by me and if my being there meant some group of girls went to school for a bit, then I was happy with that.

We also got more updates on procedures and drills. There were talks on the IED threat, which is military jargon for landmines; car bombs are tagged VBIED, for vehicle-borne improvised explosive device. They talked us through mine clearance drills and mine awareness exercises, IED types, where and when to expect Taliban to be digging them in, and the relevant drills to counter them. The Taliban often placed IEDs at pinch points on a patrol route, or used their knowledge of the terrain to predict where soldiers were likely to take cover or choose positions to lie up in. Then they dug in the IEDs, usually with a combination of pressure plate plus control wire or radio-controlled detonation system to trigger them.

Looking back, I think I must have dozed off during that lecture.

The second night they moved us into a pod, a nice air-conditioned tent with electric lighting, power-points and eight aluminium-frame camp beds with plenty of space for all our kit. The floor was black plastic decking on graded hardcore. The tent was one of thousands in Bastion and surrounded by a single level of Hesco to protect from shrapnel.

Not far away was a nice Naafi bar with a pool table and plasma screen TV. There was a shop next door to that selling lads' mags and a good selection of luxuries like toiletries, cigarettes and chilled fizzy drinks. A couple of nice civvy girls worked behind the counter.

Across the camp were purpose-built shipping containers converted into ablution blocks. They were painted olive green and had shower cubicles, toilets and sinks pre-installed. The Engineers just had to hook up water, power and drainage and they were ready to go. There were hundreds of them lined up in rows, some reserved for particular units, some for officers, and some for any old Bootneck. You got a good blast of hot water that never seemed to run out.

Not so four-star were the thunderbox toilets, just a plastic cubicle with a seat over an oil drum or integral reinforced plastic tank. They were honking, and stank worse the warmer it got. One lad was caught short and had to use one right opposite the Bastion HQ compound. He cleaned it up as best he could before sitting down. When he looked up he saw the words 'Welcome to Old Trafford' scrawled on the back of the door two inches in front of his face.

Even in October it was roasting hot and the air as dry as dust. After a day sweating about the camp and a nice hot shower, I found my skin getting dry and itchy. The Marines pride themselves on being educated infantry, and we know real men are not afraid to moisturize, so it was straight to the

Naafi for a tube of cocoa butter, which I slapped on every night. I even asked a couple of the lads to do my back for me.

We were in Bastion for three days and the forty-odd blokes from 40 Commando were mostly in transit to front-line positions so we were not required to do any work. It was different for my mate, Sgt Harry. He was going to do his whole tour at Bastion fixing up computers and doing IT for the Marines. He was going to be so bored it wasn't true. I wouldn't have traded places with him for anything. Unlike us, he was working his nuts off from day one. Motor Transport Troop at Bastion were in their own world and none of them bothered me, which suited me fine. We just went to the gym to keep on top of our phys, took showers, ate food and chilled out in the sun sipping coffee or Cokes outside the Naafi.

After three days, word came through. Transfer to FOB ROB was to be by Chinook next morning. A Corporal was coming to pick us up in a four-tonner at 1100.

'Hoofin',' I thought. 'This is it.'

3

The blast of the GPMG in Sangar Five shattered the night's silence. Tracer rounds glowed red as they disappeared over the perimeter and flew towards the enemy.

'Contact, contact, contact!' yelled Corporal Sean Helsby. 'Stand to!'

Marines left and right were grabbing body armour and helmets, kicking over cups of tea, snatching weapons and charging for the perimeter. My heart started pounding in my chest with excitement. 'Shit, this isn't a drill,' I thought.

I ran the 40 metres to my post in Sangar Four, pounding up the hill. There was a loud *zzzip* and a *crack* a few feet above my head. It was the first time I'd heard a 'lead wasp' – the unmistakable sound made by a round passing within a few feet of your head at supersonic speed. My brain took in the fact that live ammunition was flying by close to my head and ignored it. I was too busy and pumped up to worry about it. I ran on up to the sangar, shoved the black plastic curtain aside and stomped through the doorway.

I hadn't seen any Taliban since arriving and now, not only were they out there in the darkness, they were fighting back.

Bambababam. The sentry in my sangar was firing another GPMG in short bursts, spewing spent shell cases and link across the floor and top of the Hesco. The sangar commander was on the battlefield radio to the HQ compound, Zero, telling them what was going on. A second GPMG lay on top of the Hesco ready to fire. It had a massive belt of ammunition arranged neatly beside it, several hundred rounds linked up and ready to go.

Tracer was flying downrange from Sangars Four and Five. I followed it to the target in the darkness. It was weird how it seemed to slow down as it got further away. Some rounds deflected on impact and suddenly flew into the air and you could see how fast they were moving again. The deflections marked the targets and I spotted a muzzle flash stupidly close to the FOB. It was no more than 250 metres away.

I had no doubt about what I had seen. That was definitely enemy firing in my direction. We had night vision goggles but you didn't need them. I could now see clearly four or five enemy muzzle flashes out there in the field at various ranges.

Without waiting to be told I grabbed the gun,

cocked it and levelled it at the muzzle flash. I looked through the iron sight of the gun and mashed the trigger. The ammo belt leapt as the GPMG chewed it up, spitting a stream of 7.62mm rounds from the barrel, red tracer blazing away into the night. I concentrated on putting down short, accurate bursts around the flashes in the field, the gun braced tight into my shoulder and left hand over the top of the butt. If you fired long bursts the recoil forced your aim up and to the right. Too many long bursts and the barrel would become red-hot and distort, making the accuracy even worse. We had spare gun barrels in case of overheating but changing them was time-consuming and a second or two was enough for your target to bug out and disappear.

We were malleting the enemy positions, putting down hundreds of rounds between us in interlocking arcs from the sangars, catching the Taliban up in a deadly crossfire. They were shooting back at us and you could see their tracer, glowing red as it came in. The outgoing tracer would help the Taliban mark our position but I had no idea how near they were to hitting us. Enemy rounds into the sangar would not *zip* or *crack* but impact the sandbags or Hesco with a loud thunk. Thankfully, I didn't hear anything like that come near me.

My tracer was impacting right where I wanted it and I knew for certain I was hitting my man. Fire one 7.62mm round at a dustbin full of water and it doesn't just blow the lid off, the shockwave around the bullet will punch all the water out of it as well. The weapon's effect at this range would be like putting the man through a meat grinder. Sure enough, the muzzle flash in the field stopped and I moved straight on to another.

One by one, the muzzle flashes died out and the field reverted to darkness.

We ceased fire. The silence was deafening. Blood was roaring in my ears, still ringing from the muzzle blast. When I shifted my stance, my boots crunched shells and link underfoot. It felt as if neat adrenalin had replaced the blood in my veins. The rush was off the scale.

I reckoned I must have hit or killed two or three men. They had no cover and were so close it was impossible to miss. I took no pleasure in it, but I felt no guilt either. The fact they were dead was simply a relief. The attack had been stopped. They weren't trying to kill us any more and they couldn't try it again.

I didn't give them a second thought. The fact they must have been off their tits on opium to take on Marines in well-defended sangars, with no cover and no heavy weapons, made me feel no sympathy for them at all. They tied the people they killed to the backs of trucks and dragged them through villages. That's what they wanted to do to us. They were not firing AK47 rifles at us for a laugh.

It just felt brilliant to have won the firefight, for the moment at least. What I was most worried about was what was coming next. 'That can't be all of them,' I thought. 'Five men can't take a FOB unsupported and these blokes are not stupid.' The Afghan Taliban loved nothing better than a frontal assault into combat. But there was usually a method to their madness. They were good tactical fighters. They wouldn't just throw blokes away like that and I knew they must be up to something.

All the Marines in the sangars and on the perimeter were tensed up for a continuation or switch of attack. I expected rocket-propelled grenades or mortars to open up on us at any second.

I looked nervously around at the piles of ammunition in the sangar, thousands of rounds of GPMG and Minimi link, boxes and boxes of high explosive and smoke grenades, two AT4 shoulder-launched missiles.

'We're not going to run out of ammo up here any time soon, are we?' I grinned nervously in the dark.

'Nah, mate,' said the other gunner. 'Thing is, though, this sangar was hit by an RPG in the last tour.'

If that happened now . . . well, it was a few days early for Guy Fawkes night but it would make one hell of a fireworks display.

We stood to.

It was quite scary in the night. You're not the one manoeuvring or planning the attack, you're just sitting there waiting to get hit, jumping at every little noise coming out of a landscape with not even a glimmer of starlight to see by.

Seconds dragged.

The other GPMG gunner was my mate Ryan Wordsworth, or 'Jurgen the German'. Jurgen was a hoofin' Marine who was actually from Carlisle. But with his mop of dark-blond hair, blue eyes and distinctive nose, we thought he looked more German than Michael Schumacher. The nickname stuck.

We scanned our arcs with the naked eye as best we could.

'Is that the lot of them, you reckon, Jurg?' I muttered quietly. It was my first contact and I was excited. I didn't want to make any mistakes.

'Dunno, mate, little fuckers could be up to anything. I tell you what though, if there are any more I bet I get on them before you do.'

'You cheeky twat, Jurg.'

He nodded at the spent shells heaped up on the Hesco next to my fire position and added, 'Just clear some of that brass away, make sure your weapon's good, and keep checking your arcs.'

From then on I was more concerned with doing better in a contact than Jurgen than I was worrying what the Taliban were up to.

Other lads in the sangars and on the perimeter used night vision monocles and SOPHIE sight thermal imaging equipment to scan the ground around the FOB. In addition, HQ had a camera mounted on a cherry picker behind us which they called the removercam. It was equipped with some brilliant optics and the latest night vision kit. They scanned our arcs through it via remote control.

The Taliban were expert at using the local terrain, crawling up drainage ditches, through treelines, knocking holes through the walls of buildings and using every scrap of cover to get close enough to have a crack at the FOB then leg it. If the attack was about to develop we had so many eyes on, from Mark One Eyeball to a battery of the best optics known to man, that one of us must see it coming, surely?

We watched and waited. I hated it. Once it kicked off you knew what to do and time flew by. Just waiting for it was no fun at all.

'Come on then if you think you're hard enough,' I grumbled quietly.

'All sangars, all sangars,' the battlefield radios crackled. We weren't told how they knew, but the HQ compound deemed the attack to be over. The sangar commander gave his verdict: 'That lot were testing our strength. They would have tried something else if we hadn't given them such a good malleting. Good effort, lads, well done.'

I stomped out of the sangar still buzzing and went to get my head down. I'd be on watch in Sangar Four again in a couple of hours' time.

I felt OK. I'd got through my first contact and hadn't made any mistakes. I was confident in myself, the other Marines and the kit around me. We had just sent a message to the local Taliban that we were more than up for a scrap and none of our lads had got a scratch.

Early the next morning we saw people come forward into the field and drag away five bodies. The men dragging them off didn't appear to be armed and could have been locals. We just let them crack on.

On the way up from Bastion I had been sitting near the tail-ramp of the Chinook with a great view of Helmand Province unfolding beneath me. There were fourteen of us bound for FOB ROB, bergens, mail and supplies piled up along the centre of the aircraft. Our rifles were fully bombed up and held loosely between our knees, muzzle down. If you were biff enough to negligently discharge your weapon during the flight it was better the round exited the aircraft through the floor below than the rotors above. Everyone was fired up and ready to get stuck in.

I'd hated Bastion in the end, because there was too much bullshit around. I was walking back to my grot once when a Sergeant stopped me. 'You there, tuck your T-shirt in. The next time I see you, you'd better have had a shave. Look at the state of you, where do you think you are?'

'In the middle of a war, you arsehole?' was what I couldn't say.

Fair enough, Bastion was well in the rear and standards were more strictly upheld than up at the front. But we'd be in combat in a few days' time and no one had to shave or dress smart in the FOBs where we were heading.

When Bastion disappeared beneath me I was glad to see the back of it. Within minutes we were flying over empty desert. I watched the landscape abruptly transform into dried-up valleys and then mountains beneath us. Apart from the odd goat track the land was untouched. 'We are really heading for the middle of fucking nowhere,' I thought.

We touched down in a cloud of flying grit and dumped the cargo out of the back before crouching on one knee, backs to the helo, as it wound up to depart. The rotors blasted 11 tonnes of thrust in our direction enveloping us in a hail of stones and crap.

I didn't care about that. As far as I was concerned I had just been dumped in the middle of undefended hostile territory with thirteen other gravs, a load of bags and a Corporal I didn't know. All I wanted to do was get into cover because every Taliban within ten miles must have heard us thundering up the Sangin Valley and seen us set down in the middle of their backyard in open ground. I could imagine some Taliban mortar team cackling with delight nearby as they zeroed in on us with their 82mm tube. My heart's desire at that point was a deep ditch and the opportunity to lie at the bottom of it.

As the dust cleared, a bare-chested Bootneck wearing shorts and flip-flops grinned at us through an uber-chad moustache and massive lamb-chop sideys. He looked like he'd stepped out of a 1970s porn movie. The RSMs back at Bastion would have had a coronary just looking at a photo of his growler.

'Welcome to FOB ROB,' he chuckled. 'Grab your stuff and follow me.'

The FOB's perimeter was a Hesco oval shaped like a giant kidney. It was about a quarter of a mile from top to bottom and half a mile across from east to west. The HLS was on the southern edge inside the perimeter. It was huge for a FOB.

Set on a slope dominating the highest ground outside a village on route 611, a single-lane dirt road, the base controlled a section of the main supply route about seven kilometres south of Sangin town, the Taliban stronghold.

Three Pinzgauer trucks and trailers had come to collect us from the HLS, and the fresh supplies that came with us. After a quick brief at the HQ tent we threw our stuff into the back of a brightly coloured Afghan 'Jingly' four-tonner which drove us down to the western end at the bottom of the slope to a compound of mud buildings that was home to Echo Company, 40 Commando, Royal Marines.

A company normally has more than a hundred blokes in it; E Coy on our arrival had twenty. We made it up to thirty-four so they were pleased to see us. Where anyone got off calling us a company I have no idea: we were barely up to troop strength. No wonder they wanted more gravs out here.

E Coy's little compound was made up of an old mosque and its outbuildings, about 40 feet inside the perimeter directly behind the main gate. At first I wasn't too pleased because I reckoned any attempt to breach the perimeter would come through that gate and we'd be the first people Terry said hello to if he got inside.

The gate itself did not inspire confidence: it was just a load of boards bolted together to form two sections about eight feet long and five feet tall. They weren't even on hinges. Each of the barriers had a load of razor wire coiled along the top but the edge of the gates only came up to chest height. The handles of a couple of entrenching tools had been fixed to each barrier, allowing the sentries to drag them into position. Closed up, the gates formed a shallow V-shape with the tip pointing into the camp. Last man in off a patrol had to close these gates. The last 20 metres into the camp formed the steepest part of the hill so you'd be roasting and knackered, weighed down with kit, and dragging them closed behind you single-handed was a pain. Plus everyone would be watching to see if you could manage it, so you'd be struggling not to let anyone know how much of an arseache it was. There was lots of talk of getting the Gurkha Engineers to fix up a proper gate with hinges. It never happened.

The E Coy compound was a good spot in other ways, though. There were so few of us, there was plenty of room for a start. The mosque was about 50 feet long by 15 feet wide, a single-storey building about eight feet high with rendered clay-brick walls two feet thick. The walls were more than enough to stop Taliban small-arms and shrapnel and I patted the clay in appreciation. It felt hard as nails. The few windows were fitted with intricate wooden lattices carved with Islamic geometric shapes. They were boarded up on one side to stop dust getting in.

I looked at the flat surface of the clay-rendered ceiling inside. There were holes in the roof here and there that the lads had covered with ponchos to keep the rain out. 'I wonder what's holding that lot up?' I thought. 'Whoever built it probably didn't have mortars or rockets landing on the roof as part of the brief.'

I kicked the worry aside and turned my attention to the deluxe mozzie net they had issued me with. Hoofin'. It was more like a two-man tent than a net. One compartment for my cot and another for all my admin. Cushty. By the end of the tour Marines would be packed into this one room so tight their cots would line both walls 18 inches apart with a two-foot walkway down the middle of the room. For now, it wasn't bad at all.

I didn't know any of the lads here and we hadn't even started to get to know one another when we trooped outside to be allocated to sangar watches and to meet the sangar commanders. I was pleased when I saw mine was Cpl Helsby because I knew him. We had been through training at Lympstone at the same time and served in Iraq together. I'd taken a year out in civvy street and re-enlisted since then, while Sean had carried on. He was a bit shorter than me at around 5ft 10in but he was mega-fit. He was from Manchester and had his brown hair shaved tight to his head.

The good thing about Sean was that he was a natural leader. He never had to raise his voice, lose his temper or bollock people to get things done. The lads just didn't want to let him down. Part of what he did was that he never passed shit downhill. If we messed up, we knew we had earned him a bollock-ing from the Troop Stripey or HQ, but he would never let you know about it. He could make you feel terrible just by a shake of the head, which let you know he was disappointed with you. He would seem perplexed that you had behaved like a dick-head when you were capable of much better. It was worse than copping a bollocking.

The other thing was his judgement. It seemed to be spot on all the time. I never had any worries about going on patrol with him, he made you feel safe. You felt that if the shit hit the fan Sean would be able to sort it out, do the right thing and get you out alive at least. In short, I would have followed him pretty much anywhere, and most of the lads felt the same.

Sean was the commander of Sangar Four and a couple of us had just been assigned to his section. 'Great,' I thought. 'Right next to that RPG-magnet of a gate.'

'Right, lads,' said Sean, laying out a map of the FOB. 'Sangar Four has the main arcs covering the approach to the gate. You've got Afghan National Army in the compound inside the perimeter on your left—'

There were groans.

'Less of that,' Sean went on. 'They've got a decent set of NCOs keeping them in line and they are not bad at present.'

'Except on Thursday afternoons?' someone said, and some of the lads laughed knowingly. This was the time each week when some of the Afghans liked to slope off, get stoned and enjoy other unspeakable practices.

'Never mind that,' added Sean. 'The fifty cal HMG is on the roof of their compound and manned by Bootnecks covering arcs to the south-west. Sangar Three is the other side of the gate on your right. You'll be in pairs during the night and on your own during the day on two-hour watches. It's hard graft but the sangars are key to the defence of the FOB. We've got to stay alert and keep a good watch. The boss will want to know about anything that moves out there. When the order comes to engage, we need to be on top of our drills and have the weapons systems in order.'

I noticed he said 'when' not 'if' we were ordered to engage and felt a buzz of excitement.

E Coy had four sangars to man around the clock between thirty-four men and that meant two hours on and three to five hours off, day and night.

Sean took us up to our sangar, a single layer of Hesco built in a square with a sandbagged roof, on top of a small hill next to the gate. The north and western sides were open, and these were our main arcs. Off to the north the 611 disappeared up to Sangin. To the west, the ground sloped steeply away into a green zone of fields and trees. The Helmand River wound its way down the valley running roughly parallel to the road. Directly to our west a village of one- and two-storey mud-walled buildings was built up along the riverbank. Apart from the odd motorbike, the village could have come straight out of the Bible.

To the south and east the sangar had smaller windows and we were not expected to fight from these. We would have to shoot across the base to do so, and that was a big no-no.

The watchtower arcs had been carefully laid out to cover every inch of ground around the FOB with roughly equal amounts of weaponry and firepower depending on the threat. There were no chairs. You stood to against the Hesco for the duration of your watch.

Some of the lads who had been at the FOB for a while told us horror stories about Afghans sneaking up and posting grenades over the gate at night. It was a weak point in the FOB's defence for sure. I had a think about it but the stories didn't bother me. I couldn't see anyone getting close to the FOB unless we wanted them to. If they tried to charge the gate with a car or truck bomb, the sangar GPMGs would take out the drivers in seconds. Or the .50-calibre heavy machine gun would melt the vehicle's engine block before it even got close. There was more than enough firepower to fend off a human wave of suicide bombers, and the Taliban didn't have enough manpower for that. Their only option, I reckoned, was to try sneaking up close for a surprise attack. But as long as the sentries stayed awake, there was no way that was ever going to work either.

Nah. There was no way any Taliban could get through that gate. I plodded back to my grot and chilled out.

'Zero. Sangar Four. Message. Over.'

'Sangar Four, this is Zero. Send. Over.'

'Three times suspicious pax approaching the main gate. One male carrying a package. One male waving a handkerchief. Over.'

'Roger that. Keep eyes on. Do not engage. Out.'

You could hear what was in the suspicious package from about 100 metres away. It was a baby, howling in pain.

The three adults made a pathetic sight, weeping

and wailing. They were obviously very distressed at the state the child was in. I cocked the GPMG and covered them as they approached the camp. It was obvious these blokes wanted help, but we were nervous. It could be a trick.

We got a terp up to the main gate to see what was going on. It was obvious that the baby had been badly hurt but it wasn't clear how. The terp babbled away in Pashto as the three men gestured pleadingly with their arms, then explained, 'They say the baby has been scalded very badly. It has pulled a pot of boiling water over itself by accident. They want us to help the baby, it is very badly injured.'

One of the men unwrapped part of the cloth bundle to show the poor little kid's burned body, red and blistered. It must have been in agony. The burns looked very bad.

I watched from the sangar as this infant screamed its head off a few metres away, clearly in massive amounts of pain. I didn't want to help. I thought it might be a trap and the possibility was making me think, 'Go away. Stop that screaming. Go home.'

In that moment, I realized how much Afghanistan was already affecting me without my even noticing, in just a few short weeks. A civvy would look at this situation and it would be a no-brainer: 'Poor kid. Get the medic down here to treat that baby quick time.' It's the only humane reaction. If you respond in any other way, how can you hope to win over the hearts and minds of local people? In any other country I'd've been thinking the exact same thing. But this was Afghanistan and we were living in a different reality. Out here, compassion might be a stupid and dangerous reaction. The Taliban would pour a pot of boiling water over a baby in a heartbeat if they thought it would get a suicide bomber inside our perimeter. If they could take out five or six of us it would be well worth it in their book. That's the way you had to think over there, because that's the way it was.

The Afghan man doing most of the talking was obviously the kid's father. I didn't understand one word of Pashto but I could tell he was pleading for his son's life. I softened up a bit. He seemed genuine. But we were still jumpy. The baby's howls, the adults weeping – it was a very tense situation. If the three of them were strapped up with explosives, we were in deep shit.

We opened the gate and thoroughly searched the men. We took them in and a couple of the lads escorted them to the sick bay where the medic treated the baby. He cleaned up the wounds, injected antibiotics and morphine, handed out dressings and antiseptic creams. The baby was in a bad way with first-degree burns covering most of its body. The medic's main concern was to ease its pain. He thought its chances of survival were not very good.

We covered the group as they left. I kept them in the sights of the GPMG all the way back down the hill until they disappeared into the village.

Looking back on it, I think they were genuine and I'm glad we did what we could to help. You've got to hope that the Taliban wouldn't think it was worth scalding a baby so horribly just to get inside the FOB. They couldn't want a plan of our accommodation and equipment within the perimeter badly enough to be that brutal, surely?

Whump.

The ground heaved. Clouds of dust drifted down from the mosque ceiling and chips of clay render fell off the walls and rattled on to the deck.

'What the f—'

'Incoming!' yelled Jurgen. 'The shelter, quick!'

I leapt off my cot, flapping like a novice, and piled on my body armour and helmet. 'Shit!' I was wearing flip-flops. I started putting on my boots.

'Rammers, c'mon!'

'Aw fuckit.'

I flapped my way out of the mosque and ran at full tilt ten yards across the compound into the shelter, a two-storey Hesco shack topped with railway sleepers piled up with sandbags on top. Marines were piling in.

'What the fuck was that?' I asked. 'A mortar?'

'Nah, Rammers. You can hear a mortar whistling towards you before it hits. That was a Chinese rocket I reckon. One-oh-seven millimetre. They don't make that much noise as they come in.'

'Sounded quite close.'

'Yeah it was, near the bogs. Let's hope nobody was turfing one out just then.'

I looked around the shelter. I was scared and trying not to show it. The Hesco would soak up a lot of damage, but a direct hit? I looked at the railway sleepers up top. We were sitting underneath tons and tons of sand and gravel. If it was brought down on top of us it would bury us alive. This was not the glamorous warfighting I'd come out here for. Sitting in a gloomy cave, no way to fight back, waiting for the sleepers to collapse in a ball of flame, shrapnel and rock. What was I doing here?

I got a grip on myself. 'There's nothing you can do about it, just chill out,' I told myself. 'The Taliban can't aim those rockets to save their lives. Be one in a million if they manage to hit us in here.' Slowly, I got over the shock and composed myself. We were all in it together and none of the other lads seemed to be bothered.

I listened to the others talking bollocks, winding each other up and cracking jokes as we sat shoulder to shoulder on benches lining the walls of the shelter.

We had to wait for a 'soak period' to pass and then the all-clear was given. 'Right lads, Op Wideawake, let's go,' ordered Sean.

It was dark. The rocket had come in about eight p.m., just after we'd finished our scran. It was a 107mm, just as Jurgen said. There had been no follow-up attacks but now we had to begin a sweep of the area around our compound to look for any unexploded mortar or rocket rounds, called blinds, that had come in.

We found the 107mm rocket tube lying about a metre behind the row of five thunderbox toilets. We checked each cubicle because anyone using them at the time could have been seriously injured. They were all empty. Good. No one wants to see anyone die like Elvis.

The lads seemed pretty chuffed with the rocket case. It was almost a metre long, all split up at the warhead end, and it made a good trophy. We had a two-burner gas ring on a trolley outside the mosque under the shade of a cam net where we could all hang out, make a wet and heat up water in a kettle to warm our foil bag ration packs. We hung it up there. Nice try, Terry, but not good enough.

The next morning we examined the impact site in daylight. The rocket had ploughed a five-metre-long gouge into the ground that was all blackened at one end where it had exploded, about 20 metres from the spot where my cot lay. It had narrowly missed the five wooden toilet cubicles and blown up. Nearby there was a section of corrugated iron that was held vertically off the ground between two posts. The metal sheet drained into a length of guttering that fed in turn into a pipe buried about three feet into the ground. This was our urinal, the corrugated iron serving as a splashback. It was peppered with shrapnel holes like a sieve.

I looked at the impact crater, then back to the urinal. Anyone stood there taking a piss when this came in would have been turned into pink mist. What a way to go.

4

There were Afghan males of fighting age moving up and down the 611 on foot, on mules, in Jingly trucks, you name it. None of them approached the base in daylight but we were pretty sure most of them were enemy anyway. Even if they did approach, there were strict rules about opening fire. Despite all the small-arms firepower on hand, we were very careful about engaging anyone near the base. We had to be extra sure that we were looking at hostile Taliban before HQ would even think about opening fire.

Most of the lads thought HQ were being a bit too picky. The way we saw it, it encouraged the Taliban knowing we were cautious about opening fire. It was frustrating because every lad in every sangar knew exactly what he was looking at, but HQ always seemed to come down on the side of caution.

The Officer Commanding the FOB was a Royal Marines Captain named Chris Jesson. FOB bosses were usually Majors but Captain Jesson was no ordinary officer. For a start, he'd joined the Marines as a Bootie in the eighties and been promoted to Warrant Officer Class 2, a serious non-commissioned rank. He then took it a stage further to become a Senior Corps Commissioned Officer and was promoted Lieutenant. He was now in his late thirties with twenty years' experience and knew the Corps backwards.

He was backed up by CSM Bob Toomey, a married man with two young children, who was about thirty-seven. Between the pair of them they had almost forty years' experience as Royal Marines and they commanded instant respect among the Bootnecks.

They were overseeing a FOB manned by forces of at least five different nations and seven or eight different military cap badges. The British contingent alone had Marines, Army, Royal Artillery and Gurkha Engineers. To cap it all the Brits were working to different Rules of Engagement from an American unit operating from the FOB. No wonder HQ were being careful about initiating contacts.

I could see that if we shot up an Afghan civvy instead of the Taliban it would be very bad news for us. An innocent man would be dead, his family would starve without him, and the village would be threaders for all time with us. Most of his male relatives would be duty bound to take up arms against us and months of patient work with the locals by previous units would be wasted.

But some of us still felt HQ were being too careful about who we engaged. If they called it wrong and we shot up a load of civvies it was their head on the block, fair one. But if you're just going to let the Taliban carry on as normal, you might as well go home.

I was standing on watch in Sangar Four at around 0300. It was a ridiculously dark night. Most nights there would be a bit of moon or starlight and you could see quite a bit with the naked eye. Not tonight: you could only just see your hand in front of your face. Fortunately we had a suite of vision aids to hand or we couldn't have seen a thing.

I was using a SOPHIE thermal imaging device, which is just like a pair of binoculars that uses heat to make an image instead of light. You see a black and white picture and the black bits are the hottest. The desert appeared in shades of grey and looked like the surface of the moon. I could clearly make out landmarks recognized from hours and hours spent on watch during daylight. A man standing in the desert would appear as a solid black silhouette on a light grey background, the natural heat of his body enough for the SOPHIE to produce a good image.

We stayed on sentry in two-hour watches. By day you were alone in the sangar but at night there were two of you, overlapping to allow a sentry change every hour.

I swept methodically across the desert ground in

silence from the western window of the sangar. You just got into a routine, checking all the ground from point-blank range out to about 1,000m, left to right across the arcs and back again. Doing it properly was a headache and some lads took the job more seriously than others. The level of threat kept me keen. There was every chance of the Taliban attacking the FOB at night and if they were about to try anything then I wanted to see it coming and get in on the contact.

Sweeping out to about 700m, I came up against some compound walls and a couple of buildings – the outskirts of the main village by the river. I was busy working out which buildings they were and trying to make them fit into the grid I had in my head. 'Ah, that's it,' I thought as they slotted into place in the imaginary map built up by daylight observation.

I checked out the rooftops and surrounding areas of each building then swept down a compound wall.

A sudden flicker of movement made me catch my breath. A shadow had ducked behind the wall at the end of it. Definite movement. 'Probably a dog,' I thought, but excitement was surging through me.

I kept the SOPHIE glued to the spot. I checked in the direction of the compound with the naked eye, but it was so black out there I couldn't see a thing. Through the SOPHIE it was another world. The unmistakable sight of a man's head and shoulders suddenly moved out from behind the compound wall and stepped into a ditch. He was carrying something long. He stooped and struck the ground with it.

'Jurg,' I hissed. 'Got a cheeky Taliban fucker digging in.'

I checked where he was on our grid. He was working the ground methodically with a tool. How he could see what he was doing I have no idea. He looked as if he was digging in an IED at a good spot, right where you would turn a corner to come around the wall – a natural pinch point. He had really picked the wrong night to do it. If he wasn't digging in an IED then he must be after a cache of weapons or some other contraband. There was a slight chance he was off his tits on opium and thought it was a good night for gardening, but I didn't think so.

I reported the sighting to Zero and they checked him out on the removercam.

'Sangar Four. Zero. Fire a high warning shot. Over.'

'Ah for fuck's sake, we should take him out,' I thought. 'What do they think he's doing, pruning his roses?'

'Roger that. Out.'

I could see exactly where he was and relayed the grid to Jurgen, who cocked the GPMG and fired a burst. A single red tracer round in the lead salvo zoomed over the Afghan's head and disappeared downrange. It was way above him but there could be no mistaking our message: 'We can see what you're doing, now piss off.'

The Afghan leapt up and ran behind the compound wall. 'Yeah, and stay there, mate,' I muttered.

I was threaders about it. What more evidence did they want?

I continued sweeping my arcs but returned every few seconds to the same spot. Five minutes later the Afghan was back digging away without a care in the world and I couldn't believe it.

'You're fucked now, mate,' I thought.

Again, the order came from HQ: 'Warning shot.'

Jurgen gave him another toot on the GPMG and he dived behind his wall again.

'Is he trying to wind us up or does he want to die?' I dripped.

Another five minutes and he was back again. What was he playing at? This happened three or four times in total and in the end HQ ordered us to cease fire and let him get on with it. 'Nothing suspicious,' they said.

'You what?' I thought. A bloke is prepared to repeatedly risk his life under fire to do gardening at three a.m. on a night so black he must have been working by sense of touch? If we were happy to let the local Taliban plant IEDs on our doorstep then it was HQ's fault, not ours. At least they were taking responsibility for the call. What did I know? I was just a Bootneck. There was more than one reason

HQ compounds were full of people on higher pay grades than me.

I carried on dripping like that for most of the watch and stomped off to bed in disgust. It was Taliban 1 HQ 0 in my book.

Jurgen and me were leaning on the perimeter one morning watching the 611.

''Ere, Rammers, I don't fookin' believe it. Look who's coming down the hill.'

Jurgen was itching to get into a contact. We both were. Just to relieve the boredom if nothing else.

'The orange pick-up truck again,' I said. 'They're taking the piss.'

It was loaded with fighting-age Afghan males and trundling down the road from Sangin town. You couldn't see a single weapon between them.

'They need taking out, Rammers. Look at them, you can see they're enemy from here.'

'No doubt about it, mate.'

We heard the Bowman radio in Sangar Four behind us crackle and braced ourselves for the long burst of automatic fire from the sentry on the GPMG we hoped would follow.

Nothing doing.

'Aw bollocks,' said Jurgen in disgust. 'Look, Rammers, they've even got scarves pulled up over their faces so we can't identify them.'

'It's very dusty on the road though.'

'My arse. They're Taliban and we should catch 'em up while we've got the chance.'

Jurgen stomped back to his grot.

The orange pick-up used to pass the FOB on the 611 every other day. They were careful never to have anything suspicious in the back of the pick-up or on display. All the lads agreed with Jurgen: they were 100 per cent Taliban and we should take them out while we had the chance. Every time they drove by we asked for permission to engage and it was refused.

We were on the lookout for them one morning when the message came through from HQ. At last, the men in the orange pick-up had been positively identified as Tier One Taliban, hardcore fighters who would never be persuaded to chuck it in, and we were to engage them on sight.

Fair enough. Our GPMGs would shred that pick-up in a few minutes at this range. Except, guess what? The minute the order was given, the truck disappeared. It was like they knew about it and stayed away on purpose. Maybe they were listening in on our personal role radios and someone had said a bit too much. I doubt it though. The PRR is a short-range VHF radio for comms between sections on the ground and we were all careful and disciplined using it. The main battlefield radios were digitally encrypted and secure as far as we could tell. Maybe they had another way of getting information about our intent. Or maybe they just ran out of petrol that day.

It was too much of a coincidence for me. I don't know how they did it, but they must have known that if they came by the FOB that day they were dead men.

Four days later the truck bimbled over the hill to the north and came down the 611 towards us. I grabbed the GPMG and shouted a warning to the others. I cocked the weapon and lined up the iron sight just ahead of the cab of the vehicle, leading it nicely as it came down the road. The pick-up was moving at a steady speed and was a few seconds from being turned into a truck-sized cheesegrater as far as I was concerned.

HQ came straight on the radio: 'Do not engage. Repeat, do not engage.'

I made the weapon safe and wasn't shy in having a little rant about it.

The truck came on. The cab was packed. There were a few young Afghan men inside, Taliban without a doubt. But they had a load of little kids with them and were blatantly using them as a human shield. I could have shot up a truckload of children had it not been for the spot-on call from Zero. No one would want that on their conscience. I breathed a sigh of relief and said a silent thank you to HQ for the call.

HQ 1 Taliban 1.

A couple of weeks later we were on watch around midnight. It was dead quiet when the Bowman radio crackled with HQ giving us a grid reference and range to the north-west. The order couldn't have been clearer: 'Hostiles, engage.'

It was the first we knew about it. Game on.

I was straight on the GPMG, cocked it and shattered the night's silence with a short burst, fired blind at the grid position given by HQ. Another Marine was in the sangar, watching through the SOPHIE, and he directed my fire. 'Come left and you're on. There they are, about eight hostiles trying to come up behind a tractor in a field at about seven hundred metres. They're all going firm or in cover behind the tractor.'

The GPMG leapt as I let go another burst.

'You're just short, Rammers, come up a bit.'

Another short burst.

'You're on. Go for it, mate.'

The machine gun bucked and kicked in my hands as I let go in a long burst. Tracer smashed into the enemy positions around the tractor and hit the machine itself, deflecting high into the night sky. Sangars Three and Five knew immediately from the long burst that I was on and piled in with everything they'd got. The enemy were suddenly lit up as an illumination round from a 51mm mortar soared into the sky and turned night into day. Other sangars added to the light show, firing handheld Schermuly illumination flares into the night. The noise was deafening as the FOB erupted, red tracer flashing into the enemy positions. The high-pitched rip of a Minimi was backed by the *thunk thunk* of the .50-calibre heavy machine gun giving it some.

It was like a battle out of *Star Wars*.

The other GPMG gunner in my sangar began alternating fire with me to keep the barrels cool. As my burst ended, he took over malleting the Taliban; as soon as he stopped, I opened up again. By this point the rest of the lads were lined up on the perimeter wall firing whatever weapons they had to hand. The Marine on the SOPHIE sight directed us whenever the illum packed up, giving us a running commentary. We were hitting the Taliban hard. They were dragging their wounded into a ditch. The tractor was taking so many hits it was practically sawn in half.

The spent shells and link were piling up around my boots as hundreds and hundreds of 7.62mm rounds went downrange with no order to cease fire. Weeks of frustration at being held back by HQ caution came pouring out of me and I whooped in excitement as the GPMG chewed up the link and blasted the enemy.

We kept firing in alternate bursts, but my bursts were too long. The GPMG was only just usable, which meant the rounds would be drifting off target all over the shop. It was good enough – we were using the guns as area weapons not aiming at individuals and the combined firepower was having a devastating effect – but it wasn't pretty shooting.

'Fuck me, Rammers, they're evacuating the wounded in wheelbarrows.'

The Taliban were loading up their casualties in a ditch by the tractor and bugging out as fast as they could push. They hadn't got closer than 700 metres to the FOB. They couldn't touch us.

The ceasefire came and we took a breather. The firefight had lasted about fifteen minutes. I had fired more than eight hundred rounds of ammunition from my GPMG alone – a ridiculous amount. Usually I would have been more cautious but because there were seven or eight of them we just let rip.

We had given the Taliban a beating. Most of the group had been hit and seriously wounded if not killed.

I hadn't seen a single one of them before the contact. If they'd opened up on the FOB it would have come as a nasty surprise to me. There were sharp eyes at work on the other end of the remover-cam in the HQ compound.

Final score: HQ 2 Taliban 1.

5

Two of the lads lifted the main gate to one side and we waited while the first section of men, led by Sgt Dinger Bell, walked through the Hesco chicane behind the gate and out of the FOB. We let them get about 100 metres ahead of us.

We were going out on patrol to dominate the ground and show the local farmers exactly who was in charge around here. We could come and go as we pleased because the Taliban couldn't touch us. The Afghans would side with the people they thought were winning, so it was important to make a show of strength.

'OK, lads, move out,' said Sean Helsby.

We followed Dinger's section out of the base and down the hill. As soon as we were out of the gate we fanned out across the terrain, dispersing ourselves with the section spread out over about 40 metres. The staggered formation made it as difficult as possible for the Taliban to concentrate fire on more

95

than one of us at a time. If someone in the section stepped on a landmine or IED, as few of us as possible would catch it up in the blast.

The two patrols moved down the hill towards the village.

It was a clear, sunny day, mid-morning and cool, but I was redders already. I'd loaded myself up with a ridiculous amount of weaponry and ammunition and the sweat was soaking into my T-shirt beneath my body armour. If we got into a contact it would have to turn into a major battle before I ran out of ammo.

Lots of the lads took the piss out of me for taking so much out on patrol, but I didn't understand why. If having too much ammo became a problem you could dump it, preferably by expending it in the direction of the Taliban. Running out of ammo in a contact was a problem that wouldn't be easy to fix. It was something I was never going to allow to happen to me. Typically, I would load up with about 30 kilos of kit and that made me heavier than most of the lads on patrol, but if we got into any sort of a firefight they would be thanking me for it. That was the way I looked at it. Carrying the extra load was good phys anyway. I'd also attached a UGL to my personal weapon, so as well as a few hundred rounds for the rifle I was carrying a variety of 40mm grenades, high explosive and smoke.

It was brilliant to get out of the FOB. It was a real buzz in the sangars during the contacts but they were usually over in a few minutes. The reality, when it came down to it, was hour after boring hour of sangar duty when nothing at all happened. Even if we spotted something suspicious, chances were HQ would stop us from blowing it away. After all those hours cooped up there was a lot of pent-up tension and bucketloads of adrenalin waiting to be released.

I was itching to get into a scrap just to let off steam. A mid-morning dust-up against an enemy prepared to stand and fight was what we were all looking for. There was definite competition between some of us to see who could do the best in a contact. It would put all our training to the test and give us something to tell the grandkids about.

Although some of us had only known each other for a couple of weeks, the lads were all confident in our ability in a firefight. We had all been through the same training. It had turned us into some of the fittest infantry in the world. We had the equipment and the skills. Now bring on the bad guys.

The biggest fear for all of us was landmines or IEDs. In a contact you can fight back, use your superior skills, communications and firepower to win. There was no way to fight an IED. All you could do was try to detect it before it detected you.

The gravel crunched under our boots as we scanned the ground ahead for disturbance or signs of suspicious activity. The lead section was approaching a narrow footbridge across the river giving access to the village and the fields beyond. The district around the FOB was infested with Taliban and this was an ideal spot for an IED or an ambush. Any patrol into the southern end of the village would have to use this bridge to cross the river, unless they fancied a dip in the water. The local Taliban commanders must have had it right at the top of their to-do list, to dig in a load of anti-personnel IEDs right there. The sangar lookouts and HQ removercam kept this point under surveillance 24/7 for that reason.

HQ was certain no Taliban had dug anything in at the bridge and that it was clear for us to cross. But the blokes back in the FOB didn't have to test the theory with their own boots.

As the lead section approached the crossing, we went firm on the hillside about 100 metres behind to cover them. Dinger sent two lads to approach the bridge and take up fire positions either side of it. Two more went across in a pair and went firm on the far side.

All quiet.

The rest of the section yomped across and went firm covering arcs into the village. The first pair who'd gone up to the bridge had been leap-frogged and now brought up the rear of the section.

We watched it all and listened in on our PRRs.

If Dinger wanted to talk to HQ he would have to get on to the main battlefield radio and use a formal Voice Procedure to get his message across. HQ was

Zero and the Officer Commanding the FOB, Captain Chris Jesson, was Zero Alpha. If Dinger wanted to talk to either he would use his section's callsign, Romeo Two Zero, to identify himself. Our section, led by Sean, was Romeo One Zero, and the same rules applied.

The leaders of the two patrols could talk to each other via the short-range PRRs and were much more informal on this loop. Zero Alpha on the PRRs was simply 'the Boss'. The two patrol leaders on the ground would talk to each other almost as if they were having a casual chat:

'Hello, Sean. Dinger, over.'

'Dinger, Sean. Go ahead, mate.'

'All OK in the village. People out and about as usual. On you come, out.'

Our section walked up to the bridge and repeated the crossing process, working in pairs so that every member of the patrol was covered as they moved.

Dinger and his section emerged from their fire positions and continued straight on, out into the fields beyond the village before turning right and heading north. They fanned out into an arrowhead formation as they moved through the fields. It was the correct formation for advancing across open ground. If any of the men were shot at, or spotted armed Taliban, they would shout a brief contact warning and the whole section would hit the deck. Without waiting for an order the lads would then all crawl forward on their bellies to form a baseline facing the enemy. Half the section would engage the enemy while the other half would make an attempt to outflank them.

That was the theory. It went like clockwork in training.

We covered them part of the way and then began our own patrol up towards the main street of the village. We stopped just outside, split into two fire teams of four, Charlie and Delta, and checked our perimeter at five metres, looking for any disturbed ground, command wires, or anything suspicious. Once clear, two lads from each team went forward to check the perimeter at 20 metres, covered by the pairs of men remaining in fire positions. It's called 'five and twenties' and a good section does it all the time without thinking about it.

Our eyes were everywhere. The situation could change in a heartbeat. Taliban were in and out of this village all the time and we knew it. I expected a bloke with an RPG or AK47 to pop his head round every corner and have a crack at us any minute. It was tense on ground but also exciting to think enemy might be close by and we might get a crack at them. We were all on the alert for movement or clues that there might be trouble ahead.

It was hot and dusty and the lads were on edge. I took a slurp on the feeding tube of the Camelbak water carrier on my back. I was loving being out of the FOB. Just doing something different made my day.

The village's main street was hard-packed clay and grit bordered on both sides by one- and two-storey clay-brick buildings for about 200 metres. We walked up the street about five metres apart. Ideally we would have been in a staggered formation, but the street was too narrow so we just went through as a snake of men. We would have liked to spread out more but there was an ECM bubble around us and we all wanted to stay inside it. This was an electronic jamming signal emitted from a pack carried by men in the patrol. It helped to stop IEDs being triggered by remote control.

We continued up the street. The village was quiet but not deserted. I checked across the flat rooftops around us, down alleys to our left and right, into compound doorways and behind walls. We were checking every possible area of cover for the enemy. All of us were also scanning the ground around us for the little piles of rocks the Taliban leave for each other to indicate where IEDs are buried.

We had been lectured to fuck by the intelligence officers on the IED threat and what motivated the enemy. They told us that the Afghan fighter has a genuine terror of landmines. His idea of a proper war is to charge into battle and come out of it either a dead legend or loaded down with his enemy's treasure, women and weapons. Then he can gob off about his fearless prowess in combat for all time. Landmines are a total nightmare anywhere, but in an Afghan rural shithole where a bloke who can't fight will starve, losing limbs is a fate worse than death. Afghan Taliban preferred to stand and fight against the UK Task Force in Helmand rather than sneak about laying mines, which they thought was a cowardly way to fight your enemy. You've got to have some respect for that.

It was only when they had been repeatedly hammered in open battle that professional insurgents moved in to replace the Afghan Taliban killed in action. Then the IED started to become the insurgents' main armament. Every time you saw a few stones heaped on one another it made you sweat. Sometimes on patrol you could see poorly hidden or exposed command wires used to trigger a device and you could do something about it. But if devices were well hidden there wasn't a lot you could do but try to step into the footprints of the man in front.

The fact that there were a few people about in the village was a good sign for us. If the place was deserted, it would have been a strong combat indicator. If you were about to walk into an ambush, a newly placed IED or any other shit, the locals wanted nothing to do with it and disappeared.

I checked around a corner of the main street and caught my breath. An old Afghan geezer was rounding up his family, shooing them indoors. Green dish-dash, huge turban, big hooked nose and bushy grey-black beard.

I checked him out – no weapon. A local resident,

or Taliban taking a break? Probably both, I reckoned. I nodded to him and smiled. He just gave me a filthy look and disappeared inside, slamming the door. Nice. The old boys hated having a foreign army on their doorstep even if they were nothing to do with the Taliban.

The intelligence brief told us that some of the rural folk actively hated the Taliban. The insurgents descended on the villages demanding food and supplies and took whatever they wanted. The Afghans' notion of hospitality is as important to them as their passion for vengeance. If a stranger showed up at their home, some Afghans would slaughter their last animal and starve through the winter rather than live with the shame of failing in this duty. On the other hand, if a starving farmer accepted help from British troops he could expect to be brutally punished by the Taliban.

The Paras patrolled through one village in Helmand that was short of containers to store water. The village elders explained that if they took anything off the Brits the Taliban would find out and kill them. But there was a way round it: no one could object if the villagers collected rubbish and put it to good use. From then on, the Paras became the world's biggest litter louts every time they approached the village. Empty water bottles and catering containers showered out of their wagons into the desert a short walk from the village itself. The villagers gathered it all up, and it got them onside.

This made me laugh. Who could have known that in advance? You can't imagine a military planner sitting there going, 'Lads, lads, I've got the secret to hearts and minds. Just give the villagers our rubbish, that'll sort them out.'

This village was different. A few old water bottles weren't going to make any difference. We reckoned just about every Afghan male of fighting age around here was either hardcore Taliban or Tier Two – supporters of the Taliban who helped them out when required.

We carried on up the street. I checked through a compound doorway and caught sight of a young woman, hijab over her face, scurrying into a house, not wanting us to set eyes on her. Plenty of women of all ages lived in the village but you rarely saw any of them. A few kids hung around watching us, smiling away and jabbering at us in Pashto. This was a good thing. If the locals had any sort of serious shit planned for us the kids wouldn't have been there.

We had two interpreters with us and they seemed to be making all the right noises, saying hello and explaining what we were doing. A little gap-toothed kid aged about seven came towards me wearing a dirty brown shalwar kameez (knee-length shirt and matching leggings), his bare feet black with filth. A beautifully embroidered skull cap was sitting on top of his head. 'Hello, chocklat? Chocklat, hello?' he squawked.

'Don't give them anything, Rammers, you'll start a riot, mate.' It was Helsby's voice on the PRR.

'Roger that.'

'Keep watching your arcs, lads, let's keep it moving.'

I smiled back at the kids but they were wasting their time: we had no treats for them.

We carried on, Dinger's section matching our pace through the fields on our left flank outside the village, hammering home the point of the patrol: to show the locals we could come right up their high street and hang around for as long as we wanted. We were the strongest force around. We were polite and we took nothing. We could take on the Taliban anywhere they wanted and win convincingly. We were strong enough to protect the villagers from Taliban reprisals if they did start to lean our way. They'd better not think for a second about stashing weapons for the enemy down this high street because we could come down here any time we liked. We were dominating the ground, not just sitting back in the FOB waiting to cop a load of indirect fire.

I passed a miserable-looking donkey in a ten-foot-square mud enclosure munching on a mound of straw. It stared at me balefully, checking me out, then dismissed me with a flick of its ears and went back to its lunch.

Not a single window in the village was fitted with glass. The walls were about two feet thick.

Everywhere was clay brick covered in a render of mud mixed with straw. The bricks were made from local clay and fired in kilns. After a couple of hundred years being blasted by the sun every day and cooled overnight they had baked off to a point where they were as hard as rock. The result was buildings with massive strength under compression. I gave a wall a thump. It was like concrete. Excellent kit to take cover from small-arms or even RPGs. You had to hand it to the locals, to erect buildings as strong as this out of mud seemed quite an achievement.

Only a few crops were grown around the Helmand River, a bit of barley, wheat and corn for the locals and their animals to eat. Otherwise it was all opium poppy. Out here, a knackered old pushbike was a status symbol and a motorbike made you a big player. We could help these people, but the Taliban would rather choke. They wanted them living in the dark ages for a reason, so there was nothing to do but grow poppy and fight.

We weren't there to speak with the village elders or call on anyone. We wouldn't have been invited in to be fair. But the Afghan interpreters seemed fairly relaxed – another good sign. They picked up the mood and were tuned in to the locals much better than we could ever be. It looked as if the Taliban weren't going to come out to play today.

We carried on until we emerged at the northern end of the village, then recrossed the river on a two-foot-wide pipe running from bank to bank. It reminded me of the scene from *Dirty Dancing* when Patrick Swayze is leaping about on a log to improve his balance. Except this was a bunch of big hairy Bootnecks – about as graceful as Bambi on ice. Much to my surprise, none of the lads fell in.

We headed on to the 611 and marched south in staggered formation, back towards the FOB, with the village across the river to our right and rolling desert hills to our left. The section was in two zig-zag lines on either side of the road, each Marine taking a position 45 degrees off the man in front. The guys at the rear spent about 90 per cent of their time walking backwards. The formation allowed us to cover a 360-degree arc as we walked. Any contact would result in a warning shout and we would all engage and then outflank the enemy.

Both sections were nearly back at the FOB when the battlefield radio crackled into life: 'Romeo Two Zero. This is Zero. Message. Over.'

There was a few seconds' delay while Dinger responded: 'Hello Zero, Romeo Two Zero. Send. Over.'

'One times suspicious pax digging in on the 611 north of your position.' They indicated an area about 400 metres to our rear.

I couldn't believe it. The cheeky bastard must have waited until we passed by, then popped out and started digging an IED right into our footprints in broad daylight within sight of the FOB.

We turned around and marched quick time back up the road, going firm in the ditches and behind cover on either side of the road as we saw our man. He hadn't noticed us and sure enough was going hard at it with a spade right by the side of the road. Half the section had walked across the spot he was digging no more than twenty minutes ago. He must have been thinking we were bound to come back and was setting an explosive to catch us up next time round. He hadn't banked on us being back this quickly though.

I levelled my rifle at him, placing the tip of the SUSAT's needle over his stomach, and pressed the safety catch to off. Anyone not covering the arcs required for all-round defence did the same. This bloke was taking the piss and was about to pay for it big-style. There was enough weaponry pointing at this Afghan to vaporize him but he just carried on digging right under our noses. He was either very brave, very stupid or very stoned.

He had a handful of seconds left on this earth as far as I was concerned.

The PRR crackled. 'Lads, Dinger. Hold your fire. This ain't right. Me and the terp'll go and have a word with him. Out.'

Dinger approached the Afghan, who looked up and cracked a horrible toothless smile through a black, wiry beard. In a minute he was back on the net: 'Relax, lads, he's just digging in a power cable. He says he's got to dig a trench right across the road.'

I clicked the safety back on and breathed out slowly. What a wind-up. The old sod will probably never know how close he came to having his life ended that day.

Back at the FOB I grabbed a couple of hours in my grot and then spent another couple of hours alone in Sangar Four on watch through the afternoon.

Nothing moved.

Our patrol had shown the locals who was the boss and the little village looked at peace, an innocent rural community that had not changed its idyllic way of life for a thousand years.

Yeah, right.

In our compound there was one building reserved as a TV room with a DVD player and a pile of films. After handing over to my relief I headed straight there for a bit of down time. *Blackadder* and *Alan Partridge* DVDs were included in our welfare package, but our mates sent us hundreds of movies so there was no shortage of choice.

There was a Marine in there already watching the TV, Stu Green.

'Aw, Stu, you're not still watching *Alan Partridge* are you, mate?'

'What else is worth my time out here, Rammers?'

'What about a bit of *Blackadder*? Come on, mate, it's dead funny. Or there are some great movies we've not had a look at yet.'

There was no way I was winning this one. Stu was

addicted to *Alan Partridge*. He would let us all go off for the evening meal to make sure he got it on the DVD player. It would take incoming mortars to move him now.

I headed back to my grot and decided to grab a quick shower. I peeled off my desert rig and boots, grabbed my towel and washbag and headed off in my flip-flops.

'They'll be freezing by now, Rammers, you're off your nut,' yelled Baggsy, one of the few Marines in the FOB I'd known for years as he used to be in Motor Troop, and he wasn't wrong. The showers were black rubberized bags that soaked up the sun's rays to warm the water but the day was cooling off rapidly. We had a load of galvanized dustbins with kerosene heaters attached underneath for warming water. It would boil if you left the water in them long enough. You filled the solar shower bags with hot water from the bins, but I couldn't be arsed to wait. A quick splash and dash to get the grime off would do me.

The shower stalls were surrounded by a Hesco but there was no blast protection overhead. That and the cold water meant I was going to shower in the spirit of Vinnie Jones's movie title: *Gone in 60 Seconds*.

I got dressed and wandered outside into the compound. It was a nice evening, cool but not too cold. The sun was just going down behind the Helmand River. The clay render of the houses took on a honeyed colour as light from the sinking sun struck it. The green zone of cultivated land near the river looked genuinely beautiful. 'It could be a fantastic place,' I thought. I was feeling mellow and chilled out as darkness fell.

'Rammers, get down here,' hissed Sean Helsby.

I joined a group of Marines he was briefing in an urgent whisper.

'HQ have ordered a silent stand-to and triple manning of the sangars. Get all your kit, get your weapons systems up and get the GPMGs made ready. Once you're at your posts, no unnecessary movement outside your hard cover.'

Other Bootnecks were filing past us silently carrying weapons and ammo towards sangars that were only used in battle. There were no shouts of 'Stand to!' and no whistles. Something big was brewing and we were getting ready to hit it with everything we had.

I ran towards Sangar Four buzzing with excitement when out of nowhere, *whoosh*! Something making a noise like a truck dumping its air brake flew straight over my head, trailing smoke. Jurgen was in the middle of the FOB, driving down the hill from the HQ compound in a Pinzgauer truck. The smoke trail was arrowing straight for him.

It was an RPG-7 rocket-propelled grenade, and it smashed into the ground a couple of metres in front of Jurgen's wagon, exploding with a shattering bang.

'Shit that was close. Is he OK?'

The Pinzgauer lurched to the right but had missed the impact point of the RPG. For a second I thought Jurgen was going to roll the vehicle but he just floored the accelerator and roared through the smoke of the explosion, bouncing over the small crater it had made. He crunched to a halt outside our compound, ran inside without a scratch on him and emerged a few seconds later in helmet and body armour, carrying his 51mm mortar and legging it for the mortar pit behind Sangar Seven.

As I approached Sangar Four, all hell was breaking loose. The crackle of multiple small-arms fire opened up from outside the perimeter. It sounded very close. At the exact same instant the GPMG in Sangar Seven let rip: *brrraaam*. The gunners overlooking the southern approach to the FOB were hitting something with everything they'd got. They started alternating fire, trying to put down a constant maximum of rounds without melting the barrels.

'Yes, let's get some in!' I was excited and ready for a fight. I'd not been in a contact where the Taliban used RPGs before. This must be a planned attack, and that was serious.

My blood was up, but within a few seconds I was gutted. It was now properly dark but I couldn't see Sangar Seven's tracer rounds in flight or where they were impacting. The attack was developing from an area we couldn't see from our sangar. We couldn't just down tools and run along the perimeter to join in, we had our own arcs to cover and had to stay put in case an attack developed in front of us. With RPGs flying about, the order to stay in hard cover had to be obeyed.

It was mega-frustrating.

Whoosh. Another RPG roared overhead and smashed into the ground a few metres from the doorway to Sangar Three, clattering the sandbagged watchtower with shrapnel. I winced. 'Anyone coming out of that sangar then would have caught up an RPG in the chest,' I thought to myself with a shiver. Two more RPGs hissed over the camp perimeter and exploded harmlessly in the rock shingle of the desert floor.

'Come on, lads, fucking smash 'em! If we don't stop these quick time they're going to get lucky with one of these grenades.'

The RPG is the Taliban's favourite weapon after the AK47 assault rifle. It's an anti-tank grenade based on the American World War Two bazooka. It fires a 93mm high-explosive round that explodes either on contact or in an airburst a few metres off the deck. It was designed by the Soviets in the sixties and has been used worldwide ever since. As a piece of kit it is cheap and simple. Guerrilla forces in Somalia used them to shoot down two American UH60 Black Hawk helicopters in 1993. They hid in alleyways and aimed for the tail rotors as the heavy-lift helos flew over Mogadishu at rooftop level. That battle was made world famous by the book and movie *Black Hawk Down* and showed what clever use of the RPG could achieve.

It is a stupidly inaccurate weapon at anything more than 200 metres but the Taliban love it and don't care. It's a big round, and if it's coming your way it's going to put your head down and do damage wherever it lands. I heard a totally gen dit about a lad from Juliet Company of 42 Commando who saw one coming straight for him in a big contact near Gereshk, a few miles upriver from the capital Lashkar Gah, about ten months before my tour. He could see the incoming round clearly, a black dot about the size of a tennis ball surrounded by an incandescent halo from its rocket motor. He described it as looking like a mini-eclipse. He realized that meant it was coming straight for him at about 500 miles an hour and he had fractions of a second to live. He had no time to run for his life, the round had his name on it. With nothing else to do, his gut reaction was to leap straight up into the air. In mid-jump, the RPG hit the muddy ground underneath his feet, bounced about 30 metres to his rear and exploded. He didn't get a scratch.

It is the closest shave I have ever heard about. He is one very jammy Bootneck and has gone down in Corps history as the bloke who hurdled an incoming RPG. His mates loved the fact that he was one of the shortest Booties in the company.

A Schermuly flare sailed 300 feet up into the night

sky, casting a flickering half-light over the ground south of Sangar Seven. We heard on the battlefield radios that there were an estimated thirty Taliban attacking the FOB from a position we called Dicker's Walk, a ruined compound that had been bombed to rubble in a previous tour, about 300 metres from the perimeter. Every spare Bootie was in the sangars putting down rounds with their rifles. Tracer streamed out of Sangar Seven as its gunners hammered the enemy.

I was trying to think up some excuse for getting involved in the action when there was a blinding flash and instantaneous thunderclap. An RPG round had smashed into Sangar Seven and engulfed it in a ball of fire.

The watchtower was silhouetted in flame for a split second, then went dark. My teeth clenched hard, waiting for the secondary explosion that would blow the two lads and their tower into a million bits. They had as much ammunition in there as we did. It didn't come, but there were anxious seconds as we waited for HQ to raise the tower. The lads answered in the best way possible, with a long double burst from the GPMGs. Thank fuck for that.

The lads inside had been knocked about by the blast wave but were otherwise unhurt. The shrapnel from the round had been soaked up by the Hesco and sandbagging. The RPG had come within a couple of feet of flying straight in through the sangar window. If that had happened, at least two men would have been killed.

It turned out the Sangar Seven gunners had pulled off an incredible shot. They'd started firing on to a grid ref given to them by HQ without using the night vision sights. One of the GPMGs opened up with a twenty-round burst at a range of 330 metres to suppress the enemy position. The first tracer round was seen smashing into a low wall by Dicker's Walk at the exact instant a Taliban popped his head up. The recoil from the burst forced the gunner's aim up slightly and the last rounds of the burst smashed into the enemy fighter's forehead, killing him instantly.

A headshot on fully automatic at 330 metres in the dark? It was a ridiculous piece of shooting.

Jurgen, meanwhile, was a busy little bastard in his mortar pit. The sangar crew were yelling for him to get rounds from the 51 on to Dicker's Walk quick time. He also had a direct link to FOB HQ via a Bowman battlefield radio. Everyone was calling in ranges and bearings to him as he set up and yelling at him to hurry up. We had no other heavy weapons at the FOB that could be brought to bear and no light gun battery in the rear to call 105mm shells down on the enemy. Jurgen was the artillery for the moment. The clay-brick walls of Dicker's Walk were standing up to everything else the lads pounded them with.

It was horrible standing there in my sangar,

unable to join in the fight, just waiting for the Taliban to get themselves sorted and start lobbing mortars or RPGs our way. 'Hurry up,' I thought. 'Sort them out before they open up on us with something heavier.'

The mortar has a spirit-level-type bubble attached to it. There are markings alongside this bubble indicating ranges in 100-metre increments. The longer the range, the shallower the angle to hold the mortar at. There is a canvas sleeve around the tube that you grip in order to aim it, which prevents the operator from burning his hand off every time he fires. Getting rounds down on target is blatantly a knack rather than a science.

Jurgen yanked a pin from the nosecone of a shell to arm the warhead and dropped the round down the muzzle. He paused to hold the tube carefully at the desired angle and bearing, then pulled a cord to fire. There was the sharp crack of an explosion and the high-explosive shell soared up in an arc. I heard a crackling thump as it detonated 300 metres away, boiling the ground with shrapnel around the enemy position.

Jurgen loved being in a contact more than any Marine I knew. He was a true Bootneck through and through. He knew Dicker's Walk well. We'd all patrolled through it and we had panoramic photographs of the landscape pinned up in our compound identifying the local landmarks and ranges from the FOB. He knew what he was aiming at and where it was, but all he had to go on for accuracy was a range and bearing.

He tugged the firing cord again and another mortar round sailed into the air with a sharp crack. Before it had even impacted, Jurgen had another round in the tube. HQ saw the fall of shot. Captain Jesson was straight on to the Bowman: 'Drop fifty metres and you're on, Jurgen.' He'd barely finished giving the order before Jurgen had the shot away. It exploded roughly on target and then he just went for it, firing for effect. The mortar barked and leapt, spitting round after round downrange every four or five seconds as Jurgen armed the warheads and rammed the shells down the tube. It seemed he was determined to spunk every round in his possession before HQ ordered a ceasefire. The target area crackled and boiled under Jurgen's bombardment. I imagined the Taliban running around flapping under the firestorm, wishing they'd stayed at home.

It was a hoofin' effort, interrupted only by requests for illumination rounds by other forces in the FOB. After five minutes Jurgen had fired almost sixty rounds. It was an extreme rate of fire and he almost melted the mortar tube. He said afterwards he was a bit worried he'd get a bollocking for safety reasons. He didn't have anything to worry about. HQ was over the moon with him.

They were watching on the removercam and saw a couple of the Taliban bugging out from Dicker's Walk, taking their weapons with them. They gave

Jurgen a range and bearing on a Taliban fighter legging it across a field. Jurgen yanked the cord and his mortar round exploded about 50 metres away from the running man. HQ corrected his range and Jurgen let rip again. The 51mm round seemed to hit the Taliban on the head and vaporized him instantly. It was a ridiculously brilliant shot on a moving target about 400 metres away.

Meanwhile, tracer flashed back and forth across the desert between the FOB and Dicker's Walk as both sides exchanged small-arms fire at a ferocious rate. We were about an hour into the contact and we just couldn't winkle the tough little bastards out. The .50-cal heavy machine gun on top of the ANA compound would have been like a demolition tool at this range, but it couldn't be brought to bear as Dicker's Walk was out of its arc. If you moved the .50 you'd leave a big gap in the defence of the FOB. Light mortar and UGL rounds were keeping the Taliban's heads down but not doing enough damage to make all of them withdraw.

We didn't have enough blokes to put together a fighting patrol to get out and flank them and we didn't have the heavy weapons to pound them into submission.

Between ten and fifteen RPG rounds had hit the FOB. We'd been lucky. The hits on Sangars Seven and Three hurt no one. The only damage done to the FOB so far was a severed telephone cable and our shower block, blasted by shrapnel from an RPG airburst directly above. I'd been in there a couple of hours earlier but they were empty now and no one was hurt. If we let them carry on like this it would be only a matter of time before the Taliban got lucky and did serious damage to kit or people.

As we fought the Taliban, there was a massive British, US and Afghan Army attack going down about 40km north-east of us at the town of Musa Qala. The Taliban had occupied the place and were being driven out in a big battle, codenamed Operation Mar Karadad. The Americans had committed an entire Combat Air Brigade to the fight, and as a result every air asset you could imagine was circling the battlefield, just a few minutes' flying time away from us.

The Americans had an infantry unit based in the FOB who went out on their own missions, not usually having much to do with us. They were watching closely as the contact developed, and eventually got on the radio. A few minutes later we heard in the distance the droning roar of a multi-engined turbo-prop aircraft. It got louder and began circling the FOB, quite a way off.

It was a US Spectre gunship, originally designed during the Vietnam war, a truly awesome aircraft to have on your side. It was thundering overhead with a noise that suited the Americans' nickname for the plane: Spooky. If it was coming for me, just the sound of its engines would make me shit my pants and bug out. The Spectre is a Hercules C130 transport kitted out with the best surveillance optics, radars and thermal imaging equipment known to man. Sticking out of the side of it under the port wing is a dirty great 105mm howitzer. Alongside that is a massive five-barrel 'Equalizer' Gatling gun that can put down four thousand rounds of 25mm cannon shells a minute. You never forget the sound one of those things makes when it lets rip. It's not like a gun at all: it makes a deep, moaning roar, like a jet turbine at full whack with a handful of nuts and bolts rattling round inside it. The final weapon on board is a 40mm Bofors gun with a cyclic rate of 120 rounds a minute, each round packed with nearly a kilo of high explosive. The aircraft is used as a total saturation area weapon, its cargo hold rammed with tons of ammunition so the gun crews can maintain a devastating rate of fire for long periods if necessary.

Death from above, in other words.

I tried to get a view of Dicker's Walk just as the Spectre struck. It had spotted a Taliban mortar crew setting up in the rear of the attack to cover their retreat. The mortar position disappeared in a storm of high explosive that howled down from the night sky.

The FOB erupted as the Spooky gunship annihilated the Taliban position. 'Yee-hah, 'ave some of that!'

The Spectre crew could see other Taliban legging it across the fields in retreat from Dicker's Walk.

They started picking them off with 40mm Bofors rounds as they ran, explosions ripping the ground from under their feet, taking them out one by one.

We were delighted. These fuckers had come close to killing several lads that night and now they were paying the price. If there was anything left of the enemy after the Spooky attack they knew it was time to call it a night.

After the contact, a buzz started going around. The GPMG headshot and Jurgen's bull's-eye mortar strike had both been caught on video. In Jurgen's case you saw a Taliban running across a field, AK clearly visible in his hands, and then *boom*, he disappeared in a cloud of black smoke.

Jurgen was like, 'See that, Rammers? Pinpoint accuracy with an area weapon. That takes skill that does.'

I was a bit jealous to be honest. 'Jurgen, you couldn't hit a cow's arse at arm's length with that tube, you jammy twat.'

He was having none of it. 'Forget about Spooky gunships, mate, all you need is me on the 51 and you can sleep sound all night long. There'll be nothing left for you to do, Rammers.'

He never let us forget that contact, and Jurgen's shot was a brilliant morale booster. It showed what we could do with the small-arms at the FOB, and if we ever needed serious backup, air support was on hand.

We didn't give the enemy dead a second thought.

The Taliban were trying to catch the FOB on the back foot and we'd beaten the shit out of them. They had at least five dead on their side and hadn't given us a scratch. Patrols the next day found plenty of blood trails but no bodies.

'That should make them think long and hard about having a crack at the FOB again,' I thought.

6

I was chilling under the cam net in our compound waiting for the kettle to boil to heat up a foil bag ration pack. Sausage and beans, my current favourite. It was the middle of the afternoon and the compound was quiet, the lads either on the sangars or getting their heads down in their grots.

Out of nowhere, a high-pitched, drawn-out shriek filled the air above my head. Incoming. Fuck. The Taliban had obviously thought long and hard about it for two whole seconds before deciding to attack again. The whistling screech got louder, and it felt as if it was coming straight for me.

'Incoming!' someone yelled.

'No shit,' I thought. 'And I know where it's going to land.' It sounded as if it was going to impact top dead centre of my helmet.

I wasn't going to make the shelter in time. I threw myself on the ground, every muscle clenched, and hoped the blokes who made the body armour knew what they were doing.

There was a *crump* from the middle of the camp followed by the rattle of shrapnel and skittering of stones on gravel. It had landed inside the perimeter. But not on top of me. What a let-off.

I sprang up and legged it for the shelter. Having got away with it, I wasn't about to let the enemy have a second crack at me and I sprinted full pelt. I was shaken up but dealing with it. Everyone else came piling in but they seemed totally chilled out, which I found weird and a bit hard to take. If they were cool with it, there was no way I was letting the side down.

Whatever it was, it sounded a lot worse than the rockets. I knew mortars were supposed to whistle, but this was a screech.

'I didn't think mortars would make such a gopping noise,' I said to the lads.

'Nah, Rammers, mate, they don't. That was SPG9 recoilless rifle, we get it all the time round here. HQ will be trying to locate the firing position and see if we can catch 'em up somehow.'

SPG9 carried a smaller warhead than the 107mm rockets, but that wasn't much of a comfort.

I didn't know it then, but pretty much everyone in the FOB had the exact same feelings about indirect fire at first. Anyone tells you they weren't seriously apprehensive the first time they came under indirect fire is either a liar or a dumbass. At first I thought the round was going to blow me, personally, to fuck. I could almost hear the Taliban crews going, 'Look, there's Rammers lying in the dirt outside the shelter. Get the twat.' The trick was to concentrate on your drills and protect yourself as best you could. Body armour, helmet, don't flap. If you can't make the shelter then get down on the deck until a break in the barrage. We came under fire so many times, every day or every other day, that I did it without thinking in the end.

When we weren't on watch in the sangars we had quite a bit of free time during the day. Marines are always keen to keep on top of their phys, incoming or not. Pride in personal fitness is hardwired into every Bootneck's brain. We had no gym equipment to use, and with Chinooks costing about £10,000 an hour to keep in the air no prospect of them delivering a tonne of bench-pressing equipment any time soon.

We were pretty friendly with the Gurkha Engineers and the field kitchen, which cooked a hot breakfast and evening meal every day. They were happy to give us used catering tins which we filled with cement and stuck scaffold poles in to make our own weights. We made our own bench press out of scrap timber and some metal pickets. We also got jerry cans and filled them with sand to use in short relay sprints, carrying a pair of them across a ten-yard course in teams. It gave us something to do when it was quiet. Marines prevented from doing their phys are going to start dripping and causing trouble.

I spent most mornings jogging around the inside of the perimeter. About four p.m. seemed to be the favourite time for Taliban mortar or rocket attacks; most of the mornings remained clear. We were allowed to do phys anywhere we liked in the camp unless told otherwise.

It was beautiful weather early on in the tour, bright sunshine and warm enough but not roasting. Round the perimeter was a mile and a bit. Two or three laps every day or so kept me in good shape. I ran wearing just shorts, trainers and an iPod. It did occur to me halfway round the perimeter, 'What if mortars start coming in now?' Hit the deck and hope for the best was the answer. The FOB was so big and the Taliban's aim so shite it was reasonably safe.

I had Eminem on the iPod and mainly hip-hop tracks stored on it, 50 Cent and the like. I remember one Eminem song, 'Soldier', going through my head as I ran round the compound, the beat matching my footfalls. The lyrics to the tunes were angry but it just helped me get in the mood for phys.

I ran through the American compound about 300 metres from our mosque accommodation. We didn't have much to do with the Yanks in the FOB. They used to disappear into the surrounding countryside for days on end and come back looking like extras out of *Lawrence of Arabia*, bearded up and filthy. They were building themselves a beautiful wooden barracks and were really going to town on it. They'd poured concrete foundations, and every time I ran through progress had been made. The accommodation had power and proper drainage. They were even planning on aircon. It was going to make the grots in our mosque look a bit second-hand.

I did wonder how they were going to protect themselves against incoming mortars and rockets. Our shower block looked better protected against IDF. FOB ROB was probably the most heavily bombarded base in Helmand after FOB Inkerman, a few klicks up the valley to the north of Sangin town. The gravs up there called it FOB Incoming (or Stinkerman, depending on how bad their dhoby was getting). This US barracks was going to be beautiful, but it was just timber frame and boarding as far as I could see. Their defence seemed to be dispersal. The FOB was massive, most of the inside was empty desert, and the IDF rounds were all poorly aimed. Many fell outside the camp, and the ones that struck inside the perimeter had acres of empty ground to fall in. Even so, I felt happier in the mosque or its outbuildings, behind their two-foot-thick, sun-baked, hard-as-nails walls.

Cpl Helsby strode into the compound. 'Rammers, get our section together, the Boss has ordered a patrol. The whole company's going out.'

'Hoofin',' I thought, always up for a change in the routine.

The lads started grabbing kit, preparing weapons and getting their arses up to the HQ compound for a brief. We formed up on the East Gate and it felt great to be getting out and about again.

The brief was to look into a village to the south-east then return in a loop around the north of the camp on to the high ground before coming back in via the main gate. We were going out in three sections – almost the whole of the Royal Marines' fighting strength at the FOB. Again, the intention was to send a message to the Taliban: 'Don't even think about hiding shit or setting up mortars around here, this is our backyard now.'

Sgt Kevin Hazeldine was going to lead our section on this one and we spread out into a staggered formation behind him as he led us out of the gate. As usual, I was bombed up with my SA80 and UGL, a drop bag full of grenades at my side and about four hundred rounds of ammunition in spare mags and bandoliers.

The terrain heading east was undulating desert, hills rolling away from the river behind us. It was like being on the moon. The village was just a collection of mud huts in the middle of nowhere as far as I could see. Unlike the farming village by the river, I couldn't see how this lot made a living. The land around it was barren.

Our section patrolled out to the eastern flank of

the village and went firm. We formed a rough baseline facing east while another section did the same to the north. There was almost no cover. I wasn't that happy because if small-arms or mortars started coming in on us there wasn't a lot we could do about it. A mad dash into the village to get into cover was the best option, I reckoned.

The section in the village gave it a good half hour poking around, checking for arms caches or anything suspicious.

'Kevin, Dinger. Nothing doing in the village but children and goats. We're moving out. Over.'

'Roger that, Dinger. OK, lads,' he said to us on the PRRs. 'See the low hill to the north-east? We're going to head up there then loop off to the left towards North Fort.'

We saw Dinger's patrol exiting the village as we moved out. We scanned our arcs as we moved and straight away I spotted an Afghan man pop his head up from behind a wall on a hill about 300 metres away and duck behind it again. A few seconds later he popped up again. He was clearly dicking us, watching where we were headed and how much weaponry we were carrying. This was a possible combat indicator. By reporting our movement and strength he might be able to fix it for us to walk into a whole world of trouble.

He was clearly Taliban, or helping the Taliban, and I was itching to take him out. I pressed the button on the PRR transmitter, a cigarette-sized box attached to my webbing.

'Sarge, Rammers. Got one times suspicious pax, dicking us from the hill to the north-east, 'bout three hundred metres away. Over.'

'Got him, Rammers, good spot. Keep eyes on for the moment. Out.'

We kept moving at exactly the same pace. The cheeky little sod kept popping out and dicking us.

'OK, Rammers, fire a high warning shot, that should get rid of him.'

'Roger that.'

Without waiting for further instruction, I popped a 40mm high explosive round in the UGL and snapped it shut. I raised the rear sight on the rifle and aimed the grenade well clear of him. It was the first time I had used the UGL in anger and I wasn't that sure of my accuracy, so well clear meant about 60 metres from the target. I really did not want to hit him.

I pulled the trigger and the rifle bucked in my hands, emitting a puff of smoke as the grenade sailed in the dicker's general direction. The round burst in a cloud of grey-black smoke and a fraction of a second later a sharp bang echoed across the desert. It exploded roughly where I'd intended, about 50 metres to his right, out of shrapnel range but close enough to signal my intent.

I have never seen an Afghan bug out so fast. It felt absolutely great.

'Rammers, you fucking twat! I meant 5.56mm single-shot not a fucking UGL and you know it, you fucking *dickhead*!'

Kevin was the Troop Stripey and he was furious. Anywhere else I would have been in deep, deep trouble. Luckily for me we were in the middle of a patrol in hostile territory and this was no time or place for issuing beastings.

I tried to look sheepish. It was hard because the other lads in the patrol were pissing themselves laughing and failing to hide the fact. I shrugged. As I said, I had never fired a UGL in anger before and who knows, I might not get another chance. It did the trick though. The Afghan was proper gone. The Taliban would have to be worried about dicking us in future.

Kevin was a decent bloke. As Troop Stripey he was well aware of the frustrations we had suffered in the sangars and shelters under IDF. The whole section was having a good chuckle and attempting to discipline me would just have made it funnier. But he made sure I got the message loud and clear. 'Rammers, I expect much better from you,' he snapped in disgust. 'Now move out.'

I was in disgrace.

Fair one.

We continued the patrol, looping round to the north as planned. The last men in the formation, walking backwards most of the time, spotted a white pick-up truck that kept popping up to our rear and then disappearing. It was obviously following us. That meant it was a truckful of Taliban and they could be planning either to call fighters on to us or have a crack themselves.

This time there was no mucking about. Kevin ordered the two rear men to fire a series of high warning shots over the vehicle with their SA80s. He just glared at me. He didn't have to tell me I was not to fire a single round.

The Taliban in the truck knew we had seen them, they knew we were ready for a fight if they wanted it. They thought better of it and bugged out.

We continued our circuit around the camp and re-entered via the main gate.

I threw my kit into my pit in disgust. It was the last patrol we would mount for five weeks.

We spent hundreds of hours on watch in the sangars, by day on your own, at night always two of you. Off duty you were just chilling around the compound, spinning dits and talking bullshit, or else stuck in the shelter waiting for the all-clear doing the same. You got to know people inside out: where they came from, why they joined up, how badly they got beasted in training.

Jurgen travelled the length of the country from Carlisle to join the Marines. For me it was on my doorstep. I grew up in Plymouth. My mum and dad's place was only two miles from Stonehouse Barracks, the Corps HQ. As a little kid I didn't think about joining up though. My ambition was to become a martial arts expert and put Jean Claude Van Damme out of a job.

Don't laugh, I'm serious. By the time I grew up I reckoned he would be too old for the movies and I could take over. It was funny, because I was a little fat kid and wasn't at all sporty. I loved my scran and was getting chubby, so at the age of about twelve I started going to a Muay Thai kick boxing club called the Scorpions based in a gym across the park from our house. It was like something out of *The Karate Kid*. We fought proper bouts against opponents matched by weight. I was still carrying some puppy fat so usually fought slightly older kids.

I started to get quite good but was such a show-off. I'd leap through the air spinning like a lunatic in training and learned Van Damme's trick of doing the splits across the back of two chairs. I thought I was the business, but had just enough sense to know that if I tried any of the show-off stuff in the ring I would get battered.

Our club took part in regional competitions with bouts of three one-minute rounds, with gloves, shin pads and head guards. The level of contact was strictly regulated because we were so young. Despite this, and even though I was only twelve, I managed to pick up a horrendous injury in sparring. I rolled to avoid a punch and was chuckling as my opponent missed with his glove. The next instant, all I could see was his training shoe and, *bam*, he hit me straight in the nose with his shin. Pain exploded all over my face. My nose split open but didn't break. A plastic toggle on the end of his shoelace scratched my eyeball causing quite a serious injury.

The next day I was waiting at the bus stop on the way to my nan's house in Plymouth and I looked like a raccoon. I had two massive black eyes, a patch over my scratched eye, and my nose was a mess. I didn't care, I just wanted to get back into the ring. To catch the right bus I had to stop every single one and ask, 'What number's this one, mate?' I'm surprised I didn't get another beating from the drivers.

It didn't put me off the sport at all and I got better and better. Our club changed venues and started fighting out of a gym called The House of Pain. After a couple of years I won the Under-16 Grand Championship for the South-West. I've still got the trophy in the dining room.

I fought full contact from the age of sixteen, which was gloves and bare feet, no head guard. My opponents were still a bit older than me. We fought all over the south-west – Plymouth, Exeter, Bournemouth – and I loved it. My dad would drive me to competitions but my mum Jackie wouldn't come. She hated seeing me in a fight, but she supported me anyway.

I had one big fight in Bournemouth when I was sixteen. My opponent was twenty, an instructor, and ripped from head to toe with muscle. He looked pretty ninja. I was much fitter than I had been but still carried some fat. I was nervous. The fight was three two-minute rounds. My instructor told me, 'Don't be intimidated. Don't hang back. Get in there and fight him like you would anyone else.'

The pace in the ring was fast, quick jabs and left-foot strikes probing for weakness. I was trying to size him up quickly. Can he kick? Punch hard? Guard any good? Everyone fights differently and you've got to be the first one to work out a chink in the armour and exploit it. He had plenty of power and favoured maxed-out jabs that would do lots of damage if they connected.

Round two, and I'd noticed that his guard went to pieces in the jab. He was concentrating totally on landing the shot with full power. I feinted once or twice and managed to draw a jab from him. Sure enough, he was wide open.

Round three, and I had a plan. I feinted again and, without waiting to see if he took the bait, mashed all my weight on to the ball of my left foot and spun hard with a high right-leg kick. I kept my body upright and my foot where I thought his head would be if he'd thrown the jab. *Bang*. My shin smacked into the side of his head. It was a solid strike with good power and he went down. His legs had gone and he couldn't make the count.

This guy was supposed to be fitter, technically better and just plain harder than me. I'd found a way round him and won it by a knockout with a super-flash high kick to the head. Van Damme, eat your heart out. I'm not saying I was getting big-headed, but if they hadn't had double doors at that gym I might have scraped my ears off on the way out.

By the age of seventeen I'd won ten fights in a row, three or four by knockout. There was another contest in Bournemouth and I was due to fight a black guy from London. In the dressing room he came to see me and told me he couldn't make the fight. Fair play, the bloke had a hoofin' excuse: 'I've been shot.' He showed me the scar on his leg from an old wound from some trouble in London a few years earlier. He said it was playing up that night. He was genuinely apologetic. He'd travelled down to Bournemouth hoping it would clear up, but no such luck, he had to pull out.

'Fair one,' I thought.

It makes me laugh now. I was only seventeen and thinking, 'So that's what it's like in London, you get shot. Must be brave people living up there.'

An instructor came to see me. 'There's a French fighter in your weight class who can step in, if you're willing to go up against him.'

'I don't see why not. Who is he?'

'Don't know much about him. He's giving you a couple of pounds, Mark, and he's a lot older than you, but he's got good technique. Seems like a fairly even contest.'

I'd won every fight so far and couldn't see any reason not to take on any opponent in my own class. I was like, 'Sure, bring him on.'

This French guy had a lean, wiry physique. He wasn't particularly ripped but everything about him looked mean. He was fit the same way a wild animal is, not a scrap of fat on him, every ounce of his body weight there to earn its living. He was more than twice my age. He looked focused and businesslike. My plan was to try to land some hard strikes to the body early on and hope the weight advantage and age gap would start to work in my favour.

From the first second of round one I knew I was in deep shit. His workrate made me gasp. Strikes were coming in so quick I couldn't work out what he was hitting me with. He was a blur of elbows, feet, knees and hands. He seemed to be able to hit me in two places at once. Each strike had crushing power and every shot hurt like fuck.

Bam. He put me on my arse after about forty-five seconds. I think he got me with a left hook but I'm still not sure. My whole world had changed in less than a minute. I would have taken a deep breath but was already breathing as hard as my lungs would let me. I made it up after a count of about five or six. My only hope was to go defensive, weather the onslaught and try to find a counter-attack.

Boom. Arse on the canvas again, winded. The bloke's fitness and strength were awesome. His strikes were so hard, even if they didn't put you on the deck they sucked the strength and the will to fight right out of you.

He put me down three times in that first round. I went back to my corner and didn't want to come out again. Being in the same ring as this guy was so far outside my comfort zone I couldn't explain it. Every sensible brain cell in my head was screaming at me to run away.

I knew I'd lost the fight. The only way to victory after an opening round like that was to knock him out. That wasn't going to happen. He was in a different league. Everywhere I looked, strength, speed, technique, I was outclassed. I searched for my courage. It seemed to be in the dressing room, putting on its coat.

Bollocks to that. No way. 'I'm going to lose this fight, but I won't quit.'

I had a new target: survival. I would make it to the end of the fight on my feet. This bloke was of international standard and if I could stay in the ring with him for three rounds that would be an achievement in itself.

He punched and kicked the crap out of me. I got him down on the deck once. Doing my best to fend him off, I came up with a fast left-foot strike at the same time as he unleashed a powerful right-leg kick. Our legs connected and somehow his own power bounced back on him and he was on his arse. It was no more than a stumble from the judges' point of view but it was the one positive attacking moment in the fight for me. I kept waiting for the bloke to fade and give me a chance but it didn't happen. One flurry of strikes came so fast and strong I was going out of the ring over the top rope on to the judges' table. I hooked my right arm into the ropes and stopped myself. It was good to give the judges a scare. They should have got in with this bloke and seen how frightening that was.

The bell to end round three came at last. I was still on my feet. The judges' technical assessment was that he had knocked seven kinds of crap out of me.

I was so upset with myself I smashed my runner's-up trophy in the changing rooms. It was the first time I'd lost a full-contact bout. There was no need for double doors to get out of the gym any more.

That fight taught me a lesson: to have a bit of humility is a good thing. But I was pissed off. I wasn't Jean Claude Van Damme after all.

7

I was lying on my cot in the mosque when there was a shattering roar and the ground shook again. Not a rocket, not SPG9. What were the Taliban hitting us with now? It was too late to shout 'Incoming!' so I just waited for the mosque roof to fall in. No one else seemed worried.

'What the fuck was that?'

'Ha, Rammers, calm down, mate, that's us giving them some,' said Baggsy.

'What?'

'Come and have a look at the rocket launcher.'

The Royal Artillery had a hoofin' bit of kit in the camp that I hadn't noticed, as it hadn't fired since I'd arrived: the GMLRS, or guided multiple launch rocket system.

'What is that?' I asked as Baggsy showed me the launcher. 'It looks like a tank out of *Thunderbirds*.'

The GMLRS was a tracked vehicle with a massive rectangular metal box on the back which housed twelve mini-cruise missiles. The rockets were four metres long and carried 200lb of high explosive. Once launched, the missiles guided themselves to target working off the GPS system like sat nav. You dialled in the coordinates and it flew to the exact spot and piled in. It was so accurate the Army called it the '60-kilometre sniper'.

The launcher disappeared in a cloud of white smoke as a second rocket roared out of the launch tube and streaked away into the sky. Sixty-klick wrecking ball more like.

Royal Marines from 40 Commando were protecting the hydroelectric dam at Kajaki at the top of the valley. They were calling in fire on Taliban positions about 30km away from us. It felt good to watch the Artillery boys sending off the good news.

'Why can't we use this thing against Taliban mortars round here?' I asked.

'Too close, mate,' Baggsy replied. 'Got to be at least fifteen klicks away to hit 'em with that.'

We had some good kit in the FOB, including a Danish Army outfit with some state-of-the-art radars that could pinpoint enemy IDF locations as they opened fire on us. The trouble was, we didn't have the right mix of weaponry on hand to counter-attack that precise threat.

At one time the FOB had a battery of three light guns from 29 Commando Regiment Royal Artillery, and they would have been ideal. It's called a light gun but it weighs about two tonnes and can blast a

105mm diameter shell more than 17km. The remains of their position could still be seen in the middle of the FOB: three big pits with berms on one side and stacks of 105mm rounds ready to fire – everything but the guns themselves. They'd been moved to another location to support a FOB further up the Sangin valley where the fighting was more intense.

The Taliban rocket and mortar teams were firing on us from a range of about 5km. They often attacked from the middle of inhabited compounds, so there was every chance we would smash up an innocent farming family if we counter-attacked with big area guns. That would screw the hearts and minds effort. One solution offered itself when another GMLRS unit set up about 15km to the south of us at a FOB near Gereshk. Now we had a guided weapon that could take on the mortars for us.

Just a few days later, HQ spotted an SPG9 crew setting up to fire. They watched the two men readying the recoilless tube and sent the grid ref down to Brigade HQ who tasked the GMLRS to have a crack at them. For once the Taliban were operating from a trench system with no other compounds nearby and we had positively identified them as they set up to fire.

The Taliban opened fire on us and an SPG9 screeched into the FOB, smashing down inside the perimeter, harmlessly rearranging the gravel floor. As the Taliban grabbed their kit and started to bug out, the GMLRS team at Gereshk fired, and the missile was soon closing in on the enemy.

The Taliban must have heard it coming and ducked a fraction of a second before they were obliterated by 200lb of high explosive. Whooping and cheering broke out in the HQ as the area around the enemy disappeared in a small mushroom cloud.

Then from the HQ compound came shouts of, 'I don't believe it! The lucky bastards!'

The Taliban emerged from their trench, dusted themselves off and legged it, apparently unhurt. The GMLRS packed such a big punch it was usually lethal. They must have got into a deep trench some way from their firing position to survive. We were gutted.

I watched the Artillery blokes going about their business. The guided missile system was a brand-new bit of kit and the Army seemed to be well pleased with it. As I watched them work I wondered what branch I would've found myself in if I'd joined the Army instead of the Marines.

It nearly went that way.

At first I didn't fancy the military at all. I'd got ten GCSEs with decent grades and decided to stay in education to do an Advanced GNVQ in Business Studies. I had no idea what I wanted to do with life, but good business skills had to come in useful.

The course was a killer. All we seemed to do was rewrite textbooks in our own words for the teacher.

What did that have to do with running a business?

One weekend I was watching the Arnie Schwarzenegger movie *Predator*. It had a blatantly sensible plot. Arnie gets to lead an elite squad through a jungle spunking the world's supply of ammo while being chased by an invisible alien. Could happen.

Arnie's squad spent the whole movie up to its neck in swamp and bullets. I looked at the latest business studies textbook waiting for me on the table and made a decision: 'Fuck it, I'm going to join the Army.'

My dad talked me out of it. My uncle John served as an officer in the Royal Marines and left as a Captain. If I was going to have a crack at the military there was no way in my family's world it was going to be with the Pongos. Join the Army? I'd never have heard the end of it.

Our house was only round the corner from the Marines' recruiting office in Devonport dockyard and I was sixteen years old when I walked in. They talked about jungle training and showed me a video. It looked like a scene out of *Predator*, only more real. Blokes covered in cam cream patrolled through the jungle up to their necks in swamp.

The recruiter also talked about Arctic training. Someone's going to pay me to learn to ski? Then they showed me a few Gucci scenes of Marines leaping out of rigid raiding boats and diving out of aircraft in parachute training. It looked like one long adventure holiday.

'Where do you want me to sign?'

They sent me home with an information pack. There was a training guide with hints on building upper body strength and stamina. They wanted thousands of press-ups, pull-ups and ab crunches out of you. I was already fit from kick boxing but I took their advice and worked hard.

They booked me a slot on a three-day Potential Royal Marines Course at the Commando Training Centre at Lympstone in Devon. It was the first time I'd stayed away from home. Changing trains at Exeter seemed like a big deal. A little two-carriage rattler dropped me and thirty other potential recruits at the Royal Marines' own railway station, a platform with a bus shelter next to the Bottom Field assault course. I was one of the youngest there; some of the potential recruits looked almost thirty and seemed like old men to me. My first taste of Commando training was minutes away. How would they test candidates for the best infantry force in the world?

We were all thrown in a room and told to iron our kit. My mum did my ironing. I struggled through it.

We slept in bunk beds twelve to a room. The snoring and farting was ridiculous. Lights blazed on at 0600. Blokes ran to and from the showers bollocky buff. I wasn't comfortable walking around with my winkie out in front of a crowd of strange men but you didn't have time to muck about. Before I'd properly woken up we were halfway through a three-mile squad run to be completed in twenty-two minutes. Blokes who couldn't do it failed the course.

From there it was straight into the gym where they thrashed us all day long. Timed press-ups, sit-ups, pull-ups and bleep tests. Running back and forth between two points as a CD player bleeped quicker and quicker. Fail to beat the bleeps and you were off the course.

Next was the Bottom Field where they smashed us over six-foot walls, monkey bars, tank traps, zig-zag walls and under nets until we were all hanging out of our arses. It wasn't just fitness they were look-ing for, they wanted to see what it took to make you quit.

Personally, I was threaders. Where were the skiing lessons? There was no sign of being taught to jump out of an aeroplane or shoot a rifle. I didn't remem-ber anything in the recruitment video about 'we're going to smash you through the Bottom Field at 0600 and yomp you until your knees snap'. It dawned on me how much I'd have to prove before I was allowed near the good stuff.

At the end of three days I'd passed their mega-tough Commando course. I was still only sixteen. It was a good effort and had to be worth something. I was presented with a certificate. It would be followed by an invitation to join the Marines and begin full-time training. I was really proud. The prospect of being asked my occupation and one day being able to say 'Royal Marine' gave me a real buzz. The Corps was held in great respect in my home town and in my mind they were the best in the world. They wanted me to have a crack at joining them. Game on.

I ran for the shelter with the whistle of an incoming mortar in my ears. *Whump*. It exploded harmlessly well outside the FOB perimeter. A second whistle was already in the air, and a third. *Crump . . . whump*. This mortar crew was walking the rounds towards us. They were getting nearer, but even their best effort was going to miss by a good margin.

I was getting well used to it now. You could tell from the whistle if the round was falling away from you. The lads reckoned if it was coming down on top of you, you heard nothing.

What cheered us all up was the Taliban's accuracy was totally shit. They might walk three mortar rounds towards you but they didn't have the balls to stay put and adjust their fall of shot. Their approach to 107mm drills was, lean the rocket up against a low wall pointing in our direction then light the blue touchpaper and leg it before we could catch them up on the counter-attack.

The annoying thing was, now we were stuck in the shelter. It was lunchtime, the hottest part of the day. There were more than thirty blokes crammed in on benches and we would be stuck until the all-clear.

We made the best of it, cracking jokes and having a laugh or getting our heads down. Some of the lads were quite new out of training and were talking about the beastings they'd been given at Lympstone.

I hadn't been in a week before my first one. We were in the Foundation Block at the Commando Training Centre. It was February, week one of thirty, and I was seventeen years old. The lot of us were still learning how to iron sharp creases in our shirts in the manner ordered by the drill leader, a Sergeant. His job was running the two-week Foundation Course teaching us the basics. Every fortnight he put a batch of sixty new recruits through the same drills.

We'd been on the go since 0600 and hit the showers just after midnight. The pace was relentless. We were being issued with hundreds of pieces of kit and it all had to be squared away exactly as instructed. They were ramming information into our heads and smashing us through physical tests all at the same time.

I was out of the shower and a few feet from my bed in the Foundation Block. Our troop of sixty recruits was sleeping in the one room. There were a couple of guys joining us from the Army who had a few drills to make life easier. One of them was, shave before getting your head down: you avoided the queue for the heads in the morning, it saved five precious minutes at 0600, and it got you through most inspections during the day.

One of the blokes was rushing so fast he'd forgotten to rinse the sink out and the bowl was left with foam and stubble in it. The drill leader spotted it and was disgusted. The whole block normally sparkled super-clean from floor to ceiling. He couldn't believe what he was seeing. You'd think we'd killed his dog.

He came screaming into the room. 'Front, support, place!'

The sixty of us rushed to get into the press-up position.

'Arms bend!'

Halfway down to the floor, my green issue towel was all I had on. 'Don't slide off,' I ordered it.

'Stretch!'

The troop snapped back up to the press-up position.

'Bend! Right, you *dickheads* . . . Stretch! Which one of you . . . Bend! Left the heads . . . Stretch! In this *gopping* . . . Bend! Condition?'

A lecture on acceptable levels of cleanliness in the Foundation Block was screamed at us, a few words at a time, between press-ups.

Other beastings singled out individuals. For example, we had to handwash everything and dry it on hot rails. If you failed to remove your kit promptly when dry, therefore selfishly preventing other recruits getting on with their dhoby, you got to stand to one side and watch the rest of your troop getting beasted for your mistake. It was a big motivator not to fuck up.

The DL screamed at us fast in Bootneck slang. They actually handed out crib sheets to make sure we got it. Most of it was simple Navy stuff. The kitchen was a galley, it produced scran. Toilets were heads. Excellent was hoofin'. Mouldy socks didn't stink, they were honking or gopping. Tea or coffee was a wet, best served redders. Mistakes made the instructors threaders, not angry. Juice was screech. Pork pies and moustaches were both growlers for some reason.

We didn't moan, we dripped. If we stopped dripping long enough to pass out as Royal Marines we would be allowed to wear the precious Green Lid that marked us out as Royal Marine Commandos, Bootnecks, Booties or Royals.

We tried hard not to make the DL threaders with us. He didn't like the fact our gleaming boots left traces of black polish on his immaculate floor. We scraped up every last speck with bayonets. Then we cleaned the bayonets.

We were threaders and thought it was shit, but it bonded the troop. They were already forcing us to work as a unit to avoid the beastings. They were starting to turn us into Royal Marines.

The other side of the train station at Lympstone was an estuary. Low tide exposed a big area of slimy oozing mud two feet deep. A friend who joined the

Marines two years before me told me about a legendary beasting there.

His troop had fucked up big time. For punishment they were ordered to go for a run and do press-ups in the estuary mud. They came out plastered in it. The only things still clean were their eyeballs and teeth. The troop felt it was fair enough, they deserved the beasting. But it had only just started.

They were quick-marched back to their barracks, ordered inside in their honking state and made to get into bed and pull up the covers. Then they got screamed at for the shocking state of their bed linen. They were ordered to whirl the sheets around the tops of their heads. Slimy mud splattered off the sheets on to the walls, windows, ceiling, lights, floor and furniture. Naturally, they got screamed at for the shocking state of their pigpen grot. It was late Friday afternoon. The troop was told no one was leaving camp for the weekend until the recruits, their accommodation and every piece of kit and bedding were returned to immaculate condition. Even with the help of another troop, who took pity on them and volunteered to help, it took them until midnight Sunday to reach the required standard.

Nice weekend?

The Royal Marines value recruits who remain cheerful in the face of adversity. Lympstone's job is to supply recruits with adversity to be cheerful in the face of.

While I was there we got a visit from the BBC's *Blue Peter* who came down to show the kids at home what the Commando Training Centre was all about, and our troop was going to be featured.

'Right, lads, who fancies a game of rugby with a *Blue Peter* presenter?'

There was a growl of appreciation. That should be a laugh, and we might get on the telly. We were all up for it.

'Good. Low tide's in thirty minutes.'

Groans. Rugby in the estuary mud.

It was a brilliant laugh. Trying to run or pass the ball was ridiculous. We were coated in a layer of slime a centimetre thick in a couple of minutes.

I hoped no one fucked up now. I knew the danger our accommodation was in.

No one did. They lined us up in the Bottom Field and blasted us clean with a freezing cold fire hose. The telly folk got the exact same treatment so we couldn't drip about it. I just wished I was on the other end of the hose.

After two weeks we moved out of the Foundation Block and took up two floors of recruit accommodation. The troop boss was a Captain. He and the Troop Sergeant were responsible for the next twenty-eight weeks of our training. The troop was broken up into sections commanded by Corporals. One of the Corporals didn't like the name Ormrod and kept calling me Ramrod instead. It stuck. From then on I was known as Rammers in the Corps.

Lessons in the classroom were crammed into the timetable alongside marches across Dartmoor and Woodbury Common loaded with kit, followed by gym sessions and obstacle courses. The Corporals rarely referred to us as recruits, we were nods to them. We'd come straight off a march into a classroom and heads would start to nod as we fell asleep on the spot through fatigue. Instructors would creep up behind us and slam a drill stick on to the desks to keep us awake.

I was one of six blokes sharing a room right next to the Corporals' office, which was bad news. After all the physical and mental exercise of the day you'd have a load of admin to catch up on. Cleaning and storing all your kit the way they wanted it done took hours. I was up until 0100 to keep on top of it most nights. Any sort of distraction or extra chore put you further behind.

The Corporals didn't care. Any time they wanted an errand doing they would simply scream, 'Nod!'

We'd be like, 'I'm not going, I'm too busy.'

'Five . . .'

'Nah, me neither.'

'Four . . .'

'I went last time, mate, it's not my go.'

'Three . . .'

'Mate, the whole troop's going to get beasted if no one goes.'

'Two . . .'

'Aw fuckit.'

'One . . .'

Stamp to attention outside the office.

'Ah, Ramrod, go and get us a pint of fresh milk before our tea goes cold. About turn, quick *march*!'

It was character building.

One thing I'd like to point out. We were beasted for mistakes throughout training but the Sergeants and Corporals had a line they wouldn't cross. During thirty weeks at Lympstone I never once saw or heard of any NCO laying a finger on any recruit, no matter how bad the fuck-up. They were professional men to the core.

The beastings and discipline focused our minds to the point where we could be trusted with rifles and live ammunition. We'd had lectures on the SA80, or L85A2 to use its proper name, until we could strip and reassemble it faster than Forrest Gump. Accurate shooting wasn't just point and squirt. You were taught to breathe properly and control your movements.

I was nervous at first. We had a full mag of thirty rounds of 5.56mm ammunition and we'd been taught what happened when you hit a man.

In the seventies, Marines and Pongo infantry used a long SLR (self-loading rifle). It fired a 7.62mm round. Remember the dustbin full of water? If you hit the enemy with the SLR he went down and stayed down. Then the military decided that in modern warfare killing the enemy wasn't as good as wounding him badly. If a soldier was killed his mates could afford to ignore him and crack on, but if he was badly wounded, screaming his tits off, they were going to stop fighting and help him. Once in the rear he would continue to put a strain on the enemy's resources. That was the theory. So the UK and NATO decided infantry rifles should fire a 5.56mm round. If you hit a man with that it would tumble on entry causing damage but not usually killing him. We were told horrendous stories about blokes catching up 5.56mm rounds that went in through the upper leg and exited through the shoulder after an unguided tour of the guts. Then they discovered that the 5.56mm round travelled at such a high velocity it sometimes zipped straight through people without tumbling. In that case you might have to hit a man with three or four rounds to put him down. The GPMG was brought back into service. When that gun put you on your arse, you didn't get up.

So, taking a fully loaded mag of 5.56mm rounds and thinking about the slug bouncing around inside a man made you treat the weapon with respect.

I'd never shot before and expected the rifle to kick like a donkey. It was an anticlimax. The recoil wasn't much more powerful than an airgun. Nevertheless, it was a reliable, accurate weapon and it was satisfying to be able to use it competently.

We were shooting over 100 metres and my marksmanship was plain average. The trick was maintaining accuracy under pressure. During close quarter combat training we had to walk up a stream bed one at a time. Metal targets popped out at random. You dived in the best cover available and took the target out as fast as possible. Instructors watched every move. They checked to see if you had identified the best cover before they checked the target for hits.

I was average again, but enjoying it. This was what I'd joined up for.

The instructors kept ramming information into us and smashed us through the yomps, gym work and assault courses. Lessons in fieldcraft showed us how to keep clean and feed ourselves while living in the open. We were taught to kill and gut chickens and rabbits. It wasn't pretty, and it brought home the meaning of 'running round like a headless chicken'. One recruit pulled the head off his bird and let go by accident. It charged around in circles, bumping into trees and squirting blood everywhere.

On my first field exercise it hammered down with rain. I was always crap at camping and this was no different. We dossed down with waterproof bivvy bags and I woke up in the middle of the night in a downpour. I was being washed down the hill in a muddy stream that hadn't been there when I went to sleep.

The next morning we heard recruits being put through the Tarzan assault course about 100m away from us. It was the world famous high-level obstacle course. As we packed up our kit we heard a man start screaming in agony. It wouldn't stop. The screaming was joined by the wail of an ambulance siren getting closer.

'What the fuck's going on?'

'Dunno, mate. Someone's fallen off by the sound of it.'

We'd yet to try the assault course ourselves. We looked at each other anxiously.

'Ideal,' I thought. 'Why am I putting myself through all this?'

We found out later what had happened. There was a tree-trunk in the middle of the rope swing that you had to clear. The recruit was too low on the rope and hit the trunk at the fastest part of the swing. The tree smashed one of his shin bones and drove one end out through the skin of his lower leg. He was in agony and shock. Treatment was on hand and he made a good recovery, but it was a reminder that if you dropped your guard this course could hurt you.

The troop's numbers dropped steadily. Some decided to wrap and go home. Others were back-trooped, sent to join the sixty lads following two weeks behind us. A few were injured and joined Hunter Troop, where they went through intensive physio to get them back on the course. I was determined not to get backtrooped. I couldn't face doing any of this shit twice.

The lowest point of the whole course for me was when we finished a yomp in full fighting order at about midnight. I was hanging out of my arse, so the thought of having to set up Harbour Position in the woods was making me threaders. I wanted a dry bed and a hot bath.

'Wet and dry routine,' snapped the Corporal. 'Everyone in the lake.'

'Aw great. He's just taking the piss.'

We jumped into the freezing cold lake up to our chests. The icy water gripped our bollocks and made us gasp.

'Heads under.'

We did as ordered to make sure every last bit of us and our clothing was soaked through.

'Out you come. Set up Harbour Position for the night.'

We picked a position in the woods. I dumped my bergen and dragged a poncho from it. My head ached with the cold. My ears throbbed. My fingers were numb and stupid. I'd tied a plastic tent peg to each of the metal rings at each corner of the poncho before setting off. I gave myself a little cheer for my good preparation. Other guys were tearing their bergens apart looking for their pegs. Me and my buddy inserted bivvy poles and drove home the pegs to make a two-man tent. Bergens at one end blocked out wind and rain. Two roll mats went inside, webbing for a pillow.

Soaking wet, we stripped off our sopping gear and stuffed it into gash bags. We dried ourselves thoroughly and only then got into our sleeping bags. We took care to lay our weapons and gear between us under the middle of the poncho. This was a tactical exercise and the training teams liked to come round in the night and steal vital bits of kit. Lose your weapon and you were in deep shit.

The ponchos were arranged in a rough triangle and sentry posts chosen. It was a textbook Harbour Position. I slept like a dead man for a couple of hours until I was woken up for my turn on watch.

I didn't want to get out of my quite warm, mostly dry pit. It was about 0400 and pouring with rain. I looked stupidly at my plastic bag of soaking wet, freezing cold clothing. I forced myself to get a grip and dragged myself into the sopping wet rig. It felt as if the clothes were coated in icy slime. I wanted to cry.

My morale turned to shit. This was bollocks. What was the point? We weren't learning anything here except how to endure misery. I considered jogging back to our accommodation block. At least the run would warm me up. Then a couple of hours' kip in a dry bed and check out of Lympstone later in the morning.

It started to rain harder.

I told myself, 'You can do that if you want. Just give it a minute first.'

After sixty of those minutes I was still there and it was someone else's turn. I didn't care what they threw at me now, I'd take it and get through it. Otherwise that miserable night would have been for nothing.

We did field firing exercises to practise infantry skirmishing, section attacks and troop attacks. We used blank ammunition at first, then live ammunition. We learned how to fight as a team in the field, to identify, engage and outflank our targets. We practised fighting withdrawals, extracting the section while hammering the enemy with suppressing fire, and urban warfare, fighting through buildings.

We lapped it up, but after one of these exercises the Corporals decided the troop still had too much energy.

'Troop. See that tree over there to the left of the mobile phone pylon?'

It was so far away it looked tiny.

'It pays to be a winner. Go!'

We instantly knew what was at stake and legged it for the tree at top speed. This was a favourite trick of the instructors. The first one or two recruits back would be allowed to stop and relax while all the others would have to carry on. The winners of the second heat would then also be allowed to join those enjoying a break. This would be repeated for as long as the Corporals wanted. That's why it paid to be a winner.

I had a brilliant idea. My mate Sammy Whiteman and I were about halfway down the pack on the first return leg. We were approaching a natural bund line in the field big enough to hide behind. I hit the deck and dragged Sammy down with me.

'Rammers, what the f—'

'Shh, Sammy. They've not seen us. Stay down. When the troop comes back out, we'll rejoin. Only we'll be rested. We'll walk it past the lot of them and put our feet up.' I grinned.

Sammy wasn't that chuffed. 'Rammers, this better work . . .'

We kept eyes on the troop as they came out again. We jumped up and ran as they crossed the bund line. We returned with a comfortable lead ahead of the pack, but not enough to take the piss or cause suspicion.

The Corporals didn't say a word. The rest of the troop streamed in.

'Good effort, lads, well done. Take a breather. Take a seat.'

'Ah well, we're all going to get a breather,' I thought. 'At least we saved ourselves half a rep. No harm done.

'Recruit Ormrod, Recruit Whiteman, the tree and back until I say stop. Go!'

We could see forty cheesy grins beaming at us from halfway across the field. As far as they were concerned, Justice Had Been Done.

Sammy and I pissed ourselves laughing as we ran.

'Hoofin' plan, Rammers. Good effort. You twat.'

The Corporals kept us going until it got dark. The fact they'd punished us on the spot meant that was the end of the matter. But it was the sort of stupid move that could have got me and Sammy back-trooped. It was the last time I tried any tricks on the Corporals at Lympstone.

The dread of getting backtrooped drove me on. Yomps got longer and faster, and the loads heavier. The six-mile speed march became nine miles. The pace picked up everywhere you looked.

The Tarzan assault course made a good change because it wasn't just extreme phys until you puked. You had to figure out your moves, and it needed bottle. It started with the zip cord, a rope strung from a tower about 30 feet high. You slung a rope handhold over the main cable, shoved your wrists through the loops, held tight and jumped. There was a high-level ropeway, a beam about 20 feet off the ground and a jump across a two-metre gap into a cargo net. On the rope-swing I thought of the lad who'd bust his leg and kept my feet up.

I loved the assault course, which was a bonus. I was good at the rest of the training but I hated it. Every time I go back to Lympstone I get a feeling in the pit of my stomach like I'm going to puke. It's the fear of being made to go through that pain for a second time. To this day, whenever I visit the camp I expect a Sergeant to leap on me any minute and shout, 'Front, support, place!'

By week thirty of the training course, four tests stood between us and our Green Berets.

It starts with the six-mile endurance test in two parts: a two-mile obstacle course with pipes full of honking brown water to crawl through followed by a four-mile run. The whole to be completed in seventy-three minutes.

Next is the nine-mile speed march carrying 32lb of kit in fighting order, to be completed in ninety minutes.

The Tarzan assault course and Bottom Field assault course have to be completed together in thirteen minutes.

Finally, a 30-mile march in full fighting order to be completed in eight hours. On top of the load you have to carry between the troop an emergency day-sack with medical supplies and hypothermia blankets.

I completed the first three tests no problem. It was exhausting but I was coping. I could almost feel the Green Beret on my head. Then came the 30-miler across Dartmoor.

I think I've blanked out the most horrendous parts of it but I can't forget the last 800 metres. After 30 miles they decided to end the course with a hill. Rider's Hill. My legs felt like I had a pair of concrete boots on as I approached it and started up the incline. I reached the top of the rise and felt relief as the ground levelled out. Then my heart sank as I saw it was only the first in a series of inclines we had to get up.

Pain jolted up and down the muscles of my legs as I forced one foot in front of the other. My left boot squelched in a mixture of bright red blood and dirty brown water with every step. Everything hurt like fuck. I knew if I stopped moving I'd never get going again. I was like a zombie but you'd have to have knocked me out to stop me moving. This was what they meant by digging out blind.

At last I got to the true top of the hill and plodded down the other side, over a stone bridge across a stream to a load of minibuses parked up to collect us.

I sat down and couldn't get up again.

All through training we'd learned what an honour the Green Beret was for the Royal Marines. There was a superstition in the Corps that if a recruit touched a beret during the training course he'd never wear one for real. I expected the clouds to part in a shaft of sunlight and a choir of angels to lower the Green Beret down from heaven on to my head. In fact a Sergeant jammed the lid into my hand and said, 'Rammers, good effort.'

I placed the beret on my head and dressed it over to the right.

It was the proudest moment of my life.

Of our original troop of sixty recruits, sixteen passed out at the first attempt, and I was one of them. Another eleven made it after being back-trooped or recovering from injury.

After the passing-out parade everyone wanted to be a general duties Marine, specializing as a grav. The only vacancies were at 45 Commando in Arbroath in Scotland. There was a list of specialists the Corps was short of that got you a posting down south. All you had to do was choose between clerk, chef, mortarman and driver. I joined the Marines to keep out of the office, so clerking got a 'no'. I hate cooking, so chef was also off the menu. Once I'd learned the mortar I thought I'd get bored. Driver wasn't the most glamorous role but it would gain me thousands of pounds' worth of driving licences valid on civvy street. There were vacancies at UK Land Force, Command Support Group, based at Stonehouse Barracks, two miles from my mum and dad's house.

Perfect.

I started work at CSG in their Motor Transport Troop in 2002. It was regular hours with a good bunch of lads. After thirty weeks at Lympstone I was ready for some normal routine.

Almost immediately, a notice went round asking for volunteers to box for the Marines; candidates would be excused duties for four weeks to train for the Corps Championships. I thought it would be a couple of hours' sparring a day and then home to relax – a good skive in other words. I deserved what I got. A civvy trainer named Mal pushed twelve of us flat out for six hours a day. The physical side was exhausting and the ringcraft was a nightmare.

I was boxing in the heavyweight division and I expected my kick boxing to give me an edge, but the opposite was true. I had all these weapons, elbows, knees and feet in particular, that I wasn't allowed to use. I'd be halfway to delivering a strike with shin or knee and have to stop myself. It made me a worse boxer. I tried to make up for lack of technique with aggression.

After four weeks' training, the Corps Championship began. I won the first fight easily and the semi-final that followed. The third fight was the final and I was close to becoming the Royal Marines' heavyweight champion at the first attempt. It was three rounds against an opponent called Scouse. My strategy was to take the hits but give two back every time. I hoped the judges would be impressed by my aggression and workrate. As long as I could land punches, it would work.

Scouse was a decent boxer and I took more punishment than I dished out. The judges gave it to him on points and I was gutted. It was a good effort but the runner-up was still a loser in my eyes.

It was probably a good thing. If I'd won the fight I'd have represented the Corps and been put up against even better boxers who would have completely outclassed me. Without the technique, I had no hope.

I went Arctic training in Norway and finally got my skiing lessons. They taught us how to do section and troop attacks in the snow and minus 20°C temperatures, and as it was winter it was also pitch black twenty hours a day with about four hours of twilight around lunchtime. We moved on military-issue cross-country skis and snowshoes like tennis racquets. We built igloos and snowholes and slept in them.

Local Norwegian prices to a young Bootneck were ridiculous. Beer was about £11 a pint so we didn't drink much. I remember paying £16 for a standard hamburger so we also lived on ration packs for most of the time.

We were all looking forward to the 15km ski race as a diversion. We used a grippy ski wax called Klister to help get our issue skis up hills and along the flat sections. It was potent stuff and we used it very sparingly. The Corporal, Harry – the chalk commander I would fly to Afghanistan with later on – decided to have a bit of fun at my expense. He plastered my skis with Klister and stuck them together the night before the race. It was like super-glue: you only needed a tiny bit.

In the morning, the race was on and my skis were stuck hard together. I prised them apart and the Klister formed spiders' webs of gloop between them.

'I'll never clean this lot off,' I dripped.

A 'mate' gave me some friendly advice. 'There's an easy way round that, Rammers. Just put a cigarette lighter to it and the Klister will vanish in a couple of seconds. It's highly flammable and will just burn off.'

'OK, I'll give it a go.'

The skis went up like they'd been napalmed. The

rest of the section laughed their arses off as I tried to put them out.

I made it to the start line, clipped into my smouldering, blackened, superglued skis. The first section was uphill and I raced to the peak in good time. 'Nothing wrong with the skis,' I thought, leaping forward into the tuck for a downhill section. The burnt skis locked hard to the snow and I went arse over tit down the slope.

'Nice style, Rammers, when you going to the Olympics?' laughed one of the lads as I dusted myself off.

That was it. I saw red, got up and just ran with the skis on, using them like long snowshoes. The course was ten miles and I managed to finish it. I didn't come last either.

Back at Stonehouse Barracks a couple of my mates were talking about trying out for the SBS. The Special Boat Service was the legendary Special Forces unit and Royal Marines were considered excellent candidates for selection. The word was that the physical side was tough but, as long as you were fully fit, not as bad as you might expect. You were treated with respect for what you'd already achieved as a Royal Marine. The real killer was the steepness of the learning curve for the massive range of new skills they rammed into you. They were rumoured to spend so much time underwater some of the lads called them 'bubbleheads', though not to their faces.

I wasn't keen. I hated the idea of failure so much I knew that if I went for it I'd force myself to pass every test, no matter what it took physically or mentally. The reality of that commitment made me hold back.

I was a Royal Marine.

That was enough.

8

About a dozen Marines were lounging round the TV room at the FOB watching Stu Green watching *Alan Partridge* as usual. We'd all done our watches in the sangars and had a couple of hours to kill before going up for our scran.

I was flipping through a lads' magazine when I came across some pictures of three Army lads posing in desert rig with weapons and webbing, trying their best to look like war heroes. They'd sent in some pictures and the magazine had printed them with a tribute to 'Our Boys' in Afghanistan. I was outraged.

'Lads, look at these REMFed-up twats trying to look like John Rambo. They sent these pictures in from – ooh, scary – Camp Bastion in – and this is actually in here – "lawless Helmand Province".'

'Let me have a look at that, Rammers.' Jurgen grabbed the mag. 'Cheeky bastards. They've actually gone and got a Minimi for the picture. All those hot showers must have softened their brains. They want to get out here to the front and get some in. Idiots.' He threw the mag back at me in disgust.

'I tell you what, boys, if they want some pictures from the front line, let's give them some of us, eh?'

'Great idea, Rammers.'

It was only a few weeks before Christmas. We were allowed thirty minutes' internet a week so I sent Becky an email asking her to send out thirty Santa hats. If they wanted a cracking phot of warfighting infantry out in the Afghan, we would be happy to oblige.

The hats arrived with the mail and we all put them on and posed for a picture in our compound. We didn't have to wear body armour and helmets unless we went outside the compound into the base. In any case it was all quiet. We lined up for the picture in desert rig with our weapons displayed and our Santa hats on.

Suddenly, Jurgen yelled 'Naked phot!' and started stripping off his clothes.

I groaned and started getting undressed. Anyone who dared to object would be pinned to the deck and shaved bald or some other punishment for not entering into the spirit of things.

Fourteen of us posed, naked apart from Santa hats and flip-flops, holding our weapons discreetly to hide our bollocks from view. Four of the lads knelt in the front row, Jurgen among them, hiding his modesty behind his 51mm mortar. Not satisfied with that, we then scampered all over our compound taking ridiculous phots of us aiming weapons and monkeying about bollocky buff. Most of the senior NCOs were up at the HQ so no harm done, it cheered us all up.

I was going to send the phot in to *Nuts* magazine but I never got the chance.

We dragged our cots out into the sun to soak up some rays.

'Here, Baggsy, these IDF attacks are a pain in the arse, eh?'

'Yeah. I reckon we're all right in the compound though. Taliban can't hit a thing and there's lots of hard cover to dive into.'

'It's nothing compared to Iraq, mate. Mortars keep you in cover but at least the Taliban can't drop chemical weapons on us.'

I told him about my tour during the invasion of Iraq in 2003. I'd sat through a series of Scud missile attacks during the build-up to the invasion. Mortars were just blast and shrapnel; Scuds carried massive warheads and might be armed with mustard gas or any other of a number of horrendous chemical weapons.

The first thing you knew about it was a sudden shout of 'Gas, gas, gas!' and someone hammering a metal spoon against the inside of a tin can as a homemade alarm bell. The first time it happened we were camped up three miles inside the Kuwaiti border waiting for the 'go' to cross into Iraq and invade. The yelled warning and rattling tin can were the scariest things I'd ever heard and I leapt off my cot in the tent. It was not a drill and I was shitting myself. The thought of being shot or even stabbed with a bayonet I could deal with, but having your skin boiled off or your lungs melted by chemicals was something I hated even thinking about.

There was no point being in body armour and helmet, we needed full nuclear, biological, chemical protection. I ripped open the top of my bergen and pulled out my NBC suit, a bundle of rubberized material tied neatly in a roll with a shoelace knot, packed on top of a fat knapsack. Then I tore open the knapsack, grabbed the respirator and jammed it over my face, pulling the straps over my head and tightening them up. Breathing hard on the musty chemicals, I pulled the shoelace knot and unrolled my suit by throwing it on to the cot. I grabbed the trousers, shoved my feet down to the end of the rubber socks attached to the suit, pulled the waist drawstring tight and pulled on a pair of cotton gloves; then I shoved my arms into the sleeves of the jacket and pulled on a pair of heavy rubber over-boots. I fastened the jacket and the hood securely over the respirator and finally added a pair of rubber gauntlets.

Grabbing the knapsack, packed with combi-pen antidote injectors and Fuller's Earth decontamin-ation kit, I fastened it around my waist and burst out of the tent. Heat, effort and fear had the sweat gushing out of me. I stumbled five metres to my right down the steps of the trench we used as a shelter against Scud missile attacks and slumped into the bottom of it.

The Marines trained you to get into the NBC suit in minutes. We got plenty of practice back in Lympstone. They put you in a chamber and sprayed you with CS gas until you could get your respirator on and airtight in a few seconds. We used to come out of that chamber choking and cursing but I was grateful for the training in Iraq. Never mind minutes, I wanted that NBC suit on and sealed up tight in seconds.

We knew Saddam Hussein had a stockpile of chemical weapons. The chief fear was mustard gas, which we thought he had used against his own Kurdish population during the Iran/Iraq war in the eighties. It makes your skin blister on contact and offers a slow, agonizing death. Tony Blair was saying Saddam had tons of it and might use weapons of mass destruction against us.

Ideal.

There were loads of other Marines and Navy personnel in the trench, all clumping about in their suits. It was five feet deep, three feet wide and 20 feet long (I knew the dimensions well because I had been ordered to dig the fucking thing out of the hard rock and packed sand of the desert). It was lunchtime and about 50°C. There was no shade, no sandbags and nothing to sit on. Inside the suits, we melted slowly. The NBC kit was like a portable sauna with steam made out of the wearer's sweat. I was nineteen years old and as fit as I would ever be in my life. Sweat streamed out of me so badly it fogged up the lenses of my respirator.

I sat there searching the air above. Mustard gas might have a brown colour or it might be colourless. I felt vulnerable and hated it. We all hoped the threat of nuclear retaliation would stop Saddam from using chemical weapons but no one knew what the mad old bastard was going to do.

The alarm was for a Scud attack on Kuwait City, but we didn't see or hear a thing. After an hour the camp commanders tested the air for chemical agents and word went round. The lad next to me clonked his respirator into the side of my head and said 'Or keer' through the rubber.

'Thank fuck for that,' I thought. The Scud attacks were the worst on a long list of bad things about being stuck in Kuwait waiting to invade.

I stomped back to our tent, peeled the NBC suit off and hung it up to dry. We couldn't wash them because it would destroy the charcoal liner on the inside. Once the sweat had dried off the inside I would roll it up again and stow it. It was one chore I was meticulous about.

I was like, 'Bring on the invasion, it can't be worse than this.'

I was one of three Marines posted to a team of

Navy medics. Our tent was the sickbay and we especially hoped there would be no casualties because we would be out of a home for starters.

The echelon camp had been set up about two weeks prior to the invasion and there were limited facilities available. It was just a lorry park in the desert to be honest. Toilets consisted of a trench in the sand with a bench suspended above it, with three holes cut out of it for three backsides. There was a windbreak around most of it but no partition between the holes. You had to take a crap sitting next to a couple of blokes. No one liked it but you just took a seat, said 'All right, mate?' and cracked on. The bit I didn't like was the fact that the windbreak around the bench was only about four feet tall and people walking around the camp could see you from the arse up. It wasn't great having people walking around behind you while you turfed one out, but Marines are known for cheerfulness in the face of adversity. A can-do attitude had never been more useful.

We were actually lucky to have the sickbay tent. Most of the lads were sleeping on the desert floor next to their vehicles with a tarp pulled over them. The food wasn't good either. There was no field kitchen and the British foil bag rations were no fun eaten cold. We used to trade and scrounge whenever we got the chance.

I was sent with a mate back to Kuwait City to stock up on medical supplies, which was a brilliant treat for us. We were not allowed to use the main road from the echelon camp down to KC, I think so as not to offend the Kuwaitis by clogging up their streets with military vehicles. The Engineers had bulldozed a Main Supply Route straight across the desert for military traffic. The journey took ninety back-breaking minutes bouncing around in the Land Rover.

The military camp at KC was about the size of FOB ROB but with less Hesco. It was a major supply dump and was almost deserted: everyone was on the border waiting to go. We drew the medical supplies – basics such as bandages and boxes of painkillers – then we took advantage of the fully REMFed-up facilities of the camp. A long hot shower, private use of a luxury toilet, and a shave with never-ending supplies of hot water. Happy days. Then it was off to the galley where the food was superb. I sank my teeth into a juicy burger followed by a fresh salad and chuckled at the thought of all the lads stuck back at camp sleeping in the dirt.

The more I thought of them the more it seemed I should do something about it. All this stuff lying around in the rear while our mates lived rough before going into combat – it wasn't right. 'Hmmm . . .' I looked around the dining room to the rear area. I poked my head through the tent and there was a miserable-looking Pongo Corporal tidying up the catering equipment.

'Hello, Corporal, have we come to the right place?'

'What's up?'

'Colonel Green, CO of the Royal Marine field hospital, sent us down here to pick up fresh rations for patients and casualties. We've already been issued the med supplies he requested. He's all cued up for the invasion but bricking it that he won't have enough rations if casualties start coming in when the invasion kicks off.'

The Corporal looked me up and down. There was no Colonel Green, but he didn't know that. 'Wait one,' he said, and disappeared.

Two minutes later he was back with his boss, a fierce-looking Warrant Officer.

'Aargh,' I thought. 'Too late to back down now.' I explained myself again, making the invented Colonel Green more pissed off about the lack of rations. I itemized the medical supplies we'd picked up and felt I sounded as if I knew what I was talking about.

The Warrant Officer looked at me with a beady eye. I concentrated on thinking chilled-out thoughts. A bead of sweat formed between my shoulder blades.

'Fine,' he said. 'Give 'em what they want, Corporal.'

'Yes! Good effort, Rammers,' I thought to myself, and breathed a sigh of relief.

We were led to the stores like two kids in a sweet

shop. Fresh fruit, fresh milk, slabs of drinks cartons, slabs of individual cereal packets. Treats stacked floor to ceiling everywhere we turned. 'Ha, Coco Pops!' The lads were going to love it. 'Woo-hoo!' We'd hit gold: stacks of US meals ready to eat, far superior to our own foil bag rations. The ration packs themselves could be heated up individually with a chemical pack so you never needed to eat them cold. The treats in the packs were better than UK sweets as well – Skittles and M&Ms.

We filled black gash bags until they were toppers with MRE packs, crammed the back of the Land Rover until it threatened to burst, and headed back to camp. We shared out the loot among our troop and all their mates and felt very pleased with our private supply chain. Royal Logistics Corps got nothing on us.

Not only that, but we went back and repeated the trick several times. I think the WO was being nice to us because he knew we were about to go over the border. Also, there was no one left in camp and they had more supplies than they knew what to do with. He might have been a Pongo, but somehow the Army had messed up and promoted a really decent bloke to senior NCO rank. It cheered us all right up.

Two Marines named Matt and Richie were the other drivers for our three vehicles: a stripped-down Land Rover that we used as a homemade WMIK with a GPMG attached, a four-tonner truck, and a Land Rover ambulance. Our officers were

Royal Navy and we were the only three blokes they could really order about, so we copped a ton of bullshit.

The officers showed us where they wanted the vehicles parked and where to put up the tent, then one of them turned round to me and said, 'Right, we'll need a decent slit trench against air attack or bombardment. Over there. Needs to be a good size. Make it three feet wide, five deep, twenty long. Carry on.' Then he turned on his heel and waltzed off with his mates for a security briefing.

The three of us looked at the entrenching tools and shovels we had on the side of our wagons. Matt gave the ground a kick. Underneath about a centimetre of loose sand on the surface it was compacted and hard as rock.

'Twenty feet long? How the fuck are we going to do that?' dripped Matt.

Richie was equally disgusted. 'A trench that big is going to take us three days' digging at least.'

'That's if we can break the ground,' I added. 'It's hard as nails. It's going to kill the entrenching tools.'

Bootnecks were tough blokes and fit with it, but this was taking the piss.

We went through the motions of marking it out, then I hit the ground hard with a pickaxe and chipped a tiny hole. 'Bloody officers. We're drivers, not sappers. There are only three of us. How can we carve a trench out of solid rock?' This was going to be an utter bastard.

There were lots of vehicles moving about near us so the roar of a diesel engine passing by barely registered with me. But something about one of them caught my ear. I looked up. Moving down the column of vehicles towards us was a Royal Engineers JCB.

'You beauty,' I thought.

Without thinking, I stepped in front of it and waved at the driver to slow down. He was a spotty kid of about seventeen. He must have been one of the youngest lads in the Army (he'd only been in a couple of months). Not only was I two years older than him, I was one of three properly threaders Bootnecks who really, *really* didn't want to spend three days digging a hole in the desert.

'All right, mate?' I greeted him with a big smile. 'Listen, do you fancy doing us a big favour?'

'What's that?' the lad asked, looking around nervously. I think he thought we were going to kidnap him or something.

'We need a slit trench twenty feet long and five feet deep right here. Shovels are no good and it'd only take you a second, mate. How about it?'

The kid looked unsure.

I changed tack. 'Have you ever tried the American ration packs?'

'No, but I've heard about them. They're supposed to be great.'

'We've got gash bags full of them. Really hoofin' scran. M&Ms.'

Matt flashed a couple out of the back of the WMIK.

'M&Ms?' The kid's face lit up.

'You'd be welcome to a bagload. Go on, what do you say?'

'All right, lads, where do you want this trench?'

Before you knew it the JCB was gouging away at the desert. He had a shovel on the back about a metre wide and dug us a beautiful trench. We sent him away with real gratitude and a big gash bag full of treats.

'Look at that, the Trench of Justice,' Richie hooted.

'Trench of Justice!' Matt and I punched the air in clenched-fist salute.

There was one slight problem with our hole in the ground: it was a bit awkward to get in and out of. You just had to jump in and scramble out again. 'What we need is a nice set of steps,' I said. And we could finish that with hand tools, no problem.

We were just putting the finishing touches to an elegant rocky staircase to the Trench of Justice when the officers came back from their brief. They expected us to have made a small dent in the desert by now, I suppose, and to be sunburnt, hanging and threaders into the bargain. The look on their faces when they saw we'd finished a three-day job in three hours was fantastic. I was fucked if I was going to tell them how we'd done it.

'Hrrmmph, good effort, well done,' they conceded, and stomped off.

It was lucky we'd done a good job on the trench because we needed it. In the two or three weeks before we invaded we sat through seven Scud alerts. All of them were for real, Scuds fired in anger, it was just a question of whether they were heading our way or not. Some roared over our position on their way to Kuwait, others we didn't see or hear. Every time the warning 'Gas, gas, gas!' was shouted it seemed to scare the shit out of me more than it had done the last time. I hated every minute of it. The lads came to my rescue, mucking around in their NBC suits, trying to headbutt each other and making stupid noises through their respirators.

We were sitting NBC-suited one night waiting for the all-clear when there was a hissing roar overhead that sounded like a cross between a jet fighter and a rocket. It was way too close for me. I hoped it was a Coalition jet of some sort but inside I was counting seconds for the bang and the mustard gas to come on down. Instead, the all-clear came and we started peeling ourselves out of the NBC suits.

Word came back. A Scud missile had impacted about 1,000 metres from our position bang on the Main Supply Route back to KC. The Engineers and Explosive Ordnance Disposal teams were going to deal with it.

'A thousand metres.'

'Yeah, but it didn't explode. It's just a dud.'

I wanted the invasion to start as soon as possible so we could get out of this desert shithole before

Saddam managed to choke us all with Agent Orange, or whatever shit he had up his sleeve. None of us slept easy: there was hard evidence of the enemy's capability to deliver chemical weapons to our doorstep sitting out on the MSR less than a mile away. They never told us what was in the warhead either. Sitting under bombardment was shit because there was nothing you could do to improve your chances. Apart from getting into your suit properly and making sure your respirator worked, you just had to sit there like a lab rat. There was no one to shoot back at, no chance to run faster or shoot straighter. You were powerless to change anything, and it drove me nuts.

Another night there was a ground-shaking bang. It was nothing like the sharp crack of a rifle but a rumbling bass explosion that you felt in your guts. I was very quickly off the cot and halfway into my NBC suit, convinced a Scud had landed and detonated. Tragically, as it turned out, there was no need for the suit. A US Sea Knight helicopter with four US aircrew and eight men from 3 Commando Brigade – seven Royal Marines and one Royal Navy operator mechanic – had crashed into the desert and exploded in a fireball. A column of smoke about 2,000 metres from our position was clearly visible the next morning.

It was a US Marine Corps helicopter and we all felt bad for the Americans, and absolutely gutted for our own lads. Everything seemed more serious from that point on. It wasn't such a big adventure. People had been killed and the attack on Saddam had only just begun.

An investigation later suggested a mechanical failure had caused the helo's nose to drop suddenly in flight with catastrophic results. The lads' families were devastated. Their loved ones had paid the ultimate price for the invasion of Iraq.

Within hours we were packing up and getting ready to cross the border. The invasion was on. I didn't care what we came across on the other side, I was just glad to be getting away from that camp.

There must have been a hundred vehicles in our convoy. It stretched for miles, further than you could see. It was a mix of supply trucks and armoured vehicles but no Challenger II main battle tanks. The dust was horrendous. I was in our home-made open-topped WMIK with helmet, goggles and shemag scarf over my nose and mouth but it was impossible to keep the dust out. It got everywhere. You could feel it crunching between your molars, a nice mix of sand, grit and goat shit.

Our destination was the Umm Qasr Naval Base and deep-water port in southern Iraq. According to plan, 3 Commando Brigade, Royal Marines would have stormed the place and cleared it out, allowing our unit to set up a field hospital.

The Marine forces had encountered stiffer opposition than expected; RM Artillery inside the

Kuwait border had been called in to pound Iraqi troops in the port as street fighting in the city escalated. By the time we got there it was all over. We rolled up to the base and a squad of lads was sent in to clear it. They came back with a few Iraqi prisoners who turned out to be fairly friendly.

My mates in Motor Transport Troop were ordered into a stinking hangar and told to pitch tents inside for their accommodation. Matt, Richie and I quickly realized we had landed on our feet: the medical aid station was to be based in air-conditioned accommodation. It was only natural that we went and visited M/T to take the piss out of their hangar. Somewhere in there was Sean Helsby, who was a Bootneck at that stage. We asked the lads if they were warm enough in the stinking heat and could we borrow a couple of blankets because the aircon in our place was a bit fierce.

We got the medical station set up quick time and then there was very little to do. Another ambulance in the unit picked up a Marine who'd been shot during an engagement on the water near the base. Fortunately he wasn't seriously hurt and it was quickly dealt with. The rest of the time we just minced around in flip-flops and shorts waiting for someone to give us some work to do.

Despite the heavy fighting up towards Basra, casualties were not coming our way. A few weeks later we were given our end-of-tour dates and spent as much time as we possibly could sunbathing naked on the roof of M/T's hangar. I came home with the best all-over sun tan I'd ever had.

The invasion saw thousands of British troops engaged in proper warfighting. The Royal Marines of 3 Commando Brigade fought their way up the Al Faw peninsula in textbook style winning a hatful of gallantry medals and impressing military commanders of all nations. In my book, I'd contributed nothing to that effort, and I was threaders about it. Even when there was a proper war on I hadn't come close to firing my weapon. I loved being in the Marines but that tour left me wondering if I would ever see any action. For the first time I wondered if civvy street might hold the key to a better life.

9

It wasn't my experience in Iraq but the Arctic exercises that eventually made up my mind. They always came round in January, which was when my baby daughter Kezia was due to be born. That meant I was always going to be away in Norway for four weeks when her birthday came around. Family life was going to get really tough if that carried on. My girlfriend at the time, Kezia's mum Vicky, wanted us to have a more regular home life. I agreed and decided to give it a go.

In January 2005, Kezia was born, a beautiful bouncing baby girl. I was really chuffed to be a dad. I immediately handed in my chit giving a year's notice that I would be leaving the Marines.

Looking back, it was madness. The Royal Marines was all I'd known since the age of sixteen. I loved Kezia like crazy but deep down I didn't want to leave at all. Everything about being in the Corps suited me down to the ground. It was like being in a second family full of brothers.

I remembered when Sean Helsby had joined our troop along with some new lads just after Iraq. He and the others had to dress up using only a roll of gaffer tape. There were about six of them and we split them into three teams to run a catfood relay. Each team had to run about ten yards then eat a plate of catfood, a plate of ketchup laced with salt and a block of lard. This had to be washed down with six pints of cider. Sean was as sick as a dog. Last pair to finish had to snog each other in front of everyone.

At the same time we'd shaved Matt's eyebrows off for lying to us in Iraq, and he had to take part as well, though he didn't have to eat the catfood. His 'crime' was to turn up at the Umm Qasr base after a trip to Kuwait City with two giant stereo speakers and a chunky gold necklace. He was mega-embarrassed about going shopping during a war for such stupid items and we gave him a hard time about it.

'I didn't buy them, honest,' he lied in protest.

'Well where did you get them from then?'

'Er, my mum sent them to me from England.'

'No she didn't, Matt. No one would send anything so stupid out here.'

'She did. Eyebrows, she did.'

Well, if he eyebrowsed it, we had to take his word for it. He was swearing he was telling the truth, and if we found out he was lying it was our duty to shave his eyebrows off.

A couple of days later I found a receipt in the door of the Land Rover from a Kuwait City shopping mall for two hi-fi speakers and a gold necklace. Matt had to appear at a kangaroo court back in the UK and sentence was duly passed.

I know it sounds childish but it was all a great laugh and it bonded the lads together. I was going to miss all that nonsense, and blokes who'd do anything for their mates. I'd never had a civvy job and didn't know how civvies lived their lives, but I had a feeling it wasn't going to be the brotherhood I'd known in the Marines.

I didn't make a fuss about going. Everyone knew months in advance I was off and I said my goodbyes quietly. I reported to the CO of 539 Assault Squadron and was handed my discharge papers stating that I was of good character.

Leaving was a bit like getting my Green Lid. I expected the gates to open in a blast of trumpets then clang like a church bell as they shut behind me for the final time. In the end I just threw my stuff in the car and drove home.

I had absolutely no idea what I was going to do with myself. The thought of working in an office for a local firm, taking orders from some sixteen-year-old sprog just because his dad ran the company, sent chills down my spine. I needed to be outdoors and active.

In the end the work chose me.

One of my civvy mates, Dave Parker, ran a firm providing doormen for pubs and clubs around Plymouth, Ivybridge and Tavistock. He was a serious bloke and ran the firm properly. All Dave's doormen wore a black 'uniform' of boots, trousers and shirt topped off with a bright red tie. They had to undergo the proper training and courses to get their Security Industry Authority badges. Dave kept up good relationships with the businesses he worked for and with the police. The money was OK and I thought it would just fill a gap while I figured out what I wanted to do.

During the training we learned how to read body language and spent most of the course practising how to defuse tense situations. We did role play where members of the group took it in turn to act like drunken arseholes. The focus was on spotting trouble before it happened and restraining violent people instead of getting into a fight with them.

Plymouth is a lively town of a weekend and we had a busy time on the doors. At first it seemed like a bit of an adventure. You never knew what was going to happen from one night to the next. After a few weeks I began to realize that although thousands of people would come out and have a great night every weekend without a hint of trouble, there was an unending supply of arseholes who couldn't go home without taking a swing at someone, usually the doormen, at the end of the night.

One incident was typical.

I was on a door in Plymouth when a young woman came running out of the club to say four blokes were knocking the crap out of each other inside. I sprinted into the club and sure enough the lads were rolling around on the floor whacking each other. I was on my own but dived in and pulled them all apart. They explained they were all good mates and they were just mucking about and having a laugh. They always did this sort of thing, it was just playfighting. None of them was hurt.

They were all drunk and I started talking to them like I was their mum. I told them if they wanted to act like that they should go out to the park and do it there. They were in a nightclub not a playground and were expected to act like it. 'I'm not going to throw you out this time, but if you start acting like idiots again you'll be asked to leave,' I warned. I was within my rights to chuck them out straight away but didn't want to act like an arsehole myself. Everyone deserves a second chance.

They settled down and I felt as if I'd just ticked off a bunch of schoolkids. I thought nothing of it and went back to the door. There were two doormen outside for security and I was in charge of taking the entrance money inside.

I was getting on with my job when, *wham*. Everything went black. I saw stars and fell against the door. Blood spurted from my nose. One of the kids had sneaked up behind me, smacked me in the face as hard as he could and tried to leg it. His shot connected on the bridge of my nose but didn't break it.

He ran straight into the other two lads on the door and was still trying to get past them when I caught up with him. They'd seen what had happened and we were all furious with the little dickhead. I lost my temper, walked straight up to him and smacked him in the head once. I didn't really put any power into the shot, I was more annoyed with his stupidity than anything else. It was me that was left bleeding afterwards, not him.

That was enough, he wasn't going to fight, but he did go and get the police complaining that I'd whacked him. Despite my bloody nose, the officers took a very dim view. The local police were quick to stamp on any violence on the doors and if they suspected a doorman was there to get into fights they came down on him like a ton of bricks. They started off on the basis that every doorman was a big dumb bully until presented with solid proof to the contrary.

Luckily for me, a hen party of women in their forties had been in the queue and seen the whole thing. They leapt to my defence without being asked and explained what had happened, how he'd crept up behind me and attacked without warning. The lad disappeared, and that was the end of that.

This sort of drunken behaviour started to get me down after a while. You were only allowed to use reasonable restraint against a drunk, which usually amounted to grabbing his wrists. If he tried to butt or kick you, what was classed as reasonable restraint might end up being decided afterwards, in the cold light of a courtroom, with you in the dock, not him. You walked a tightrope between defending yourself effectively when a drunk started swinging and being able to defend your actions to the police if the drunk decided he'd been attacked when he sobered up. There was good banter on the doors and Dave's team were a top bunch of lads, but as a career there was just too much aggro involved for me. The way I saw it, one day you were either going to get badly hurt or end up in trouble with the police for defending yourself too well.

My relationship with Kezia's mum wasn't going well either. I thought I was digging out blind to support our family, doing a tough job as well as I could. She thought I was an arsehole for any number of reasons. We decided to call Endex on the relationship and go our separate ways. Although I was determined to see as much of Kezia as I could and to be the best possible dad in the circumstances, I knew it was going to be tough.

Working the doors had one brilliant outcome. About ten months after I split up with Kezia's mum I was on the door at a nightclub called Reflex and Flares that ran a seventies and eighties night that was really popular with students at the university. A beautiful girl with long brown hair and a lovely

smile came out of the club one night and said she'd
lost her phone inside, would we have a look for it?
We gave her a number to call the next day to see if
we'd found it. I made sure it was my number she
took away with her.

We never found her phone, but Becky and her
mates were regulars at the club. Every time I saw
her queuing up to get in we had a chat and a joke
and I kept asking her out. 'Go on, drop me a text.
Let's go for a drink. Why don't you call me?'

She was like, 'Yeah, yeah, whatever.'

There was a definite spark between us. I kept
letting her in for free and blatantly hoped she'd call.
She told me later she really did fancy me but was a
bit unsure about dating a doorman. Becky's a bright
girl and was studying Public Service Management
at the uni. I guess the 'big dumb bully until
proved otherwise' attitude made her a bit wary as
well.

She wasn't like lots of the girls who came in. She
was never raucous or drunk. She was a really classy
girl but easy to talk to. Tony Soprano would have
approved: she was gentle, not loud. Sweet soundin'.
We had a good laugh whenever we saw each other
at the club.

After about a month of her not calling or texting
me I decided to go for it. 'All right, Becky,' I said
one night, 'if you don't drop me a text this time I'm
going to have to ban you from the club.'

'What?' she yelled, doing her best to sound

furious. 'How long for?' She was trying not to laugh, and that was a good thing.

'Lifetime ban. You'll have to wait outside and talk to me until your friends have finished inside. Nothing I can do about it.'

She was outraged, but with a twinkle in her eye. It did the trick. A couple of nights later we went out for a drink and had a great time. We went on more dates and never looked back. I knew she was someone special and I couldn't believe my luck.

We'd been going out together for a couple of months when we ended up taking a DVD home with a couple of bottles of rosé wine. I wanted to tell Becky something. She looked absolutely beautiful and I was pretty sure she was the one for me. Every time I was about to come out and tell her I thought better of it and took a gulp of wine. I hardly noticed it going down. I was pretty steaming by the time I finally blurted out, 'I think I've fallen in love with you.'

Becky looked at me, saw me grinning lopsided at her with about three pints of pink wine sloshing around inside me, and said, 'Oh, right.'

That was it. Not quite the response I was after, but I knew her. She was bluffing and secretly chuffed about it.

She didn't say anything more for about a week, and then she told me she loved me.

Told ya. We've been together since New Year's Eve 2006.

* * *

During the time when I was trying to persuade Becky to come out on a date, I was doing a lot of research on the internet. I thought with my military background and experience I would make an excellent bodyguard for serious close protection work and that it might provide a proper career to get me off the doors. I wanted to get the very best training and qualifications available, and that meant going on a world-class course.

There were plenty about, but one in particular looked very good, a five-weeker run by a firm in South Africa. They provided accommodation overlooking the beach in Hout Bay, a few miles down the coast from Cape Town. What appealed was that you could do every aspect of the course – weapons training, live firing, tactical driving, paramedic training – in one place; other courses suggested flying to Gibraltar, say, for weapons training and then back to mainland Europe for other elements. It was expensive, £4,000 all in, but the qualifications and coursework offered were to the highest standards available in the industry.

I had some inheritance money from my gran and a small amount of savings. I talked it through with my mum and dad. They could see I'd made up my mind to do the course and were right behind me as usual.

There were seventeen students on the course and fifteen of them were ex-British military. I was one of two ex-Marines, the rest were ex-Army. A group of eight former soldiers were setting up their own private security firm and were taking the course together. The other two students were South African. One of them was my roommate and a qualified pilot. He didn't say why he wanted close protection expertise as well as being able to fly, but he was a bright bloke and took it all very seriously.

During unarmed combat training they taught us how to disarm blokes coming at you with knives or sticks. They had a dummy knife blade and coated the 'sharp' edge of it with bright red lipstick so that everyone could see where you had been 'cut' if you failed to disarm the knifeman effectively. The technique was to aim light taps with your right hand at the forearm or wrist of the hand your opponent was holding his weapon in. The idea was to dummy the assailant into striking and then seize his forearm or wrist, forcing him to drop the weapon.

Other techniques were brutally efficient and concentrated on disabling your opponent as quickly as possible. A full-power two-fingered jab to your enemy's eye socket was a favourite strike. They pointed out areas behind the knees that could be slashed with a knife to disable an attacker and suggested shooting assailants through the wrist to prevent them taking any further hostile action against you. This brought laughs from the Brits who all said there was no way they could legally use such crippling techniques in the UK. The two South African students paid close attention to the instructors. It looked as if they could think of plenty of situations when they might have to do exactly what was being taught.

'Special Weapons and Tactics' taught us effective use of pistol, shotgun, carbine and rifle, and I was bog average at all of it. My military training came to the fore when they decided to distract the students by letting off firecrackers under their arses during the middle of a session on the range. You've got to remain focused on the fact you have a loaded weapon in your mitt that can do all sorts of un-intended damage.

The close quarter battle techniques they taught were interesting. The Marines taught you to assault buildings on the basis that there was no doubt they were occupied by armed enemy. You battered down the door and filled the room with grenades and automatic fire. The CP course focused much more on movement and techniques for advancing through buildings that might or might not be occupied by an enemy. It mainly focused on controlling your body movements to a set of rules that created minimum exposure to attack.

I loved every minute of it.

They taught us tactical driving on the skid pan. We learned to do handbrake turns, J-turns and 180-degree spins to get yourself straight back out of trouble if ambushed. All good fun. After that the driving took on a planning element, learning to operate in small convoys and the tactical roles applicable to each vehicle.

We moved to a racetrack to carry out protective driving drills. I was on the back seat of one car and had to keep a watch to the rear; just like the last man in a section patrol I spent most of the time travelling backwards. The aim was to spot an instructor who was going to appear on the course in front of us and attack the lead vehicle. Our job was to place our car between the threat and the target with a handbrake turn. My role was to take the attacker out with a paintball gun as we spun by him. I saw him in good time and let him have it.

It was a brilliant shot. I got him right in the nuts. It was an accident, I was just trying to hit his centre of mass, but the paintball shot between his legs just winged his privates. He must have been wearing a cricket box or something protective because he didn't even drop to one knee, and those paintballs sting like hell. He was a gentleman about it and we all had a good laugh at his expense. I was really pleased that I'd hit him though. No one else on the course made the shot.

The paramedic training they gave us was astonishing. The organizers operated private ambulances in South Africa that were licensed to take us out on real shouts as trainee medics. We were going to be putting what they taught us into live use immediately after learning it.

The drills were complicated and quite tough to learn. When you needed this stuff you wouldn't have time to check the book to see that you were doing it right, you had to have the correct procedures in your head. Was the casualty showing signs of internal bleeding or a heart attack? If he's stopped breathing and has a suspected neck injury, what do you do? There was a lot to take in and get right. And when you're practising CPR and all the other drills, the fact you'll have to do it for real in a few days' time makes you pay attention.

Me and another student were assigned to an ambulance with two instructor paramedics from the course. We were going to be on duty for one shift on a Saturday and were warned we would probably be quite busy.

They weren't joking.

We got the first shout a few minutes after arriving for work. We climbed into the VW Transporter that was stuffed with up-to-date medical gear, with room for four crew and two stretchers.

'What's the job?' I asked. 'Nothing too bad I hope?'

'Well, the casualty's still alive, but he's been shot three times so it's touch and go.'

I couldn't believe my ears, or my eyes. We arrived in the middle of a shanty town near Cape Town and there was a massive crowd around a man lying on his back in the middle of the road next to a truck. He was still breathing and they ordered me to stabilize his head and keep his airway clear while they went to work: they weren't sure if he had spinal injuries or not and wanted to make sure his neck didn't move at all while they worked on him. The danger was he could start to asphyxiate if his airway closed up and then there'd be no point to what they were doing. He was lying at an awkward angle and I had to crawl under the truck to hold his head the way they wanted it.

He had taken three rounds – one in the arse, one in the arm and one in the ribs which had gone through him and passed out the other side. There wasn't that much blood that I could see, which surprised me.

I was way out of my depth and didn't have a clue what was going on. The paramedics gave me orders and I did as I was told.

We got him stabilized and into the wagon then roared off to hospital. He was still alive when we got there.

'Good effort,' I thought. 'What's next?'

Within the hour we were en route to a petrol station. A black guy had been carjacked by attackers who'd stabbed him with a big blade and driven off in his vehicle. We found him lying on the deck at the petrol station with a gaping hole in his chest.

I got an oxygen mask on him and started sorting out pain relief. Meanwhile, one of the instructor paramedics spotted that one side of the victim's chest was starting to swell up badly. That was very bad news for the casualty. The knife had punctured the guy's lung and air was leaking out of the wound and filling his chest cavity with every breath he took. The air couldn't escape from the inside of his chest: there was no route to the outside and it couldn't go back inside the lung. The build-up of pressure was crushing his injured lung and suppressing blood flow to his heart. If we didn't do something, in about three minutes the bloke was going to suffer a massive cardiac arrest.

The instructor knew what to do but it was quite a risky procedure. If he fucked it up he could cause serious lung damage, but the casualty was in deep shit. He was going to die in a few seconds unless we intervened. The medic felt down from the guy's collarbone to the area between his second and third ribs at the top corner of his chest. He swabbed the skin to the side around the pectoral muscle with iodine and inserted a hollow needle through the sterilized area, piercing the muscle wall and pushing it into the chest cavity between the two ribs. After the initial insertion he changed the angle of the needle to avoid stabbing the injured lung, and got the tip of the needle into the pocket of trapped air. He opened a valve and the needle hissed as the air rushed out of the guy's chest, which subsided like a leaky balloon. The bloke's lung would not reinflate completely, but thanks to the successful chest decompression his chances of survival had just increased massively.

We got him on board the ambulance and took him

to a shitty little hospital that looked to me as if it might finish him off. I hope he made it.

We weren't done for the day either. Next shout was to a luxury mansion in one of the suburbs near Cape Town. The place had wall-to-wall marble floors and was bigger than any house I'd been in back home. These people were millionaires as far as I could tell. Screams were coming from an upstairs room where the woman of the house was in the final stages of labour. Her husband was nearby and relieved to see us. They didn't speak English and were babbling away in what I took to be Afrikaans.

I spent the whole time running around getting bits of surgical kit, hypothermia blankets and a stretcher.

The baby was born and made a gopping mess of the bed that made me retch. We cut the cord, cleaned Mum and baby up and took them to a hospital. It was the smartest medical unit of the day by a long way.

That was the last shout, and the instructors thought we'd got off relatively lightly. You what? If that was a let-off, I didn't want to be around for a busy day. I couldn't believe it. What a crazy place, and what a crazy way to earn a living. We'd saved two critically wounded men and delivered a baby.

To this day I don't know if it was a boy or a girl.

Part of the course involved trialling the taser stun gun. This was shaped like a pistol and fired two metal darts attached to wires into a target up to 15 feet away. The darts punched through clothing to hit the target's skin and complete a 50,000-volt electrical circuit that stunned the victim into submission without causing any lasting injury.

The taser course was an extra £180 to include in the training. If you volunteered to be blasted with the gun they waived the charge. One lad volunteered, a Brummie, one of the ex-Pongos. They stripped him to the waist and fired the taser into his back. He went down instantly, vibrating like a hammer drill and roaring his head off. Fuck that for a laugh. When he regained the power of speech he said it was the most pain he had ever experienced in his life. There were no other takers.

We completed the training and were given our results. The South African pilot I shared a room with came top. I managed the second highest score and was happy with that. Good effort.

We all went off to a bar in Hout Bay to celebrate the end of the course. Most of us were flying home the next day. After a few drinks I got a bit carried away. I collared one of the instructors. 'Come on,' I yelled in his ear. 'Get your taser gun and blast me with it. I don't reckon it's that bad. I'll be angry with myself if I go home without doing it.'

'Are you sure, Mark?'

'Yep.'

'Right, you're on.'

The instructors went and got the kit from the back of the car. They stripped me to the waist and stood either side of me.

'Firstly,' they said, 'we will demonstrate the way you will fall when hit.'

They laid me down, full length on to my belly.

'Secondly, this is my credit card,' said the instructor, placing it on the ground roughly where my forehead was due to hit the deck in a few seconds' time. 'If you can grab the credit card after you're hit with the taser, you can keep it.'

There was a growl of anticipation from the other lads. It was shaping up to be a good night's entertainment.

'Right Mark, ready?'

'Ye—'

Kazzap.

Burning pain sent my back into a spasm and I pitched forward. Nothing I could do, I was going down. As I dropped, it felt as if it wasn't hurting as much as I thought it should. It turned out one of the darts had not made a solid contact and I was getting an intermittent blast of juice. I went down and grabbed the credit card just as the instructor caught up with me and rammed one of the taser terminals into my backside to complete the circuit. He tasered the fuck out of me, and that did hurt. But I'd got his credit card and wasn't letting go.

I was helped to my feet and instantly put the card behind the bar and ordered drinks on the house for the night. The other lads were cheering like crazy, having a great laugh.

I started to feel a bit sick and had to make my excuses. My head was spinning and it felt as if I would chuck up at any minute. I went and got my head down ready for the flight home the next day. After I'd gone, the instructor told the boys that the first people he would recommend as bodyguards to potential employers were the blokes who'd volunteered to take the taser hit. In his view, it showed they had the Right Stuff to do the job at a high level where they might one day have to stop a bullet for the person they were protecting. That did it. Suddenly they were all volunteering. The instructors were getting three lads at a time wired up to zap them in batches. It turned into a bit of a circus at the end of the night.

I thought the course was excellent and well worth the money. The weapons training, driving, strategic planning and paramedic training taught me a load of stuff that was very different from the Marines' way of doing things. I was well pleased with it and started working out who to approach for work as a bodyguard.

There was as much work on offer as anyone could handle, as long as you didn't mind living in Baghdad. Private security firms were crying out for close protection staff in the Iraqi capital, and the money was excellent. I thought about it but wasn't happy. If I was going to be in that environment I

Recruit Ormrod in a formal pose halfway through training at Lympstone. We'd been issued with rifles but note the black training beret; I still had a way to go before earning the right to a Green Lid.

Below left: Aged about six or seven, I'm getting some early practice in for the Tarzan Assault Course by the look of it. My twin sister, Leanne, is in the background.

Below right: One of the proudest days of my life. Being formally presented with my Green Beret at Lympstone in 2001. The cap comforter on my head was issued at the start of Commando training. The Green Beret in my hand showed that I was now a Royal Marine.

The Kuwaiti desert in 2003, a few days before the invasion of Iraq. Three of us were able to 'borrow' a digger from the Army, in exchange for extra rations . . .

. . . after being ordered to dig a 20-foot slit trench (*above right*) in rock-hard ground, by hand. This was our shelter from Scud missile attack.

Right: On watch in Sangar Four, Forward Operating Base Robinson, Sangin Valley, Afghanistan in October 2007.

Below right: Marine Ryan Wordsworth, aka 'Jurgen the German', and me in Sangar Four.

Below: My GPMG after the tractor contact. Note spent 7.62mm ammunition and link on top of the Hesco *after* I'd cleared most of it away. Red tips to live ammunition indicate tracer rounds.

Kneeling during our first patrol to the west of FOB ROB to investigate the village by the river, a couple of months before Christmas.

Getting some evidence of my uber-chad 'tache. Becky doesn't like this picture and I can see why.

Striking a Rambo pose for a laugh during a quiet spell at FOB ROB. I wouldn't have been allowed near a contact in this state.

Right: Bench pressing about 45 kilos in our home-made gym at the FOB. It wasn't heavy enough so we had to do extra reps.

Below: 'Naked phot!' Having a laugh three days before the accident. I was going to send this picture in to *Nuts* magazine but never got the chance.

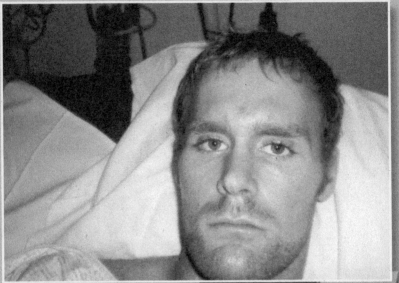

At Selly Oak hospital after being moved out of intensive care on to the Burns and Plastics ward.

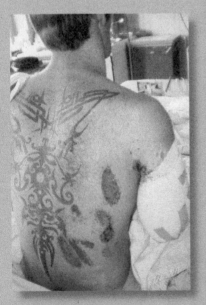

I got Becky to take this picture so I could check the damage to my tattoo. The scarring was caused by shrapnel. The tattoo didn't get a scratch.

Standing upright for the first time at Headley Court Rehabilitation Centre, about six weeks a the explosion.

Left: I spent two weeks learning to walk between the parallel bars before I could stand unaided

Below: Having my picture taken for a disabled badge. I pulled the curtain across and Becky burst out laughing. I thought the picture was hilarious. It was my Facebook photo for a while.

Bottom: First time back at my full height of six foot one. I was winched into place by a crane that broke when we first tried it.

Above: Another proud day. Standing shoulder to shoulder with the men of 40 Commando to receive my Operational Service Medal for Afghanistan, less than five months after the blast.

Left: Me with Marine Ben McBean at the 40 Commando medals parade. He lost an arm and a leg in a similar mine strike two months after me.

Below: Princes William and Harry visiting us at Headley Court. They showed a genuine interest and spent a lot of time talking to the injured lads.

Left: Home from Headley Court at last. Me and Becky at my nan's house in Plymouth.

Below: Tandem parachute jump with Sgt Reg Green of the Black Knights Royal Artillery display team seven months after the accident. This raised about £3,000 for SSAFA, a charity which provides excellent family accommodation for injured personnel at their Norton House facility near Headley Court.

Left: I kiss the bride on our wedding day, 2 May, 2009.

Below: Covered in confetti after the ceremony at Manadon House on the outskirts of Plymouth.

Below: Achieving another important goal – to walk down the aisle with Becky on my arm.

Right: Dancing with Becky to 'Amazed' by Lone Star. Not a dry eye in the house!

wanted to be part of a military effort. As a Marine, you know exactly what training and experience the men alongside you are relying on. If I was going to work in Baghdad I wanted to be with a troop of Bootnecks. Working with a bunch of people I didn't know who might or might not turn out to be bull-shitters or idiots just didn't appeal to me.

I looked for close protection work in the UK and Europe but couldn't find a way in. It was very much 'who you know not what you know' getting into that world. So from a career point of view it turned out to be a waste of time.

Or did it?

The course crystallized one thing for me: I didn't know how much I missed the banter and camaraderie of the British military until I joined the course. Almost everyone on it was fresh out of the Army or Marines and they were great to work with. I should never have left. I'd only been out for a year so I wouldn't have to go through CTC at Lympstone a second time.

I was going to re-enlist with the Marines. The thought alone put a smile on my face. As soon as I'd made the decision I knew I was going back to where I belonged.

10

I looked into the options and discovered that the Military Police carried out close protection work and I could train as a bodyguard within the Marines with them. I checked the idea out with my family and friends.

My dad didn't pull any punches. 'Mark,' he said, 'I think you're crazy.'

'Look, I don't want to join the Military Police, it's only a means to an end. They'll give me close protection training.'

'I'm telling you, son, if you join the Scuffers your mates won't want to know you. None of the Bootnecks will talk to you. Can you cope with that?'

'Well . . .'

He'd given me something to think about. I'd set my heart on re-enlisting either way so I went back down to the recruiting office in Devonport to ask about rejoining as a general duties Marine. I needed to complete some tests to prove I still had the key skills from training but they weren't tricky and I couldn't wait to get stuck in.

Military people have to take the Basic Fitness Test once a year. Compared to the CTC it's a piece of piss. I got a date to go up to Lympstone for it and the familiar feeling got a grip on my guts. I expected to be ordered into the estuary mud at any second. No such drama occurred. There was only me and an RM officer taking the test. All we had to do was a 1.5-mile run with a PT instructor and then twenty press-ups, fifty sit-ups and five pull-ups. We both passed and I was asked to come back the following week for the Weapons Handling Test. I showed I knew all the procedures and could still strip and reassemble the rifle – not quite as fast as Forrest Gump, but at least without leaving any parts on the table.

Another week passed before the Annual Percentage Weapons Test. Instructors checked us out as we fired about sixty live rounds at various ranges. I hadn't gained or lost any accuracy. Still average.

Finally, it was into the NBC chamber to be tear-gassed. Iraq had hard-wired the respirator drill into my brain. I could have done it in my sleep.

There were two choices for the draft, CTCRM at Lympstone or 40 Commando at Taunton. I'd asked around and it was a no-brainer. For the moment I was going to be a driver again, and the lads doing the job at Lympstone said it was the worst in the world. It was all lastminute.com, carting recruits about the countryside as the instructors rammed them through the course. You'd be getting ready to go home on a Friday night and find yourself ordered up to Woodbury Common to wait for the instructors to stop beasting some unlucky troop until dawn.

Thanks for the tip, lads. Hello 40 Commando.

Within a matter of weeks I was in OPTAG training for Afghanistan. The Operational Training Advisory Group was responsible for constantly updating training packages for troops about to deploy to theatres such as Afghanistan or Iraq. They incorporated the latest intelligence and insurgent tactics into the package to bring all the lads up to speed while putting them through live firing exercises, convoy drills, interaction with locals, enemy motivations, all that.

The exercises took place across the country and I remember going down to a range package in Kent driving one of two four-tonners rammed with Booties for the exercises. I was about to put in a request to transfer to the grav role. I was a bit gloomy about my chances of success because there were only a few months to go before deployment. I didn't want to spend the tour missing out on all the action like my Iraq tour. With my mind on all this, I forgot my four-tonner had a glitch. If you turned off the ignition it wouldn't start up again. You needed a jump start to get going.

'Aw bollocks,' I swore as the engine died. I'd turned it off without even thinking.

There were a couple of Land Rovers parked up nearby with some Pongo officers milling about. I went to the back of one. 'Er, scuse me, sir, any chance I could borrow your slave leads? I need to jump start the four-tonner over there.'

While they were sorting the leads for me I noticed a young officer with ginger hair sitting quietly in the back of the Rover on the right. I recognized him straight away.

I went back to the four-tonner with the leads and told the other drivers, Stu Green and a fellow Marine called Rookie, what I'd seen. 'Here, Prince Harry's sitting in the back of that Landy.'

'Yeah, Rammers, course he is.'

'Eyebrows, he is. Go and have a look for yourself.'

Rookie went over and confirmed I was telling the truth, so they wouldn't have to shave my eyebrows off.

After that the Prince realized there was no point in lying low and got out of the Landy for a leg stretch. At the time, almost no one knew what Prince Harry knew: he was going to serve in Afghanistan for real and was doing his OPTAG for a reason. I didn't give him a second glance. I presumed I'd never see him again, so why would I?

I thought about the pre-deployment training as I sat in the shelter at FOB ROB. It all seemed so long ago, it might as well have been another life. The range packages and live firing exercises were not much use to me at this moment. I was bored stupid and couldn't move.

The Taliban were taking the piss out of us. We'd been under rocket or SPG9 attack for almost five hours straight – pretty much the whole working day. It was the worst period of sustained bombardment of the whole tour. As soon as one soak period ended and we trooped out into the compound there was a warning yell of 'Incoming!' and we were straight back inside. After three incoming rounds and three soak periods I was resigned to staying in the shelter for the rest of the day.

'Bollocks to this,' I thought as the all-clear sounded. I grabbed a couple of boxes of foil bag rations and went straight back inside the blast-proof building. 'I'm staying in this shelter until they have well and truly finished.' The rest of the lads were surprised to see me heading back inside. They couldn't wait to get out. 'You'll be back,' I said. 'See you in a minute.'

I stretched out, trying to relax. It was a few hours until I was due in the sangar, the afternoon was roasting, and I was going to get my head down under hard cover. The Taliban were bound to open fire as soon as I nodded off and this way I wouldn't have to move when they did.

Five minutes later I was dozing off when thirty

sweating Marines came charging back into the shelter swearing and dripping.

'Told you so, lads. Ration packs over there, boys. Help yourselves.'

I'd already grabbed a foil bag with sausage and beans. There was also beef stew and dumplings which was a favourite for many. We had no hot water kettle to warm them up with or to make a wet but it didn't matter, we were used to eating them cold. As long as you didn't end up with corn beef hash, most people were happy.

We called it corned beef gash. There were three methods for dealing with it. You could drown it with tabasco sauce to make a weird sort of curry and disguise the taste. That worked if you were starving. Otherwise you could ignore it and go hungry. Or you could try to beg, steal or trade an alternative. And good luck, mate, you'll need it. Some lucky, lucky units were blessed with a guy who actually liked corned beef gash. These men were born without tastebuds, obviously, but were treated like royalty. Anyone prepared to swap sausage and beans for corned beef gash got well looked after by his unit, and that was only fair.

During the day's bombardment the Taliban successfully landed five or six SPG9 rounds inside and outside the FOB perimeter. No one got a scratch and nothing was damaged, but it seemed as if we'd been in that shelter for most of our lives and it was bad for morale. We were there to take care of business, not to sit pinned down in a bomb shelter all day long while the Taliban tried their luck against us without penalty.

At last, when we walked out there was no immediate screech of another mortar overhead and we completed Op Wideawake. The Taliban mortar teams had finally decided to pack up for the day and go home.

I decided to phone home myself.

The HQ compound was the communications centre of the FOB. We were allowed about thirty minutes' worth of phone calls and internet access from there a week. There was one computer and it was so slow it drove you nuts. The good thing was that all you had to do to use it was book a slot and turn up. It was way better than nothing.

The phones were Paradigm satellite units and there were a couple we could use. They were set up inside a shipping container that had been lined inside with wooden panelling. There were a couple of partitioned cubicles made out of plywood, almost like a rough-and-ready work station in a civvy office, and a couple of plastic chairs to hand. On an old-fashioned plastic desktop telephone you punched in the number on your phone card then dialled direct to any telephone number in the world. That was the theory.

The satellite service was patchy, and ringing home nearly got me in trouble one day. SPG9 and 107 had been coming in for a while – not as bad as the afternoon we'd just been through, but every couple of days. The Taliban were refusing to fight us when we went on patrol and seemed to have decided that assaulting the FOB was a mug's game. I just couldn't take it when nothing happened; it made my head ache with the frustration of it. This was the real thing and it wasn't supposed to go quiet. I wanted to be in the thick of the action, to get out on the ground in contact with the enemy and spunk the world's supply of ammunition. I'd done my phys. My weaponry and admin were sorted. I was itching for a scrap and the Taliban didn't want to know. I decided to have a good drip to Becky about it. I always rang Becky, trusting her to pass on any news to my parents.

I punched in the code on my card and dialled. Becky picked up the phone.

'All right, Becky? I'm missing you, babe.'

My words echoed through a hiss of static.

'Mark? Hello? What?'

'I said, hello, Becky—'

Static, and the link dropped out. Dial again.

'Becky, it's me.'

'Hi Mark, I can hear you—'

Click. Static.

When this happened for a third time I just went nuts and started beating the crap out of the phone booth, smashing the receiver into the wooden panelling and trying to rip the little desk away from the wall. The frustration, the rockets putting us on edge, the lack of action, and now this. I lost the plot. Before I knew what I was doing I slammed my fist straight through the wooden lining of the ISO container which gave way with a splintering crunch.

I didn't realize the phone had reconnected itself and Becky could hear the whole thing. All the banging and smashing sounded like a full-scale battle on the other end of the line.

I heard a tinny scream come down the phone. 'Huh?'

'Mark, tell me you're all right! Oh my God! Mark? Has the shooting stopped? Have you been shot? What's happening? Is there an attack?'

All the tension drained out of me as I burst out laughing and tried to explain what had happened.

The FOB sentries scanned the ground around the base during the hours of darkness with a suite of night vision aids. The HQ compound backed us up by scanning our arcs ceaselessly with the remover-cam, and one night this vigilance paid off.

A Royal Artillery Lieutenant in charge of the GMLRS rocket launcher was the duty watchkeeper in the HQ compound and he spotted a large group of men moving purposefully down from the direction of Sangin on our side of the Helmand River. There were twenty-six men in the group, evenly spaced, moving towards the river from the 611. They began fording the river which was toppers at this time of year. It was no mean feat to get across and not something you would attempt for the fun of it.

The Lieutenant called for Captain Jesson, who was doing a bit of phys at the time, it being about 2200 and fully dark outside. There's not much else to do at a FOB.

The officers tracked the group's movement. They crossed the river and patrolled up through a steep rocky area by the riverside. A section of eight men broke away from the group and headed in the direction of a known Taliban stronghold further down the valley. The remainder headed to an isolated building by the river and posted two sentries outside while the others went inside.

'What's going on here then?' Captain Jesson wondered out loud.

He called up Brigade HQ and reported the sighting, requesting air support to investigate further. With Operation Mar Karadad still in full swing around Musa Qala there was plenty of air power about.

Before we knew it the Americans had sent over a Predator unmanned spyplane, an A10 tankbuster, an F15 warplane and the deadly Spectre gunship.

HQ spent the next two and a half hours pinpointing the correct grid reference of the building involved, which was difficult. It was pitch black outside and views of the target from the aircraft were very different from the view from our night vision aids on the ground. The Americans were not sure our lads had correctly identified the target. No one wanted to be responsible for bringing down the Spectre's awesome firepower on the wrong building. But Captain Jesson was certain of his facts and stuck to his guns.

Eventually the Spectre called in to say he had thirty minutes' fuel remaining and if there was to be a fire mission they needed to crack on. With so many American assets involved, Brigade handed the operation over to US forces at this point and they brought up another bit of kit, a Humvee patrol vehicle equipped with a laser on a retractable mast. They used this to 'sparkle' the building identified by Captain Jesson, highlighting the target for the various air assets overhead.

On the ground, the Taliban popped in and out of the building in ones or twos to take a pee or whatever, blatantly unaware of the threat that surrounded them.

The Americans ordered the Spectre to engage the building with 105mm precision munitions from the aircraft's howitzer, instead of bombing it. The accuracy of these weapons is amazing considering they are unguided. They take into account wind-speed, air pressure, humidity, you name it. But at the end of the day you are still firing an artillery shell out of the side of an aircraft travelling at 300mph.

The first round screamed down and missed, but only just, exploding five metres from the building.

The Taliban froze inside; they must have been wondering what the fuck was going on. Ten seconds later the second shot went straight through the roof. A third followed and a fourth, and suddenly two massive secondary explosions ripped the building apart. The double blast sent a mushroom cloud of smoke, brown dirt and clay masonry hundreds of feet into the night sky. The boom rolled up the valley and shook the ground under the FOB.

Once more the FOB erupted in cheers and wolf whistles. 'Yee-hah! Have some of that!'

The Spectre kept firing into the ruined building, sending down three or four more 105mm rounds into the smoking rubble. The walls collapsed inward into what was left of the structure and the aircraft ceased fire.

About ten minutes later, HQ couldn't believe their eyes. A guy came running out of the remains of the front door, took a look left and right, and jumped behind a rock. There were cries of astonishment in the HQ compound. 'How the fuck did he get out of there?' The officers couldn't believe he'd survived the 105mm barrage, secondary explosions and the building collapsing on top of him.

The bloke's miraculous escape did him no good. He should have kept his head down. Under American Rules of Engagement he was associated with the arms cache and a legitimate target, and the Spectre took him out with a 40mm round from the Bofors gun. Bullseye.

The FOB had spotted and correctly targeted a massive Taliban arms cache, and the Yanks had blown it away.

The next morning there were loads of people digging on the site. Three or four big weapons systems were being dug out of the ground. The Taliban were salvaging mortar barrels and 107mm rockets from underneath the ruined building then bugging out with them slung across the petrol tanks of their motorbikes.

The Americans decided to hit the place again. Their forward air controller dialled up a B1B bomber and we heard the distant roar of its jet engines approaching about twenty minutes later. The FAC shouted to the HQ compound, repeating the warning he'd just been given by the B1B pilot: 'Off hot, twenty-five seconds.' It meant the aircraft's ordnance was away and a 500lb bomb would impact the target in less than half a minute.

We watched from the sangars, making no effort to hide our delight. The Taliban must have been doing too much on the smack pipe to think they could run an arms dump under our noses like that. They were going to cop it now, big style.

A fountain of black smoke shot up from the ruined target at the second predicted by the FAC to more whoops and hollering all around the FOB.

Two days after the engagement there was a prominent new addition to the local graveyard. A burial mound was adorned with dozens of little

flags and one massive banner flying from a flagpole
– a sign that a man of great importance to the locals
had died. This confirmed the intelligence officers'
view that we had just taken out a senior Taliban
commander, some of his key lieutenants and most of
his warfighting assets.

All because of a vigilant watchkeeper by night.

I couldn't see the Taliban trying to hide any sort of
ordnance near the FOB again. They must have felt
we had eyes in the back of our heads.

We were penned into the shelter again as rockets
and SPG9 crashed in. I hardly noticed them now. I'd
reached the point where they'd become a nuisance
not a threat: they never hit anything. It was simply
an inconvenience that interrupted your day.

We'd heard the whistle of SPG9 coming in. It
sounded close, and it was. We heard the smashing
thump of the impact and knew it had landed inside
the perimeter. We weren't that alarmed, it probably
hadn't done any damage. In any case, it was
nowhere near our shelter.

After the soak period we couldn't believe our
eyes.

The American forces had finished their beautiful
accommodation that morning. It had survived
untouched for only a few hours. After a direct hit
the building looked like a Portakabin that had been
dropped off a cliff. All the windows and most of the
walls were smashed and thousands of dollars'

worth of laptop computers and weaponry had been incinerated in the blast.

Our first reaction was to laugh. I'm a bit embarrassed about it now, but we were like, 'Hah! That's what you get for building fancy accommodation out here!'

I gave the mud walls of our mosque an affectionate slap.

Within a couple of seconds the same terrible thought hit the lot of us and the laughter stopped dead. There might be people in there.

'If anyone was inside they've caught up a shitload. Let's go.'

It turned out that every single member of the US forces contingent at the FOB had been either out on duty or in the dining hall at the time. Not one of them got a scratch. It was a fantastic piece of luck.

I wished we could let the Taliban know about this. After all their weeks of trying, they finally got a direct hit on unprotected accommodation in the middle of our camp and still no one got a scratch.

Knowing for sure it was only government property that had taken a hit made it OK to have a good laugh at the Yanks' expense and gob off about the freshly demolished show home in the middle of the FOB.

The Chinook clattered into the base and a new section of gravs came charging out the back of it chucking cargo and bergens on to the ground behind the helo. They knelt in the rotor blast wondering where the fuck they were while I signalled them to dump their bergens in the back of the Pinzgauer.

The mosque was getting busy. I was an old hand now, more than a third of the way through my tour, and had moved into superior accommodation. Outside the mosque was a low outbuilding with four rooms that the first Marines to arrive at the FOB had naturally bagged as soon as they got there. Each room had two blokes in while everyone else slept in the mosque. I got on with the occupants of one room, Marines Baggsy and Ski, really well. I knew Baggsy from Motor Troop and Ski had given me the UGL for my rifle. He just saw it as less weight to carry and wasn't bothered about being the UGL man in a contact. He worked in the stores in the UK and we'd bumped into him all the time back then and got along well. I happened to mention they'd got a great room, and on the spot they invited me to come and join them. 'Can't have you dossing down with the sprogs, Rammers.' There was plenty of room for the three of us, one cot against each wall and the fourth wall for the door.

I showed the new arrivals into the mosque and invited them to make themselves comfortable. Accommodation was automatically allocated on sprog routine. Newest arrivals had to make do with the worst of it, of course. You could tell the new arrivals because lots of the blokes who'd been there for a while had taken to growing ridiculous moustaches and lambchop sideys. Some of the boys looked like they'd walked out of an Asterix book. The new lads had all been harassed into immaculate turnout at Bastion and looked almost fit for a parade.

With the new gravs, Echo Company now had enough men to man the sangars full time and go out on patrols. While they settled in, word came down from HQ that the OC wanted to take advantage of the company's reinforced manpower and mount a patrol. We hadn't been out of the FOB for five weeks during which time we had been pounded to fuck by the Taliban. It must have looked like we didn't want to come out and fight and were happy to sit behind our perimeter soaking up the rockets.

It was Christmas Eve. Time to show them who's boss.

11

I felt a rush of excitement at the prospect of going out on patrol and ran back to my cot to sort out my kit. Desert rig, Osprey body armour, Mk6A helmet, PRR and headset, SA80A2 rifle, with bayonet and UGL attachment. Over the body armour I strapped webbing and a Camelbak water carrier with a feeding tube coming over the top of my right shoulder. The 51mm light mortar was close to my cot. I looked at it, then at my UGL. 'You never know your luck,' I thought to myself, and shoved the mortar tube, baseplate and one round of HE for it into a daysack which I strapped to my back over the camel bag.

Ammunition? Eight magazines containing 240 5.56mm rounds for my rifle. Plastic bandolier with a further 120 rounds. Three 40mm HE grenades clipped to the front of my webbing. And still I wasn't satisfied. There was a drop bag for collecting empty magazines as you expended ammo in a firefight and I filled this with about twelve more

40mm HE and smoke grenades for the UGL. All up in that rig I must have weighed 120 to 130 kilos – around 20 stone. That was enough, but I dished out a load more 51mm rounds for the mortar to other lads who were going to come out on the patrol. 'The worst thing the extra load can do is make a boring patrol good phys,' I thought to myself. The new gravs would be thanking me for it big time if we got into a serious contact. In the meantime they could take the piss out of me as much as they liked. I didn't care.

'Let there be some sort of a scrap out there today,' I muttered.

We sat down on benches outside the HQ compound. Cpl Sean Helsby was leading our section and I was second-in-command. Quite a few of the new arrivals were coming out with us.

Captain Jesson outlined his plan for our first patrol in over a month. It was time to show the locals that the Taliban's best efforts with rockets and SPG9 couldn't even touch us. We still controlled the ground around the FOB. The patrol was also going to familiarize the new lads with all the local landmarks and our Limit of Exploitation, an imaginary line surrounding the FOB that enclosed our area of operations. Beyond this we would not normally expect to engage the Taliban.

The plan was simple. Two sections would patrol in a figure eight with the FOB at the centre of the two loops. Our section, callsign Romeo One Zero, would patrol out of the back gate, down through the village we'd looked at when I fired my UGL warning shot, then up and round to the north of the FOB in the direction of Sangin, before returning via the front gate. We would then walk through the camp and complete a similar loop to the south. A second section, Romeo Two Zero, would patrol in the opposite direction around the figure eight at the same time.

Piece of piss.

'Move out.'

We patrolled across the ground in staggered formation. It felt great to be out of the FOB and on the ground again. If the Taliban dared show themselves, we'd smash 'em to bits.

We patrolled past an old shipping container we used for target practice. Holes had been gouged out of it by weapons of all calibres. The jagged steel and pockmarked walls showed the punch our small-arms delivered.

We began the ascent towards a rock landmark we called North Fort. As we reached the top of the high ground we heard gunfire coming from the direction of Sangin, about seven kilometres off to the north. It was definitely rifle fire, probably Taliban.

Our section was split into two fire teams, Charlie and Delta. As section 2 i/c I led Delta team.

'Rammers, take Delta and get them into fire positions up there,' Sean ordered, pointing at the bowl. 'Get the GPMG on the main arc to cover the village and Two Zero's approach.'

'Roger that,' I replied, already on my way.

Dinger's section was close to completing the southern loop and would be crossing low ground to our front any minute. Our job was to cover them and engage any Taliban coming south from the firefight.

I made my way up a waist-deep trench that ran across the slope of the hill and into the bowl-shaped depression at the top of North Fort. The ground up there offered excellent arcs over the local terrain, a commanding position any infantryman would be happy to get control of.

We were doing our five-and-twenty checks automatically. No sign of disturbance, no suspicious rockpiles, no problem. I stomped purposefully into the middle of the bowl, hefting the load on my chest and back. I placed the lads where I wanted them, indicating which arc belonged to which Marine. I moved around all over the inside of the bowl, checking out their arcs over their shoulders.

Turning back, I noticed that when we went firm, taking cover in the prone position with our belt buckles in the dirt, we couldn't be seen from the FOB. None of the sangars, not even the removercam on its cherry picker, was high enough to see over the southern lip of the bowl. No matter how vigilant the men in the sangars or behind the cam, the inside of the bowl was permanently hidden from the FOB's view. But I was too busy sorting out my fire team to think about the full significance of that fact.

Happy I'd got the lads into decent positions with interlocking arcs, I unslung my rifle and took a step forward. My boot sank into a layer of drying mud. My full body weight plus 30kg of kit loaded on to the few square inches of soil beneath the ball of my left foot and closed the contact on a pressure-plate detonator buried beneath the surface.

Boom.

The blast wave and a cone of white-hot shrapnel hurled me into the air and smashed my body to pieces. The enormous power of the high-explosive charge gouged a massive crater out of the hill; it was measured later at eight feet deep and 15 feet across. Shrapnel tore up my back, burning the skin as it ripped the rear plate of my body armour away, along with the Camelbak and daysack. Weapons and ammunition were blasted in all directions. The extra layer of mud washed over the IED by heavy rain may have soaked up a vital fraction of the blast that might otherwise have killed me, but I'll never know.

As I lay there struggling to take in the extent of my injuries, pure rage swelled up inside me. Shitty thoughts were flashing through my brain at unnaturally fast speed. I totally blamed myself for catching it up for no good reason. These were horrific injuries and we weren't even in a fight. I got more and more distressed as I realized I had just completely fucked my whole life for nothing. My little girl Kezia and my girlfriend Becky were going to pay a massive price for my stupidity.

Thoughts of me turning up at Kezia's school in a wheelchair with stumps poking out all over made something snap inside me and I came to a decision. I was in shock and battered to fuck but my head was clear.

When Sean came over the lip of the bowl I saw him take in my injuries and stare back at my face. We'd been through training at Lympstone together, served in Iraq together. I had massive respect for him as a Marine and as a bloke. I couldn't have wished for a better man to do what I was about to ask him.

'Sean.' I looked him in the eye. 'Shoot me.'

Kezia wouldn't want a freak for a dad. Becky was only twenty-one and stunning with it. She'd find another man, a whole man, not some freaking midget stuck in a wheelchair for all time.

I shouted at him, 'Shoot me!'

All the anger I was feeling came tearing out of me. I couldn't face the life on offer if I survived this and wanted it over with now. My bloody stumps weren't hurting, but they'd bring a world of pain with them if I lived. It was Endex, big time. Just do me a favour and get it over with.

Sean was one of the fittest Bootnecks in the Corps. If anyone could, he would understand what it meant to have that fitness ripped away for ever. I instinctively knew that in a shitstorm Sean would have the balls to do the right thing. I waited quietly for him to unholster his sidearm and plant a 9mm round into the back of my head. I could never wake up from this nightmare. There was only one way to end it. Please. Put me to sleep.

Do it now.

I wasn't wrong about Sean. 'No way, Rammers,' he snapped in a command voice. 'We're going to get you out of here. Sit tight and don't even talk about fucking wrapping. The helo's on its way.'

He wouldn't stop talking to me after that. I resigned myself to it.

'Just stop gobbing off and hurry up,' I groaned.

It was ridiculously weird that I stayed alive long enough for them to get to me. My bodyguard training in South Africa told me that I should have had blood spurting out of me at about a litre a minute. I should have bled out in four minutes and died a couple of minutes after that. The medics reckoned that the massive physical shock of being ripped to bits caused tiny muscles in the walls of my blood vessels to go into spasm and contract. That and a massive drop in my blood pressure kept just enough blood inside me until Dave the medic arrived with tourniquets and field dressings.

Meanwhile, the FOB sprang into action as a unit to get me off that hill. The Americans put up a road-block on the 611 stopping traffic to give the Supacat a clear run when they got me on board. They also formed a protective cordon in case the Taliban decided to initiate a contact while so many people were concentrating on trying to sort me out.

The lads had got the other injured Marine, Stu, into the front passenger seat of the Supacat. The FOB doctor was working on him. Stu's injury was nasty but he was now fully conscious. The doctor thought there was a possibility he might lose his arm, the wound was so bad. Stu, who we called Milky because of his white skin, was having none of it. He had a hoofin' attitude and was determined he wasn't going back to the UK for treatment. He wanted to get himself patched up at the field hospital at Bastion and come straight back on duty.

They'd got a drip into me and Bob Toomey was hanging on to a bag of fluids as well as driving the Supacat. The warmer he kept the fluids, the more easily they'd flow into my blood, so he had the bag of liquid under his arm as he drove. When the Supacat piled up the hill towards the gate and got to the steepest part of the slope Bob knew that if he didn't maintain speed the vehicle would bog down and stop. There was no way he wanted to lose precious minutes taking a second run at it so he stuck his boot right down. The automatic transmission mashed down a gear and the vehicle leapt forward, tipping up to the new incline. It was enough to tumble the medic straight out the back of the vehicle. Bob instinctively threw his arm back over his shoulder and grabbed me to stop me sliding out after the doc on my stretcher. He got hold of me by the stub of my femur bone, which was sticking out of the remains of my shattered thigh, and kept the accelerator pinned to the deck. He held on to me with an iron grip until we were safely through the gate.

I don't remember him doing this, which I'm quite pleased about. I don't think Bob will ever forget it.

By the time we made it to the HLS, the Chinook was circling the camp two minutes' flying time away and Bob was in direct communication with the pilot, telling him exactly where he wanted the helo to put down. The rotors slapped the air as the beast flared over the perimeter wall and lined up for a tactical approach into the HLS in a whirlwind of dust.

A paramedic came out of the helicopter and did a quick assessment of me before running back and using hand signals to relay my condition to Lt Col Jeremy Field, the consultant anaesthetist in the back of the helo. The paramedic swiped his hand across his legs in a chopping motion and then drew his hand across his throat. The message he intended to send was 'Both of the casualty's legs have been blown off'. Lt Col Field read the message as 'The casualty has lost both his legs and is dead'.

The stretcher party ran me up the tail-ramp and dumped me on to the deck of the helo before legging it out again, bent double beneath the spinning rotors. The Chinook's turbines roared as it wound up to full power and lurched into the air.

Having failed to find a pulse – the vibration of the Chinook airframe made it difficult to tell, but if I had a pulse it was extremely faint – the medics placed an oxygen mask over my nose and mouth. If I was breathing, moisture should collect on the inside of the mouthpiece. None did.

Lt Col Field thought I was dead. He lifted one of my eyelids and saw my eyeball move. He'd been a bit hasty, I hadn't gone yet. Game on.

My blood pressure had collapsed to the point where there wasn't enough oxygen getting into my brain for it to remember to tell my lungs to breathe. There was no point doing CPR on me: if you blew air into my lungs, there wasn't enough blood left for it to carry oxygen up to my head; if you massaged my heart, it had nothing to pump. Unless they got my blood pressure back up in a matter of seconds, I was browners.

The EZ-IO drill went into my right hip and one of the medics started pumping syringe-loads of fluids into me 50ml at a time. Lt Col Field put a second EZ-IO drill-bit into my left hip and another medic started squeezing a bag full of warmed-up Hartmann's solution – a mixture of water, salt, lactic acid and Fentanyl, a synthetic morphine-type drug – in through the new insertion. The bone marrow acted like a big sponge, soaking up the fluids and dumping them into my bloodstream. My left leg then started oozing blood, so the team readjusted the tourniquet and packed new bandages over the wounds.

'No point filling a bath unless the plug's in,' Lt Col Field commented.

During the eight-minute flight they forced about three pints of fluid into me through my hip – twenty syringe-loads plus half a bag. It doubled the amount of liquid in my bloodstream. The medics saw my breathing pick up on its own as my blood pressure returned and knew there was a chance they might save my battered arse after all.

As they got me off the Chinook and loaded me into the ambulance Lt Col Field heard me groan and start to complain about having 'sore buttocks, an itchy nose and being thirsty'. He was astonished. Lt Col Field is a regular in the Army and has served in the Balkans, Afghanistan and Iraq during a medical career spanning twenty-five years. He told me afterwards he'd never treated anyone so close to death who made it. To hear me talking coherently ten minutes after he'd thought I was browners freaked him out a little bit.

Back at the FOB, as the Chinook clattered away down the valley morale had turned to shit. Most of the lads who'd seen me reckoned I was a dead man. The next day was Christmas.

Thanks, Santa, nice one.

Other lads were wondering how you could fight an IED. All of them could come to terms with catching up a round or even a chunk of shrapnel. I was probably going to die, but the bloke one pace behind me didn't get a scratch. How can you train or prepare yourself for that?

The senior NCOs and commissioned officers in the camp went out of their way to make Christmas Day as much of a treat for the lads as possible. The Sergeants all took sangar watches from 1200 to 1400 so the whole of Echo Coy could sit down together and have Christmas lunch with no worries. The officers served them dinner – a tradition in the Marines – and the food was great. The Americans had received fresh beef in an airdrop from a C130 Hercules. They were good blokes and donated it to the lads who enjoyed roast beef, veg, gravy and all the trimmings for Christmas lunch followed by a cream gateau and pecan pie for pudding. Bob Toomey dressed up as Santa and dished out a Christmas box that Captain Jesson had been hoarding for the boys, and afterwards they all played a bit of football.

Stu's arm was in such bad shape after the blast that he did have to go back to the UK for treatment at Selly Oak Hospital where he made a full recovery. He demanded to be sent back to FOB ROB as fast as possible and was able to rejoin Echo Coy to finish his tour. He could easily have put his feet up and stayed at home but he was determined to get back where he belonged. His return was 'worth its weight in gold' to Echo Company as far as the seniors were concerned and helped everyone put a nightmare Christmas behind them.

Getting me and Stu away from the FOB quickly and safely was a massive team effort. Everyone involved responded magnificently, and without a doubt I owe them my life. I would like to put down here a massive thank you to everyone, particularly the lads of Echo Company, 40 Commando, whose skills and courage got me off that hill alive that Christmas Eve.

Three consultants, a neurosurgeon, an orthopaedic surgeon and a general surgeon worked on me at the Camp Bastion field hospital. They cut back into my wounds until they got to healthy tissue and bone and left as much of it in place as they could. There were concerns over my right arm. They worked hard to make sure they didn't have to amputate my shoulder, which is a nightmare to live with apparently. Clothes won't fit and your body shape goes to shit. Within an hour of getting me on to the slab in their operating theatre my shoulder was safe, and they'd done all they could to stabilize and clean my wounds.

I was moved to an intensive care bed where they kept pumping blood and other products into me, including a clotting agent called Factor 7A. It costs thousands of pounds per dose but they pumped it into me like there was no tomorrow. The medical care I got all the way down the line was state of the art.

As the intensive care nurses got me ready for the

transit back to the UK the 3 Commando Brigade machine set about letting my family back in the UK know what had happened to me. My girlfriend Becky was at home with her mum and dad in Staines in Surrey, wrapping presents for the following day. She'd got me an Armani watch which she'd spent a fortune on. She had also gone to the trouble of having it engraved with the words 'Forever and Always' on the back.

At the very moment she wrapped the present 'Forever and Always' had almost turned into 'Fugeddaboutit' for me. I was smashed to bits but hanging in there, floating around between life and death like something out of the movie *Gladiator*. I was answering questions lucidly yet knew nothing about it. I had wanted to die, but people were acting like the Numidian, telling me, 'Not yet, mate, not yet.'

Becky, of course, knew none of this until her mobile phone rang that Christmas Eve. She took the call in the garden because the service was patchy. It was my twin sister Leanne, and she was in shock. There were two Royal Marine officers round at my nan's house in Plymouth where Leanne was, and they had given her the news.

'Mark's been injured.'

She spoke to Becky in a weird, monotone voice. Becky's mum Dawn was watching and suddenly saw the blood drain from Becky's face. She shouted a warning to Paul, Becky's dad, who ran out into the garden and grabbed the phone from her. Becky burst into tears.

The message had come through that I had lost a leg in an explosion, which was a big enough shock but not quite the whole story.

Becky wanted to drop everything and get straight to Selly Oak Hospital. Her parents pointed out that I wouldn't be there until about lunchtime on Christmas Day and she and her dad made plans to drive up to Birmingham in the morning.

About nine p.m. that night my father spoke to Becky's dad and explained the full extent of my injuries. Becky was devastated. She didn't sleep a wink with the worry of it and was all for heading for the hospital at the crack of dawn.

In the end they arrived in the hospital car park about midday and bumped into my family: mum Jackie, dad Paul, Leanne and some aunts and uncles, who had just arrived from Plymouth. Becky had met my folks before and been out with them a couple of times. We'd been going out together for just under a year but she still didn't really know them that well. My lot are an emotional bunch – I think my dad might mist up watching *Bambi* if no one was looking – so I was glad I wasn't in the car park. The lot of them cried their eyes out and were all hugging each other, trying to get a grip on themselves.

Becky was coping with it because she was absolutely convinced that when she walked into that ward it was going to be some other poor Marine lying there. This denial mechanism was so powerful that she actually felt sorry for this other lad's family. It was going to be horrendous for them as the hospital explained how the wrong relatives had been called to their boy's bedside.

The problem with her denial was that it didn't work 100 per cent of the time. Every now and then her brain let in the possibility that this really was happening to us, and then she was overcome with terror. She knew that a big landmine had blown off both my legs and my right arm and she was very frightened by what else it might have done to me. What was going to be left of my face after an explosion that had inflicted so much damage to the rest of my body? She was worried sick that I'd have brain damage, or that I'd suffered a change in personality. She loved me and thought of me as a good-looking bloke. She was going to find it really tough if my face was all mangled up and I'd come home a different man from the one she'd fallen in love with.

Becky is a brave woman and I love her to bits. She promised herself then that she would stick by me whatever happened. She could see everyone around her was struggling to cope with the nightmare. All of them wanted to be told it simply wasn't happening. But she kept her chin up and her fears to herself. If I'd been there, I would have been very proud of her.

They all went into the Alexandra Wing of the

hospital where two ladies from the Red Cross looked after them. I arrived at the hospital at about one p.m. The doctors stabilized me in intensive care and at about three thirty p.m. the family gathered outside.

Becky didn't want to be the first one to go in to see me because she was frightened of the mess I'd be in. Mum and Dad came in first. Mum was in a state of utter shock and disbelief. I don't think she stopped crying for four days after she was told the news. She kept thinking she was in the middle of a bad dream and would wake up any second, saying, 'Oh thank goodness, Mark's OK.' She was like that for months afterwards. Mum was struck by how big I seemed to be after all the thoughts of how much of me was missing. My shoulders still seemed to fill the bed, almost touching the rails at both sides. The heavy bandaging to my stumps filled the space. Even my good left hand had caught up an ugly piece of shrapnel that cleaved the palm to the bone. They were able to save the hand but it too was bandaged up like a boxing glove.

Dad came out wiping the tears off his cheeks and reported back to Becky, 'He looks OK. He just seems to be asleep. Go and see him. It's all right, he's still our Mark.'

Becky came in, still believing that everyone, even my parents, had made a mistake. She saw my face, which was unmarked, and that was it.

'He's still gorgeous,' she said out loud.

My chest and face were untouched; everything else was bandaged up. I looked pretty much the same as the day I left for the Afghan, apart from the sun tan. She had been dreading the shock of seeing me, so the fact I still looked like the bloke she had fallen in love with, from the neck up at least, came as a mega-relief. From that moment on she hasn't looked back.

Our two families will never forget that Christmas Day, and I'm glad I wasn't awake for it. I wouldn't have enjoyed the pain on their faces as they looked at me.

The next day the doctors moved me into a room of my own on the ward. They were going to gradually reduce the dosage as I recovered from surgery and I'd start to come round. They warned the family that for a couple of days I would probably think I was still in the Afghan and was likely to shout out orders or callsigns or any old gash from the FOB. 'It's completely normal,' the houseman told my parents. 'It's just the morphine making him dream, please don't worry about it. Just comfort him as best you can. If it gets too much call the nurse and she'll check him over.'

The surgeons were working so fast in response to changes in my condition that there was a delay in information getting back to my family about exactly what they were doing. Lengths of my legs and arm were getting cut off me faster than Mum or Dad could keep up with. They were initially told my left leg had been amputated through the knee. This was important. It'd be much easier for me to learn to walk again. The next thing they knew, I was returned from theatre and my left stump was shorter than my right, which they knew had already been amputated above the knee. My mum was like, 'Please don't take him away again, there won't be anything left of him if you carry on like that.' Watching her son disappear in front of her eyes was really difficult, but she coped. I'm proud of her too.

The surgeons had no choice. They kept taking me away to theatre and sending less of me back. It turned out there was a bone fragment that had lodged in the thigh muscle of my left leg and it was causing infection. There was dead and dying muscle tissue around the fragment that they had to cut away and not enough muscle to support my left femur all the way to the knee. It had to be shortened by four centimetres as a result. The humerus bone in my shattered right arm also had to be taken up. Although I started with bone in place almost to the elbow joint, I was left with a high amputation pretty close to the shoulder.

By the 28th, although there was more surgery still to go through, the injuries had settled down and I started to come round. The first thing I heard was Becky's voice. My proposal came out as a croaking whisper. Becky could barely hear me and was not sure what she had just heard.

'Did you just ask me to marry you?' she asked.

I managed a smile and a nod.

My aunt came into the room and Becky said, 'I think he's just asked me to marry him. Is that right, Mark? Did you just ask me to marry you?'

They both listened as I repeated, as clearly as I could, 'Will you marry me?'

My aunt caught it this time and told Becky, 'He did, he did!'

Becky let out a quiet shriek and said on the spot, 'Yes, yes, of course I will.'

I smiled, nodded and passed out. The effort had left me totally drained. But deep in my drugged-out brain my proposal and Becky's answer were logged. It wasn't just that she had said yes, it was the instant response that made me feel good. Her answer was full of conviction. She wasn't just saying it to make me feel better.

While I tanked back into unconsciousness, Becky got a load of teasing from my family about the marriage proposal. It was all 'You mustn't take him too seriously, Becky. He's off his nut on morphine. He doesn't know what he's saying. He might change his tune when he comes round.' They could see that Becky thought I was serious and her answer had been genuine. They were worried that I'd wake up and say, 'Get married? Do me a favour.'

Becky was brilliant though. She knew what they were saying was right but she was convinced. Before the explosion, our relationship had been heading that way in any case. Becky had written letters to me in the Afghan every other day at least, for almost three months.

What surprised me was that she hadn't given my condition a second thought. She didn't stop to think about the implications of what she was taking on or how our life was going to be. Where would we live? How would I earn a living? None of this even crossed her mind. Her big worry, she told me later, was that I hadn't meant what I'd said because I was off my tits on drugs. Her only fear was that when I sobered up, I'd change my mind. What a girl.

She didn't have long to wait for an answer. The next day I woke up for a bit longer and was properly with it for several minutes. Becky made a bit of a joke of it to cover herself. 'Mark, do you remember what you asked me yesterday?' She had a big cheesy grin all over her face. If I didn't remember, she was going to laugh it off.

'Yes, I do,' I said, looking at her. 'And I remember your answer too.'

I wasn't about to let her off the hook.

Becky just beamed at me.

Over the next two days I started waking up for longer periods. It was a ridiculously weird experience.

My room was about ten feet square. In the wall at the foot of my bed was a window looking on to the main intensive care ward. To the left of the bed was a smaller window looking into a little ante-room you passed through to get in and out of my room. The risk of infection was high, all my wounds were swollen and inflamed; visitors had to wash their hands and put on an apron in the ante-room before coming in to see me. I was sober enough to recognize my parents and Becky in the room, but the drugs were doing strange things to my head. I was tripping my tits off. I'd be talking to my mum and over her shoulder, through the window, forklift trucks would be charging around the intensive care ward. The drivers were Marines intent on loading ammo crates on to the beds. It seemed the correct thing to be doing. I would watch this for a little bit, turn and speak to my mum, then look back at the forklift boys working like crazy. It was messed up. Once I looked back at my mum and she had streamers made from rolls of toilet paper growing out of her head like hair extensions.

After Becky had double-checked that I'd meant what I said about getting married, my mum triple-checked.

'Mum,' I dripped, 'I'm getting sick of this. I want to marry Becky and she wants to marry me. Tell everyone. I don't want to be asked about this again.'

The hallucinations started to freak me out. Becky was chatting to me by the bedside one time when I started tutting and getting irritable.

'What's wrong, Mark?'

'How am I supposed to hear you?' I replied. 'Take

that stupid bucket off your head, it's not even funny.'

There was no bucket. I just came out with this random garbage all the time. I feel genuinely sorry that they had to sit there and listen to me in that state. I would have walked out on myself in disgust.

It was upsetting for the family, but it shows how powerful the painkillers were. I was like that for three days. I remember a couple of midgets moving a giant bottle of ketchup through the ward at one point. There's a movie called *Dude, Where's My Car?* which has two 'Nordic alien dudes' from outer space in it played by Christian Middelthon and David Bannick. They kept popping up in the little wash room, hanging up aprons and keeping it tidy.

No wonder Becky was worried about whether I was serious about marriage.

Three days after coming round for the first time I could feel all my fingers and toes and didn't realize most of them had gone. I could feel the bandages, I knew that I had some damage to my hands and feet, but that was it. I remember dreaming that I was scratching my balls with the fingers of my right hand. Then I pulled away and looked at my right arm. With a shock, I saw that it was just a heavily bandaged stump that stopped before it even got to the elbow. There was no forearm, no hand and no fingers. I panicked and thought I was having a nightmare. It was very confusing.

I saw a nurse and thought I had just woken up. I

told her drowsily, 'I just had a dream that I'd lost my right arm.'

'Er, Mark, that's right, you have lost your right arm. It's an above-the-elbow amputation. You also have serious injuries to both legs. You've had a double amputation, one above and one through the knee.'

The words clunked home into my head. I tried to take on the news at the same time as working out what was real and what was a dream.

A terrifying thought then struck me and my stomach turned over. I'd dreamed I was scratching my itchy balls with the fingers of my right hand. But the fingers of my right hand didn't exist any more, and that meant my balls might not exist any more either.

OMIGOD!

In a panic, I shoved the sheet aside with my bandaged left arm and had a good check. Thank fuck for that. I hadn't got a scratch down below. I slumped back and breathed out heavily. Every few seconds I checked again to make sure I wasn't dreaming. My legs were a mess, but between them everything was exactly as it should be. I fell into a restless sleep, my bandaged left hand automatically moving to my crotch every now and then.

They were giving me heavy doses of morphine, which is in the same drug family as heroin. I tell you now, I feel really sorry for smackheads. I was aware that I had no legs and only one arm left, but the morphine made it all right somehow. It chilled me out about it and just made me really not care. It was like, 'Yeah, yeah, lost my legs, whatever, sleeping now.' For a smackhead living in some filthy flat, I really get why he takes the stuff. The flat might as well be a palace because you don't give a shit about anything around you and just feel OK. I have no idea how anyone ever gets off it. It soon got to the point where they handed control of the amount I needed to me, so that when I was in pain I pressed a button on an IV drip. The aim was to use as little as possible.

At one point I heard Becky and my parents talking to the nurse. She was warning them about me properly understanding the nature of my injuries. I just started yelling, 'Becky, Becky!' at the top of my voice, in quite a state.

She came running in. 'What is it, Mark, what's the matter?'

'Don't start gobbing off to the nurse about it, Becky, it's not her fault that I've lost my legs.'

I was being a bit dumb and had lost the plot. I thought the family were shouting at the nurse because they'd only just found out and were blaming her for the state I was in. I had quite a lot of catching up to do.

I didn't want my sister or Becky to see my right arm. The doctors had inserted a drain to take off fluid from infection around the stump. It was like a green brillo pad on the end of my arm with a tube coming out of the middle of it. It wasn't a pretty sight and I tried to hide my arm under the sheet when they came in. I had no idea they'd both seen almost every bit of me as I lay unconscious for three days after Christmas, but hey.

Becky was really thrilled about something. It turned out the doctors had carried out a CT scan of my head, checking for damage done during the blast. They found a completely undamaged brain, for a Bootneck anyway. I was given the all-clear. This was a big relief to Becky as to her my injuries were now 'what you see is what you get'. She could cope with that.

I was itchy all over, and asked my dad to scratch the inside of my leg. I drifted off again but apparently kept murmuring 'Higher ... higher' until I came out with a satisfied 'Aaaahhh'. My dad turned to Becky, his face twisted up, and whispered through gritted teeth, 'Becky, I'm scratching his balls!' I've had a good laugh about that one ever since.

Thanks Dad.

Later on in the recovery I did get anxious about whether everything was in working order down there. I knew it all looked normal but I also knew that morphine and other opiates play havoc with your sex drive. You might laugh, but if you're a bloke and you ever have reason to doubt your abilities in that area, you won't be smiling. Becky had to help me get to the bathroom on the ward, so we had an opportunity to find out. I'm pleased to report everything was in perfect working order. In that sense at least I was every bit the man I used to be. It was quite a relief.

The family helped me recover in different ways. Leanne was my twin sister and she had a brutal sense of humour that made me crack up. We'd fought like cat and dog as youngsters. I knocked her tooth out when she was about eight. She never let me forget it. When we were kids she used to beat me hollow at snap and one day I was so chuffed when I took a single game off her that I jumped up in the air and landed on my mum's glass coffee table. It smashed to pieces, gashed my lower leg open, and it took fifteen stitches to put me right. I was stupidly proud of the scar but it wasn't very pretty.

Leanne knew just how to make me stop feeling sorry for myself. She was sitting by the bedside at Selly Oak during one of my more lucid moments when she suddenly came out with, 'There is one good thing about all this, Mark.'

I frowned. 'Are you sure? What?'

'Well, your legs have gone but at least that horrible coffee-table scar went with them.'

She ran out of the room laughing as I looked around for something to throw at her. When she'd gone all I could do was smile and shake my head. Cheeky cow.

By New Year's Eve I was becoming more lucid. Becky wanted to be with me at midnight so we could see in our second year together. Visiting hours ended at 8.30 p.m. but the nurses made an exception. She smuggled in a can of Foster's beer for me and a WKD alcopop for her.

I had a TV in my room and we watched the count-down. I just about made it to midnight. Becky gave me a long kiss and handed me the can of beer. I managed only a single sip. It tasted disgusting but it was a lovely thought.

A year earlier Becky and I had properly started our relationship and we thought of New Year's Eve as our anniversary. But things were going to be very different from the way we'd planned.

I looked down at my smashed-up body. Then I looked at Becky and the tears started to come. It was unreal. I'd never given the possibility of getting hurt a second thought in Afghanistan, never mind approaching a New Year mangled to fuck.

Becky kissed the tears off my cheeks and told me she loved me. I wondered bleakly what the New Year had in store for us.

12

It was redders on the ward and I was way too hot. I couldn't sleep. The sweat was trickling off me. I'd made it out of intensive care on 2 January and been moved into my own room on the Burns and Plastics ward at Selly Oak, but I wasn't comfortable.

Lots of body heat is lost through the soles of your feet and palms of your hands. I only had one palm left and that was wrapped up in bandages. I was steaming. Your legs are also covered by a huge amount of skin, and every square inch of it vents off heat if you get too hot. I was such a compact unit now that my body was having difficulty keeping me cool. I had almost the same amount of blood in me as before the accident but only half the body to pump it around.

The red-hot shrapnel burst that had ripped off my body armour had burned my lower back on the right-hand side. The burns were itchy and sore and I hate sleeping on my back anyway. The only good news was that the shrapnel had missed the tattoo on my back which I loved.

The muscles around my stumps were swollen and very tender. The surgeons kept opening them up to clean bits of dirt and shrapnel and bone out of the wounds and I was undergoing a series of skin grafts to patch up my left leg stump. They were shaving donor skin from sites on the outside of both thighs, the top of my right arse cheek and lower back and grafting it on to the underside of the stumps. The surgery left my thighs and upper arm purple with bruising all the time. Just touching the stumps or donor sites lightly with a fingertip would send jolts of pain through what was left of my arm or legs.

I had asked the nurses to drug me and knock me out at night. I was desperate to get my head down for a few hours, but they said they couldn't do it.

Not being able to sleep made me really crabby during the day. I was hanging out of my hoop. It made me snap at Becky and my mum and dad. My moodiness hurt them, and they had been brilliant. They would come to my room every day at nine or ten in the morning and wouldn't leave until 11.30 at night.

It was bad for them seeing me in the state I was in. I'd always been such an active bloke. They were still very tearful and finding it extremely difficult to come to terms with what had happened to me.

My mum Jackie had been allowed to give me the odd cuddle while I was unconscious, but now I had come round I wouldn't let her near me. She kept wanting to give me motherly kisses and I was like, 'Mum! No! Get off!' Every time she looked at me she was fighting to keep the tears at bay. She spent every day in a daze, wanting to wake up from a living nightmare, but it never happened.

The doctors weren't keen on anyone cuddling me at this time because the biggest threat to me was from infection. Another reason I was so hot was because I was fighting off a bug that almost all wounded pick up in the Afghan. There's an organism that lives in the sand called acinetobacter and if you get a flesh wound there's almost no way to avoid it getting into your bloodstream. It is fairly easy to beat but the doctors were worried about it developing a resistance to antibiotics and they just didn't want any other infection setting in on top of it.

I can't imagine what it was like for my parents to see me lying there, obviously in pain, grumpy, moody, not even able to turn on my side or sit myself up. No one knew what to say to them or me. What can you say? We all did a lot of crying, but in the end, tears are no use.

Imagine you've lost your legs. If you shut your eyes, you can probably feel them still there. That doesn't mean anything. I could feel my fingers and toes for weeks after the explosion. Open your eyes and take a look. Still there? Good. Now, imagine if every time you opened your eyes to check your legs, all you saw was a pair of stumps. No matter how many times you opened your eyes, still stumps. You are not going to wake up and find it was all a bad dream, ever.

As I saw it, I had to cope with it and move on. It was like, 'That landmine nearly finished me off but I'm still here. Am I going to wrap, or am I going to make the best of it?' No matter how hard I tried or how hard Becky or Mum or Dad wished for it, my legs and arm were not going to grow back. We all had to accept it. Just deal with it and crack on.

That's the way I was trying to approach it, but sometimes I admit I struggled. One time I was on my own, wide awake and threaders. I had to get on to my left side and try to get my head down but I just couldn't do it. 'Maybe I should get a nurse to try to roll me over and get me a bit more comfortable,' I thought to myself. 'No way. There must be something I can do for myself.'

I took a look around the bed. There were detachable rails down each side to stop me falling out during the night. I thought through what I was going to do.

My remaining hand was still heavily bandaged, two weeks after the blast. There was a big hole in it. The shrapnel had cut open the palm from my index finger across to my little finger, right down to the bones. I could only move my first two fingers and use the lower part of my palm because it was too sore. I reached across and gripped the rail as best I could with those two fingers, keeping the injured part of my palm clear of the rail. I tensed my arm. My body rocked slightly. It was painful and I was so weak it disgusted me. I pulled with all my strength, tensing my stomach muscles and trying to roll on to my left side without brushing my stumps against anything. Slowly, my body turned, and I managed to balance myself on my side. I laid my arm down on the sheet beside my body. The exertion had left me sweating heavily and breathing hard. It was the first time I had been able to move myself since the blast and I couldn't believe the amount of effort it took.

If it was that hard just to roll over in bed, my life was going to be a fucking nightmare. I thought about that for a while. It didn't help me sleep.

My dad Paul came in one morning and decided he was going to give me a shave. It would make me feel good to tidy myself up a bit. He started on one side of the bed, lathering up my face and neck. It was slow work as he carefully drew the razor across my cheek, throat and the bit under my left ear. Then he moved to the other side of the bed and as he worked I heard him struggling to keep himself together. Tears started rolling down his face. The fact that I couldn't even shave myself any more suddenly brought home to him the massive impact the injury was going to have on my life. It was as if his son had turned into a great big grown-up baby. I was helpless, and I know he was desperately worried about how I was going to cope with every-day life.

I looked at my old man and tried to reassure him. 'It's all right, Dad,' I said. 'You'll see, next time I'll have a go at shaving myself. It'll be OK.'

'That's all right, Mark,' he said. He wiped his eyes with the back of his hand and gave a big sniff. 'I'm lucky to have you back here needing a shave at all.'

The days were better because I had so many visitors. Family, friends and almost everyone from the unit came to see me at some stage while they were on leave from the Afghan. The hospital had done every-thing it could to make me comfortable. I had a TV and a couple of chairs in the room for guests, and an ever-increasing pile of DVDs to watch.

The last time I'd seen my mate Jurgen was when he called in the nine-liner radio message to bring in the medevac helicopter a few seconds after the explosion. It was good to see him but we were both a bit awkward. I hadn't known him before FOB ROB and we'd just hit it off in the Afghan because we had such a similar attitude. If there was a contact going on we both wanted to be right in the middle of it, so we'd ended up reacting in the same way and competing to see who could get themselves into the best firefight and do the most. Looking at me must have reminded him of what a close scrape he'd been through when he dragged Stu out of the trench past the IEDs exposed by the force of the blast. What do you say to a bloke in my condition anyway? 'Chin up, Rammers, good effort, you'll be fine, mate'? Not really.

It was good of Jurgen to take the time out to see me, and I was glad of his visit. He was on his mid-tour R and R and was going back to the Afghan the next day. I told him to take care of himself and give the Taliban a good malleting for me. I was jealous not to be going back with him.

There was one visit I really fucked up though. One day the nurse came in to say there was a bloke outside waiting to see me. I was in a bad way and didn't really want to see anyone, but if someone had made the effort I felt it wasn't right to turn them away. It turned out it was Stu – the nurse had taken his surname and told it to me. The problem was, I didn't know Stu by his real name; I couldn't have told you what it was. I just knew his nickname, Milky. Stu was a cracking lad and we'd both been hurt by the same IED, of course I'd want to see him. But I confused his proper name with another Marine we'd nicknamed the FOB Knob. This other Bootneck was always going on about what a brilliant grav he was and how excellent his drills were. If he shut up and got on with his job he was about average to be fair. The thought of him sat at my bedside gobbing off about how great he was – it was just too much. I asked the nurse to make an excuse for me and the visitor left.

Later on, when I found out it was Milky I'd turned away, I was absolutely gutted. He'd made the effort to come to see me and I'd been such a dick. I still haven't bought him the pint I owe him for that one, but it's on my list.

The room was full of people most days. With so much support my attitude was improving. I wanted to show them all that I could move on and make progress. I was not going to be some sort of wrap hand, all twisted up and bitter about what had happened. It's military life. You choose your branch and you take your chance.

My mate and old boss Dave, who owned the door firm I used to work for, came up soon after I managed to roll myself over for the first time. He'd heard what had happened to me and knew the extent of my injuries but did not call to let me know he was coming. A nurse just suddenly said, 'There's a Dave Parker to see you.'

To be honest, I could have done without the visit. It was still early days and I was having a really bad time. But I couldn't send him three and a half hours back down the road to Plymouth if he had come all this way.

When he saw me, the shock was written all over his face. He tried to say hello but the sight of me made his eyes flood with tears and he couldn't speak. That set me off. I was trying not to cry but tears were just rolling out of my eyes. We were blubbing like a couple of girls and trying not to show it.

He got a grip on himself and just started yapping.

Talking about the lads we knew in his firm, everything that was going on. Sniffling away. By the end of the visit we were both fine. He promised to bring a bunch of mates up to see me next time, and he was as good as his word. A week later he brought Paddy, an ex-Bootneck I knew from the Marines who was working the doors for him, and three good lads: Ben, Kev (I used to share a place with them) and Lee (who I used to work the doors with). The boys just chilled in the room, yapping away.

Dave was looking out of the window. He used to be a hospital porter, and something had caught his attention. 'Here, Rammers,' he said. 'I like your view, mate.'

'Why's that?' I asked. All I could see was a nondescript building.

'You're right opposite the morgue, mate. Looks as if they're ready for a delivery too.'

Sure enough, an ambulance rolled up and a stretcher came out with a body on it. The person was covered head to toe in a shroud of some sort. The ambulance crew wheeled the stretcher into the building.

'Great,' I thought. 'That's hoofin'.' The lads were all laughing, checking out Rammers' inspirational view of hope. 'If you end up browners they won't have to wheel you very far will they, mate?'

I watched them pushing the corpse into the morgue. Game over, mate. Endex. It got me thinking. That could have been me on that stretcher covered head to toe in a sheet. But for whatever reason, I had survived. It made me feel grateful to be there, even if I was in a shit state.

The hospital let the physios loose on me before the surgeons had even finished operating. My stumps still hurt and needed further skin grafts, but the physios were determined to stop the tendons and muscles seizing up and set about me in early January. First task was to get me to sit up.

'One . . . two . . . *three*.'

My dad was on one side and my physio, Captain Paul Rennie, a really good bloke, on the other. The physio locked my left arm into his right and they heaved me up into a sitting position. My arse wobbled around under me on the soft bed, I tried to stick out arms and legs to balance myself, and the blood drained out of my head. My vision went, the room spun and I blacked out.

Hoofin' effort, Rammers, well done.

They started again as soon as I came round and held on to me as they raised me into a sitting position.

'Easy, Mark.'

Paul let go of my left arm. It felt as if I was sat on a water bed and was going to tip over any second. My balance was way off because I had been lying down for so long. My heart had got used to pushing blood sideways to reach my head instead of fighting gravity at every beat. I was still anticipating movement with the full weight of my arms and legs in mind. Trying to put my right arm out to balance had almost no effect. Putting my left arm out would topple me over.

I grabbed the bed rail with my left hand. The thought of falling off the bed scared the crap out of me. My stumps were still so tender I could not imagine how much it was going to hurt to hit the deck from here. Just sitting up was a struggle using all of the muscles I had left. It was a real sweat.

Paul was brilliant. He could see I was trying as hard as I could and that the desire was there. He was complimentary about the effort I was putting in, and that helped.

Becky watched, biting her lip. I was frustrated it took so much effort to do so little. Just sitting up in one place was so difficult. I could see she was trying not to cry, keeping it together for me.

I was waiting for the last of my operations, a skin graft to patch up my left stump. I was expected to go down to theatre first thing in the morning, so at about eight p.m. they put a warning in my notes and a sign on my bed, 'Nil by mouth'. I absolutely love my food so this made me more grumpy than usual.

By breakfast time I was starving and for some reason my op was delayed. I didn't get into surgery until about two p.m. Having had nothing to eat for dinner, breakfast or lunch, my stomach was growling like a bad-tempered dog.

I was taken in at last, and Mum and Dad knew I would be famished when I came back. They knew I loved pizza and tried to get Domino's to deliver to the hospital as a special treat. They tried two or three branches with no dice, until they got the Red Cross nurses in the Alex Wing to try their luck. They laid it on with a trowel: 'Wounded soldier, Afghan veteran, multiple amputee, loves your pizza, have a heart . . .' Meanwhile Dad went out and got a load of Kentucky Fried Chicken in case the pizza didn't make it. But it did.

When I got back to the ward there were about four boxes of pizza and a pile of KFC boxes. I was in junk food heaven and crammed it down. Anaesthetic puts some people off food, but not me. I felt as if I could have eaten the lot.

My stump and the graft donor site were sore and itchy but the hoofin' scran made up for it. On top of that, the operation turned out to be my last one of six, so the healing process could start for real at last.

Paul the physio and I worked out our drills fairly quickly for getting me to sit up. He knew what he was doing and I trusted him. He might have been a Pongo officer but he seemed more like a mate and you could see he wanted me to succeed. He gave me confidence to get on with it.

After I learned how to sit up without toppling over, we decided it was time to get me into a wheel-chair. I was always pushing, wanting to try something new as soon as possible. One morning

Paul came in and put me through a series of stretching exercises, helping me on to one side and
stretching my thigh muscles back and forth. Then
we went through the sitting up routine, locking my
left arm in his, hauling up and getting steady, sitting
on the bed. It was frustrating but a necessary
exercise or I would not be able to keep myself
upright.

Paul brought the wheelchair to the side of the bed
and used a board to bridge the gap. Then he placed
a blue plastic sheet on top of the board to help me
slide on to it. He helped me turn, lift and bum-
wiggle my way on to the sheet. My stumps were
swollen and hurting like crazy and I tried hard not
to knock them, and the bed had a piss-proof
mattress on that made it quite grippy and difficult to
slide about on. By the time I got on to the sheet I was
sweating with the effort again. I had not even got off
the bed yet and I was hanging already.

I was so weak it made me angry. Two weeks
earlier I had been six foot one, 15 stone of lean
muscle and bone, the fittest I had ever been in my
life with a hoofin' sun tan to go with it. Now I was
just some stumpy midget who could barely sit up in
bed on his own.

I thought about that for a minute.

Paul held me up while I bum-wiggled my way up
the sheet on to the board (try sitting on the floor and
attempting to move just by swinging your arse
cheeks and you'll get a good idea of what I was

doing). I was breathing heavily. Getting across the board half an inch at a time. Eventually I was able to lean backwards, grab the chair with my left hand and drag myself slowly down the board.

From starting my stretching routine to sitting in the wheelchair had taken an hour. A whole hour. I looked at Becky. How was I ever going to be a decent husband to her if it took me an hour just to get out of bed into a wheelchair? The sheer frustration of it was too much. I felt useless and beaten. She would be better off without me. I couldn't stop it, I just started sobbing my heart out. Becky grabbed me and she was crying her eyes out too.

I thought that was it for me, that was my life from that point on – an hour just to get out of bed. Becky wouldn't be a wife, she'd be a nurse. It made me feel guilty that I had burdened her with all this. She was only twenty-one, beautiful and bright, and had just got a good degree. She had her whole life ahead of her and it was unfair of me to inflict myself on her. We'd only been together a year. Wouldn't it be better if I just ended it?

I loved her, and we held each other tight. But I couldn't look at her.

'It's all right,' she said. 'I love you. Mark, you can do it. I know you can.'

My Marine training helped me get through it in some ways. I remembered week twenty-six of the

Royal Marines Commando Training Course at Lympstone. There is a landmark fitness test, the six-mile speed march. If you pass this point the Corps allows you to bin your training beret and wear a green Cap Comforter. This is both a mark of achievement and an official recognition that you have begun the Commando phase of training. The six-mile march is tough, carried out in full fighting order with weapon and webbing coming to more than 30lb of kit. I used diving weights in the webbing to bring up the load, but you can use anything you like, within reason. They weigh your kit at the start and the finish to make sure you haven't binned any along the way. You have to complete the course in less than sixty minutes. It's rough terrain, up hills and through rivers. Ten minutes a mile sounds like a fairly easy pace, but the load and the terrain punish you. If you start dropping behind it's a killer to make up the time.

During my march, by the time I got to mile four I was hanging out of my hoop. More than anything else in the world I just wanted to sit down and wrap. They could take their speed march and wedge it up their arse. There was only one thing that stopped me: the thought of being backtrooped. I couldn't stomach even the thought of being put back two weeks and doing it all over again.

This was the way I dealt with things at Selly Oak. If I gave up getting into the chair now I would just have to start again from scratch in a little while. It was so important to me to keep moving, even if I was digging out blind and getting almost nowhere. I was alive, I was breathing, and this was my life now.

'Whatever you do, don't wrap,' I ordered myself.

Paul and I practised getting from bed to chair over and over again. It was always a real struggle and quite painful on my stumps and burns, and my bandaged left hand. But I got better, and it got a bit easier and a bit quicker each time.

One morning Paul wasn't there and I wanted to get into the chair. I asked two nurses to help me. We hadn't been through this routine before and I was a bit nervous. They were too, to be fair. Paul was so good and knew me so well. He would anticipate my moves and see if I was losing my balance almost before it happened.

The nurses helped me up and I sat there getting myself ready. They moved the chair to the side of the bed and put the brakes on. The bed sheet seemed more grippy than usual for some reason and I was having trouble moving around. Before I knew it, my balance disappeared. I over-corrected and started falling, out of control. The nurses couldn't stop me. I couldn't break my fall or affect my balance. I've never felt so scared or helpless in all my life. I thought I was going off the bed to smash my stumps into the floor. It was going to hurt. I just hoped I didn't get any more messed up than I was already.

I fell on to the side of the bed and somehow managed to throw out my left arm to stop myself pitching off. I was shaking all over. None of my family were there. I started blubbing and the nurses gave me a hug. They were upset too and were only doing their best.

It is hard to describe how bad it makes you feel when a little thing like that has become so frightening. I was a kickass warfighting gravel belly and supposed to be scared of no man. When you can't do a simple thing like sit upright on your own bed, it chokes you. I was on the brink of total despair. I wanted to wrap there and then but knew I had to try to get into the chair.

The nurses got me upright again and I concentrated as hard as possible on remaining stable on the bed. As I sat there the nurses got ready to turn me so that I could wiggle backwards on to the board. It was, 'One, two, three, *twist*.' Pain exploded from everywhere, legs, arms, body core, the lot. I roared out in agony and tears filled my eyes and poured down my cheeks. The nurses let go of me. My bum had sort of got stuck to the sheet and half of me had tried to twist and the other half not. Everywhere was so badly bruised and tender you could not even press your finger on my stumps without causing a ridiculous amount of pain. The twist left me gasping and in agony.

I took five minutes to compose myself and get over it. The pain ebbed away in waves. I tried to relax.

It had all gone tits. I was scared to carry on. I didn't want to try getting into the chair in case I ended up on the floor on my back. I didn't really trust the nurses. I shuffled myself backwards and prayed I didn't end up on the deck.

I did get into the chair but I was badly shaken and upset. It felt like a massive step backwards. They drummed it into you in the Marines that what they wanted was determination, courage, unselfishness and cheerfulness in the face of adversity. They could ram it. I had just run out of all four for the first time in my life. I felt miserable and sorry for myself, and that made it worse, because self-pity is something the Marine Corps has little time for, as men or as an organization.

Me too. I felt shit about feeling shit.

Paul came back and set to work on me. He talked me round and gradually cheered me up. He persuaded me to practise again and I got back into my stride, so to speak. But it was still such a pain to get into that chair. I was really down about it. I'd been given a second chance when that mine failed to kill me, I knew I was lucky to be alive and a lot of people had worked their tits off to save me and pull me through, but what's the point if you've been turned into a midget who takes an hour to move a few feet?

I thought that maybe if I could get outside once in a while it would help so I started bugging the nurses to let me go out in my wheelchair. I was on at them every day for a week. 'Come on, please? Look, I'm doing great. It takes me so long to get into that chair, when I'm in it I want to get out and about a bit.' They were nervous that I was pushing it way too fast – this was only about three weeks after I was blown up – and worried that I would go wheeling off somewhere, fall out of my chair and bash up my stumps, which needed all the help they could get to heal. But every day I was on at them: 'Can I go out today? I feel great. Let me out.' I drove them nuts, and after a week of this they finally agreed that if I could get into the chair independently they would let me go.

I love a challenge, and now I had something to aim for. If I did it fair and square there was no way they could stop me. Game on!

Paul broke it down into stages. I practised them all with him and Mum, Dad and Becky for a couple of days. It was the first real test. Bursting into tears, blubbing like some gopping cry baby, was just not me.

The first challenge was to sit up by myself. I wiggled over to the left-hand bed rail, extended my arm down by my side, grabbed the rail and heaved myself upright. My shoulders, bicep, forearm and core muscles strained with the effort. I slumped my shoulders forward for balance and took a minute to get used to wiggling and wobbling around on the mattress. My core stability was honking but it would get better when my stumps weren't hurting so much. In time, I wouldn't need to protect them from knocks and bumps so carefully.

Once I was up and stable, I asked them to park the chair at the left-hand side of the bed and make sure the brakes were on. I lowered the bed rail and picked up the board. I placed one end into the seat of the wheelchair, the other on to the mattress beside me. I unfolded the slippery sheet and spread it over the board. Paul helped spread the sheet, but no one had said that was a disqualifying offence.

Next I had to complete a turn 90 degrees to my right, leaving my back facing the chair with my bum on the edge of the sheet. That was quite hard because of the mattress. If you went too far in the turn you would wobble over. It was just wiggle round a bit left, right, left, right on your bum cheeks. Bit by bit, I completed the turn.

If I could get on to the sheet I was in the chair – that was how I looked at it. It would be downhill from there.

First, I put my right leg stump down and transferred my full weight on to it. Pain throbbed up my stump in waves. It was ridiculous but I had to do it in order to lift my left bum cheek on to the sheet.

'Take ... the ... pain,' I told myself. 'If you're on the sheet, you're in the chair.'

I swapped my weight on to my other stump, sweating hard, breathing in gasps, and lifted my other cheek on to the sheet.

'Good work, Mark,' said Dad.

'Be careful,' said Becky.

'You can do it, love,' said Mum.

Now I could slither myself on to the board nice and slow, moving a tiny distance each time so I didn't slide off on to the deck. Slowly down the board inch by inch until I was near enough to the chair to look over my left shoulder.

I reached out and grabbed the arm of the wheelchair. I pulled myself into it and burst into a grin. I'd done it. I was too knackered to punch the air but it felt brilliant to have made it on my own. The best bit was that I'd done it all in twenty minutes flat. Becky threw her arms around me with a smile that made me feel like a man again.

I was going to get out of there for a bit, at last.

13

Dad pushed me out of my room on the Burns and Plastics ward in the wheelchair for the first time in a month since the explosion. Just getting out of that little room felt like freedom. I couldn't believe we were going outside at last and I was going to get some fresh air.

We got into the lift and we went down one floor. Intensive care was on the left as I came out and I gave it a wary glance. I still hadn't recovered from seeing ketchup bottles and space aliens in there on morphine.

The corridor ahead of me was about 75 metres long and outside the winter night had just fallen. All I could see was darkness at the end of a brightly lit tunnel.

We were on the way to see the flat where the family were staying. It was about 800 metres from the hospital in a block laid on for the relatives of injured military personnel. It means people can spend a few days or weeks visiting from around the country without having to travel every day, or run up hotel bills. Dad and Mum, Becky, my sister Leanne, my uncle Chris, aunt Karen and my cousin Lauren were all staying there and they were really pleased they didn't have to cram into some poky hotel. There were three good bedrooms and a fold-out sofa bed in the lounge to spread out in.

'Just wait until you see the flat,' said Becky. 'There's plenty of room. The seven of us got in, no problem. It's brand new, just been decorated, and guess what? The interior's been designed by Laurence Llewelyn-Bowen off the TV.'

'Oh yeah?' I said unenthusiastically, like I cared. I was just glad to be out of my room.

'It's very tastefully done up, since you ask, in magnolia,' Becky carried on.

'Magnolia? They must've painted over whatever he did to it then.'

She was really impressed with the flat they had been provided with. I couldn't have cared less. I just wanted to be out in the fresh air.

We got to the end of the corridor and the hospital doors slid open automatically. It was a gopping night. Swamping down with rain.

'They knew you were coming out today, Mark, they ordered the weather just for you.'

'Yeah, right,' I said. I didn't care. 'Just get me out there.'

The rain splashed on to me. I was surprised at

how good it felt. I turned my face up to the sky and let the drops spatter on to my skin. It made me feel like part of the world again. The rain didn't care I had no legs, it would soak me the same as it did everyone else.

'Put your hood up, Mark, you're going to get drowned.' I was wearing a grey hooded sweatshirt top that I'd pinched from one of the lads back at camp.

'Nah, leave it, Dad, it's OK.'

It felt great. The fresh, cold air on my skin made me feel alive. I laughed out loud.

Dad rang the buzzer to the flat and wheeled me through the communal entrance, tipping the chair to get it up the step. Their place was the first on the right and he pushed me through the door into an L-shaped hallway.

Everyone was there and they were all chuffed to bits to see me out of the hospital. It was great. They were all smiling and congratulating me on getting out of the ward for the first time.

I wanted to get into the lounge on the right to check out the decor. I wheeled the chair with my left hand. 'Oh,' I said, and my face fell. The doorway was too narrow for the chair. There was no way I could jiggle it through. I wheeled around and took a look at the rest of the hall. The doors to the kitchen, bathroom and bedrooms were all the same size. This was the only bit of the flat I was going to be seeing. I couldn't get out of the chair; I had only just learned to get into it. I was devastated. No one really noticed I was upset because they were all so pleased to see me out and about.

All my family started bustling around, getting the kettle on and chatting away about how I was getting on, how big the flat was, what was on telly and what we were going to have for dinner. They split themselves between the kitchen and the lounge and were just yapping away, shouting questions out to me in the hall.

I watched everyone through the doorways, catching glimpses as they moved about. It made me feel pathetic. It was like being a homeless little street kid looking through the window at a happy family indoors that I couldn't be a part of any more.

I looked at my stumps, heavily wrapped in bandages, and I started to fill up with tears again. I couldn't stop them. This wasn't how it was supposed to be, it was all going wrong. I was too hot, sweat from my legs was making me itchy and irritable in the chair, and I badly needed to use the toilet. My chair wouldn't go in there either.

Becky handed me a hospital bottle and I took a pee right there in the hallway.

I was crying quietly, overcome by what a state I was in and how crap my life was going to be. 'Oh yeah, invite Mark round, he's a great laugh. If he can't get in the bog he'll just piss in a bottle in your hallway.'

Becky could see me getting in a state and she

came and put her arms around me. She knew what I was feeling and she just kissed away the tears, tried to cheer me up and told me it was going to be OK. We had a good cry and it went quiet in the flat.

I pulled myself together and tried to compose myself. 'That's it,' I promised myself. 'The next time I come up here I am getting in that front room if I have to smash a hole through the wall to do it.'

I started working on a plan with Becky the next day. She had an idea about using a commode wheelchair that was used on the ward. It was narrower and would fit through the doors. We could put it in the flat then get me over there in my normal chair. I could swap over inside and wheel through the doors, no problem.

It was a good plan, and it would have worked. It was just the idea of travelling by a toilet on wheels. It wasn't exactly going to make me feel great about myself. Then again, Dad could just lift me out of the chair and carry me into the room, like a $10\frac{1}{2}$-stone baby. Likewise, not a great plan on the feelgood front.

There had to be a better way. A self-respecting Bootneck way.

'Yep, that's it,' I thought. 'I'll just jump out.'

'If I could get out of the chair,' I said, 'I could lower myself on to the floor and then sort of bum-walk my way across the floor.'

'What if you fall out and bust your stumps?' asked Dad.

'No, I reckon I could let myself down slowly on to the deck. Anyway, if it all goes tits we haven't got far to go for help. If I do get a knock, you know how to bandage me as well as the nurses. I think I can do it.'

'That's it,' said Becky. 'Let's go for it.'

But she looked worried.

Three days later and it was just Mum, Dad, me and Becky at the flat. I got back through the communal entrance, back through the front door, wheeled my chair up to the front room doorway and put the brakes on, bracing it up against the doorposts. I grabbed the armrest tightly in my hand and slid my bum forward on the chair. I leaned back and pointed my stumps straight at the floor then eased myself down as far as possible, waiting to feel the touch of the carpet.

I hung there and asked, 'Are my stumps near the floor?'

'You're still about three inches off the deck,' said Dad.

I was fully extended and thought about just letting go, but my stumps were still too painful. I pulled hard and inched my way slowly back up into the chair. It took a massive effort, like trying to bench-press your own body weight. My arm and shoulder were throbbing by the time I got myself into a sitting position again and I was sweating like a dog.

'If you get me a big cushion maybe I could just flop on to that.'

Dad sorted it out and we tried again. I felt the tips of my stumps brush the top of the cushion, pointed them up as high as I could and let go, landing with a thud on my arse but quite nicely balanced.

'Hey, the Eagle has landed,' chuckled Dad.

'Right, time for a little walk.'

I took it slowly. I raised my stumps to point them as high as possible, aiming for the ceiling, and sort of bum-walked forward on the bones of my backside. It was hot in the flat and I could feel sweat running down my back already. As I wiggled forward, the friction of the carpet started to irritate the back of my legs. It felt like prickly heat. Everything hurt.

After about five minutes I got over to the sofa, which was covered in beige fabric with a red trim. Nice one, Laurence. I leaned my left arm on it and Becky sat down beside me.

We watched TV and tried to chill out. But I was too uncomfortable. I was in pain and too hot, bad-tempered and snapping at everyone. Mum and Dad went out to get some burgers for our tea. The carpet was itching me. I decided I was getting off it and on to the sofa. I started sizing the furniture up, trying to work out a plan of attack. The sofa cushions were soft but there was a hard back behind and if I reached up I could grab it and pull myself up.

I threw my arm up, managed to get a hold, and heaved. It was a massive physical effort again, pulling with every last ounce of strength. I knew if I let go and wrapped I wouldn't have the strength for a second attempt. That would be me on the floor for the night, and no way was that going to happen. I wiggled one leg stump over the lip of the seat cushion and flopped on to my belly on the sofa. Panting hard, I pushed myself up by my left arm and just about managed to wedge myself against the arm at one end of the sofa.

The sofa was soft and the fabric covering made it difficult to move. I was wobbling around again and worried about pitching back on to the floor. My breathing soon started to return to normal but I looked at the distance covered and it was no more than six feet from the door to the sofa. It was just shit. The effort involved was ridiculous. I felt as if I'd just been twelve rounds with Mike Tyson, and for what? To move two metres from a chair to a sofa.

If it took that much just to get into a room and sit down, my life might as well be over. Again, fear and anger overwhelmed me. I couldn't keep it in and let out a roar of humiliation and rage. Exhaustion, frustration, painful stumps and burning irritation from the carpet tore the tears out of me. The fact I couldn't stop crying made it worse. In another life I had made it through Commando training as one of sixteen lads out of sixty to pass every stage at the first attempt. Excelling at one of the most gruelling physical tests on the planet had come naturally. Now I was reduced to crawling across a floor on my arse inch by inch and having the fight of my life just to get on to a sofa.

I looked bitterly through my tears at the pathetic distance covered. If this was going to be my life, I didn't want it.

I wished Sean Helsby had finished the job on North Fort and shot me in the head when he had the chance. It would have saved us all this grief.

I turned to Becky and whispered, 'Will you help me?'

She could see the state I had got myself into and was crying her eyes out herself.

'Of course, Mark, what is it?'

'I don't want to be here any more.'

'No, Mark. No, please don't—'

'I wish I had died in Afghanistan. It should have happened. Look at the state of me. I don't want to be here. I want to die. Will you help me?'

14

Becky's reaction didn't look like much at first. We clung to each other on the sofa blubbing our hearts out, and eventually I drifted into an uneasy sleep.

I was woken up by Mum and Dad coming back with a load of takeaway burgers and chips. I didn't want them to see the state I'd got myself into. I couldn't look either one of them in the eye. Neither could Becky.

We must have looked a right state, red-eyed, silent and miserable, but if Mum and Dad suspected something was wrong, they didn't let on. I munched my burger in something near total silence, then announced I was going to bed. After the effort of getting on to that sofa I wasn't going anywhere else for the night. Dad fetched some sheets and blankets and I kipped right there.

The hospital was already OK with this. I'd been badgering them to let me stay in the flat overnight for a couple of days. The nurses weren't keen because my stumps were still raw, but the infection was almost beaten. The flat was only a few minutes from the hospital if something went wrong, and in the end the doctors agreed, mainly to stop me giving the nursing staff grief, I think. I knew my attitude was going to play a massive part in my recovery from this point on.

My first night out of a hospital bed since the explosion was supposed to be a mega-boost to my morale. In reality, it was the worst day of my life.

I woke up next morning to find Becky sitting nearby, already up and dressed. We didn't mention what we'd talked about the night before. After breakfast, Dad carried me to my chair and we went back to the ward where I settled into my bed.

Mum and Dad went off for a break. Becky and I were alone in the room.

'Kezia really loves her dad,' she began. 'And I really want you as my husband.'

She was on a mission, and she wasn't taking prisoners. She reminded me that Kezia would need a daddy through every stage of her life, childhood, teenage years and as a young woman. She made me think ahead to a time when Kezia maybe had children herself. Didn't I want to be there for that?

Then she really started on me.

'You're still the man I fell in love with,' she told me. 'I couldn't be without you and I don't want anyone else. You've been torn to bits but you're still the man I want to spend the rest of my life with. I don't care about your injury. Your personality hasn't changed a bit. We've still got so much going for us. We're both lucky that you survived the explosion and that we've been given a second chance to be together.'

Becky wouldn't let me off the hook. She talked about our own wedding, about starting a family of our own and growing old together. She reminded me of the love of my parents, how desperate they were to see me make a decent recovery. She spoke about all my mates, in the Marines and civvy life, how much they wanted to see me make it and how gutted they would be if I was gone. She told me how Paul the physio was blown away by the effort I was putting in and by the pace of improvement in my condition. She listed almost every possible thing I had to look forward to and everything that could still be good in my life.

I was surprised at how much there was.

She promised me things would get better. That I would walk again, that I would drive a car, have kids, that I could do anything I wanted to in time. It would take effort and patience but it was all possible.

Finally, she made another promise that made me think: if things didn't improve and I was still determined to end it, she would do whatever I asked of her to help me.

Becky didn't leave my side for more than a

few minutes for the next forty-eight hours. She instinctively knew when to drum home the message and when to lay off and give me a break. I didn't realize it at the time, but she was getting me through the most dangerous hours of my life since I stepped on the landmine. You might call it a cry for help and say there was no way I was really going to top myself. I feel mega-embarrassed admitting that I even thought about it now. But back then I was feeling a bitter hatred for my condition. The weakness, it made me puke. It wasn't so much the effort or the pain, it was the limit on achievement, the almost total loss of ability. If crawling across a floor measuring progress in fractions of an inch was what life had to offer, then screw that, I'm outta here. Better all round to call Endex and get it over with. That was the way I was thinking at the time, and Becky was worried. She knew what a stubborn and determined sod I could be once I'd set my mind to something.

As I said, I feel embarrassed about it now and didn't tell my mum and dad about that night for months and months. It was the lowest point of my life. Becky got me through it without a scratch. Her response over the next few days was magnificent. She instinctively knew how to dig me out of the shitty hole I'd fallen into.

Coming back from that low was tough, but Becky kept up the pressure, pointing out all the little improvements in my condition every day. I laser-beamed in on these positives, and that pulled me through.

I'd spent a good amount of time thinking through the way I got from bed to chair, and with Paul the physio's help we worked out a new routine. It cut minutes off the time and was less exhausting, and it was something that I'd done for myself. I tried to find something every day that was a little better than the day before, from feeding myself to sliding from my chair on to the toilet seat in the ward bogs. I think Becky sensed that if she could get me past a certain point I would suddenly go for it and not look back.

The prospect of learning to walk again got my attention. Becky had been doing quite a lot of research on the internet about Headley Court, the Defence Medical Rehabilitation Centre, the military's world-class rehab facility in Surrey. There wasn't that much information available but she was checking up on modern prosthetic limbs. We had a rough idea of what was out there but had no idea what was in store for me as an individual.

A few days after I got back from the flat, a bloke came to see me and introduced himself as an NHS prosthetics expert. He had no military connection but he was a proper health professional who spent his working life with amputees. He knew what he was talking about and I was hanging on his every word. I was desperate to learn what the limits of my recovery would be.

He was in his fifties I guess, with grey hair and a grey beard. He looked a bit like Father Christmas but there was no 'ho, ho, ho'. Truth was, he was a miserable git. He was used to dealing with civvy amputees and patients a good deal older than me, judging by his manner. He described the basic NHS prosthetics, false arms and legs, some still made of wood. He droned on at me, and what he had to say boiled down to 'NHS prosthetics are crap, but unless you've got fortunes they are your only option'. Then he took a look at my injuries and seemed to be weighing them up. 'Of course,' he said, 'for someone in your condition, it will be two years before you walk again, if you ever can. You might have to accept that you'll never be able to walk again.'

I think he was trying to be honest with me and spare me the bullshit about the nature of my injuries. But never walk again? No way. I was devastated and outraged. I wanted to smack him in the face, the miserable twat. I was fuming. He left.

Becky was furious too. She knew from the internet that the bloke had been talking bollocks. She also knew that he couldn't have had much experience working with military people. 'Mark, don't listen to him,' she begged. 'He's talking rubbish. He's talking about men in their sixties, or blokes who've lost a leg to heart disease. You're not like that.'

'He's the professional, Becky, he knows what he's talking about,' I snapped, blinking away tears.

'No, he doesn't. Military people like you aren't like civvies. You're a Royal Marine, you'll try harder, you'll do better.'

'No, Becky,' I yelled. 'He's the expert, you're just a civvy. He sees people like me all the time. Two years or not at all, that's what he said, and that's the truth.'

'He's wrong, Mark.'

Her faith in me made me angry, because I thought it was bullshit. 'I'm going to be in a fucking wheelchair all my life,' I shouted at her. 'I've got to deal with that, and so have you.'

I hated yelling at her, but what did she know? He was the professional and he'd just given me the good news, right between the eyes.

Becky didn't push it any further but she refused to back down. I could see in her eyes that she was convinced she was right.

I sat in bed looking at the wheelchair and tried to imagine spending the rest of my life with my arse glued to that seat.

The next day I had another visitor, a Royal Marines Colonel who came especially to brief me on the Rehab Centre at Headley Court. This was the place where I would learn, or fail, to walk again. I wish I'd seen the Colonel the day before the NHS guy and saved myself a sleepless night.

Just as Becky suspected, things were much better than I'd been told. He explained that Headley had its own prosthetics department where experts made their own kit to order. They had access to the best prosthetics on the world market and if there wasn't a product out there to suit then they made one themselves. He didn't pull any punches. Headley was a military environment and certain standards were expected. He warned me I would have to work my arse off, but that if I listened to the staff he would expect to see me up and walking about within a year. They would start with the most simple prosthetics available to get me standing and take it from there.

'Now you're talking,' I thought to myself. 'If he thinks I can walk again then there's nothing to stop me.'

He picked me up just when I needed it, a real antidote to all the crap of the previous day. Becky had an 'I told you so' sort of look on her face.

Fair one, Becky.

The following week I had a visit from Mick Brennan. Mick was a talented soldier with the Royal Signals Regiment who made Sergeant at the age of twenty-five. He was really going places in the Army. After a day spent clearing landmines near Camp Dogwood in Baghdad in November 2004 he was blown up by a suicide bomber. He lost both his legs in the blast, went into a coma for two weeks, and underwent around forty operations. He was still in the Army when he came to see me, and training as a Paralympic oarsman under the guidance of

Matthew Pinsent. He wasn't exactly sitting about feeling sorry for himself.

His visit was a brilliant morale booster for me. For a start, he walked into the room. I couldn't believe my eyes. It was just over three years since he'd been blown up. He had a natural gait. If he walked past you in the street you would never know he'd lost a limb, never mind both legs.

He walked to the side of my bed and sat down on a chair. I was struggling not to gawp at him. I knew he had lost both legs but that fact was not computing with the reality in front of me.

Mick was brutally honest about what I could expect in the future. He was so matter of fact, it really chilled me out. He sat down and showed me the prosthetics he had walked in on. Without any embarrassment, he rolled up his trousers and took one of his legs off. It was held in place by a carbon-fibre suction cup called a socket that had been moulded to fit exactly on to Mick's stump. There were no straps. The leg itself was a hoofin' piece of kit. It looked like something straight out of *The Six Million Dollar Man*. It had a decent training shoe on the foot and glittered with polished stainless steel and carbon fibre.

'It's called a C-Leg,' Mick explained. 'They're twenty grand apiece, state of the art. It's hard work learning to use them, but once you get it, they're brilliant.'

'I didn't think a false leg could look like such a

cool gadget,' I thought, without interrupting Mick.

'As a double leg amputee,' Mick went on, 'you'll be getting a pair of these when you're ready for them.'

He explained how they worked. 'A micro-processor in the leg at the knee here controls this hydraulic system. It's all powered by lithium-ion batteries, bigger versions of what's in your mobile phone.' He showed me how the mains charger plugged into the legs to juice up the batteries overnight. During the day, the computer memorized your ideal gait, depending on speed and whether you were going uphill or downhill. The computer controlled the on-board hydraulic system to throw the foot forward beneath the fully mobile knee joint as you walked. It also adjusted the angle of attack of the false foot, depending on the slope. A Bluetooth key fob allowed Mick to select different modes as he walked and to put a brake on the knee joint when he wanted to just stand in one spot. A stainless steel column linked the knee and foot in place of a shin bone and could be adjusted to match the wearer's natural height.

The thought of being able to stand at six foot one again and not only walk but do so without a limp blew me away.

Mick told me there was every chance that in time I would be wheelchair-free. That was a concept I'd not even considered. Binning the wheelchair and walking everywhere. Hoofin'.

Mick was brilliant. He answered every question I could think of and told me the C-Legs were so good that eventually I would be able to walk up and down stairs on them. For the first time I was speaking to a military man who had survived pretty much exactly what I had survived. He'd been through what I'd experienced, and worse. He knew exactly what was around the corner for me, and a lot of it was good. I was very grateful to him for taking the time to come and see me. He turned it all around for me.

Watching him walk out of my room on the Burns and Plastics ward was a boost. He wasn't bobbing from side to side or throwing his hips around to swing his legs forward. I could see my future self in him, and it looked good.

I was determined now. I was going to walk. Not in years, but in months. My target was no longer simply managing a few steps to prove the NHS guy wrong. They had the technology and I had the willpower. With a pair of bionic legs like Mick's I was going to leap out of the wheelchair, and one day I wouldn't need it at all.

Two visitors came to see me who made me sit up straight in bed. The Commandant General of the Royal Marines, Major General Garry Robison, had travelled up to Selly Oak with the Corps Regimental Sergeant Major, Baz Dawe. These two formidable men had risen to the highest ranks achievable within the Royal Marines as commissioned and non-commissioned officers respectively. Even God called them God as far as I was concerned. From their point of view, this was the only proper attitude for a lowly Marine like me.

Bearing in mind the circumstances, they were all smiles. 'How are you doing, Marine Ormrod?'

I was like, 'Excellent, thank you, sah.' I did everything but throw a left-handed salute in bed.

Mum, Dad and Becky looked at me strangely. This was a side of me they hadn't ever seen before. Outside the Marines I had a fairly chilled attitude and referred to almost everyone as 'mate'. Seeing me trying to sit up straight and saying 'yes sir, thank you sir' was very odd for them. My mum was a bit uncomfortable with it. She shoved past the Corps RSM and said over her shoulder, 'Scuse me, mate.'

I winced. Calling the Corps RSM 'mate'. It was wrong on so many levels.

The RSM shook my left hand and said, 'I'm not sure if we've met before.'

'That's probably because every time I saw you I crossed the road and legged it round a corner,' I thought to myself.

He was the RSM at Stonehouse Barracks when I was there, and we had met before. RSM Dawe had called me in for some misdemeanour or other and he hadn't liked the look of my beret. He had a thing about regulation berets. He knew some Marines liked to cut the lining out of them to achieve a slightly sharper look when the Green Lid was dressed to the right side of the head. He could spot this illegal alteration across a parade ground at 100 metres. Through fog.

'Let me have a look at your lid then, Ormrod,' he'd growled at me as I stood to attention in his office.

I handed it over and he turned it inside out.

'Hah!' he said in triumph, and nailed the offending lid to his noticeboard with a drawing pin. 'You have got three minutes to get yourself to the Quartermaster and draw yourself a regulation beret, Ormrod, then get back here quick time. Do not remove the lining from your new lid.'

It wasn't said in a nice way. You had to hear the unspoken 'or you will cop a beasting to within an inch of your miserable fucking life' to appreciate the menace behind the order.

As I sat in the bed at Selly Oak I told him this story and we had a bit of a laugh about it. He seemed to be a different bloke outside the disciplined RM environment, but I was still wary of him and Major General Robison.

I didn't think the RSM would think anything of my story, but he came back to Selly Oak a couple of weeks later and presented me with a brand new beret. I was genuinely chuffed up about that. This legendary disciplinarian made a 400-mile round trip just to hand me a new lid. It's the sort of gesture that makes the Corps like a second family.

Major General Robison just wanted to see how I was getting along, but it was all a bit odd for me.

'Is there anything I can get you?' he asked, quite concerned. 'Anything you need?'

It suddenly seemed like a daft question. Before I knew it I'd come out with, 'A new pair of legs please, sir?'

We looked each other in the eye. I thought it best not to laugh.

Things got better by the day. My stumps were healing, the inflammation and swelling died down. The skin grafts took, the donor sites healed and became less sore. I came off the morphine drip and moved on to painkilling pills.

Paul the physio got me down into the little gym at Selly Oak and started working on my core stability, abs and glutes in particular. One day I came in and he was blowing up a balloon.

'We having a party?' I asked.

I sat on the floor and he handed me a table tennis bat. We played ping-pong with the balloon for about twenty minutes. It massively improved my balance. My brain was so occupied with hitting the balloon that my core muscles had to get on with the job of keeping me upright by themselves.

It was around this time that Becky and I started to discuss our wedding plans. Things were moving forward well with my recovery so it seemed a good time to start looking to the future. We were both excited, and I decided to make it a bit more real. Becky was missing an engagement ring for a start. There's not much to spend your wages on in the Afghan, or in hospital, so for once I had a bit of cash to do things right.

'There's a cracking jewellery quarter in Birmingham. Let's get me out of here and get your engagement ring sorted.'

That put a big smile on Becky's face.

Once the nurses found out what we were up to they made a fuss of me. They kept coming up with information they had downloaded from the internet about gemstones. Before I knew it, I was getting lectures on the 'three Cs'. 'Carat, clarity, colour,' said the ward sister. 'That's what you've got to check in every gemstone you look at.' I think they were more excited than Becky.

I decided to make it a family trip and to take Mum and Dad along for backup. We hired a people carrier from the hospital and set off with the wheelchair on board.

I was blown away by the jewellery quarter. There were hundreds of shops; the place went on for ever. Lots of stores had security men on the door and I got chatting to a few of them. Some of the shops stocked a load of top-notch bling worth tens of thousands. Armed robberies were quite common; they needed men on the door to stop blaggers running riot. In another life I could have found myself doing their job for a bit. I would have got bored if there weren't enough robberies.

Becky stopped at the second shop. She'd seen something she liked and I was going to be cool with whatever she chose. She deserved it. The shopkeeper came to the door and offered his help.

'Have you got many more rings inside?' asked Becky.

'Oh yeah,' grinned the manager. 'It's a real mine-field in there for a young man.'

That was priceless. We burst out laughing. I was roaring my head off and tears were running down my cheeks, I couldn't help it. It was just the timing and the look on his face. He must have thought we'd all gone nuts. 'What did I say? What's so funny?'

I composed myself and looked up at him from my wheelchair. 'Well, mate,' I explained, 'how do you think I ended up like this?'

The poor bloke went bright pink. He was horrified at what he'd said and came over all apologetic.

'Don't worry about it, mate, that was the funniest thing that's happened for a while and it's cheered us all up. Are you going to show us some rings or what?'

He gave us the red carpet treatment after that and Becky picked out a fantastic square-cut diamond ring with four smaller diamonds set on each of the corners. It cost a lot of money.

'Are you sure, Mark?'

'It's going to be on your finger a long time, darling.'

She was over the moon. The whole family was buzzing and feeling good.

Back at Selly Oak the doctors were checking me out. After six weeks at the hospital they had done what they could for me. The surgeons were finished. The stumps were clean and stable but still tender. The acinetobacter infection was beaten. I was getting a little stronger every day and now the gym facilities at Selly Oak were not sufficient for the sort of rehab I was going to need. Everyone had been great, but it was time for me to move on.

The hospital made arrangements for me to be transferred to Headley Court.

15

We drove past the gatehouse and parked in front of a red-brick manor house where some of the most seriously injured combat veterans in the history of warfare were being helped to rebuild their lives.

Headley Court in Surrey was the country home of a Governor of the Bank of England during the First World War and then the HQ of Canadian forces in Britain during World War Two. It was bought by the RAF in 1946. Some people think it is a beautiful stately home. Becky didn't like the feel of the place: it looked like a haunted house to her. I didn't care what it looked like, I was just itching to get stuck in.

The Headley motto is *Per Mutua*, for the joint effort needed from medics and patients to 'break the shackles' of injury. About two hundred medical staff run the place with therapists specializing in everything from physio to brain injury. It has gyms with equipment designed to tackle almost any form of disability. The only thing the place lacked then was its own therapy pool. They used to take veterans off to Leatherhead swimming baths until a group of patients got a load of abuse from local dickheads who didn't like the sight of smashed-up soldiers, some of them amputees, swimming in public. The Help for Heroes charity raised money to provide a pool at Headley, and once that is in the place will be mega.

I was given a room to myself for high-dependency care next to the nursing station where they could keep a beady eye on me. The morning of my second day they took me down to the prosthetics department.

I still hadn't got to know the place and I didn't know anyone there yet but it was good to be back in a military environment. 'Crack on' was the order of the day, and that suited me.

The first thing the prosthetics people did was remove the bandages and take a look at my stumps. They were healing well, apart from a bit of over granulation. My body was trying to make the wounds heal too quickly and this caused the skin to blister up.

They covered the stumps with a sheet of clingfilm and then started winding plaster of Paris bandages around them as if they were setting a broken leg. Once the plaster hardened off they took the casts away and used them as moulds to make hard 'plugs', solid replicas of the ends of my stumps. They used these to shape two clear plastic 'sockets' that would fit exactly over what was left of my legs. By the time I'd had my lunch they were ready to try out.

It was brilliant. I hadn't been there twenty-four hours and they'd done so much. I was used to lying on my back for most of the day doing nothing and it had been driving me mad. It felt great to be making so much progress so fast.

Two guys from the prosthetics department helped roll silicone 'socks' on to my stumps. They sprayed the outside of the socks with an alcohol-based lubricant then fitted the clear plastic sockets on top of them. All the air was driven out of the gap between the silicone and the inner wall of the plastic socket. With an exact fit moulded to the shape of the stumps, the sockets stayed on by suction alone.

I was sitting on a plinth about three feet off the ground, with a headboard section that could be raised to the vertical. I shuffled round to face the headboard and grabbed it with my left hand. Leaning forward, I shifted my weight on to the two sockets and slowly straightened myself up.

I turned round with a smile ten feet wide on my face. I was standing upright for the first time since the explosion.

'Way to go, Mark, how does that feel?' asked the technician.

'They feel great. The stumps are a bit sore but the sockets are nicely cushioned. You've done a hoofin' job, lads.'

'We're just going to mark the sockets where we can see the fit's too tight or too loose, then we'll adjust them for you. Can you stand still for a couple of minutes?'

'Happy with that,' I said, but inside I was thinking, 'Stand still? The bloke's just asked me to *stand* still?' It was only a couple of weeks since the NHS bloke had told me I might never walk again. I couldn't wipe the grin off my face.

I shifted my weight from thigh to thigh. Mum, Dad and Becky were there clicking away with a camera and wiping away tears. I was over the moon. The explosion had knocked me down hard on my arse. Six weeks later I was standing up again. Battered to fuck, but not down and not out.

Headley went by in a whirl. The team just seemed to attack everything at 100mph. Different departments looked after different aspects of my care. They assessed my strength, fitness and general physical ability. It was the first time they'd dealt with a triple amputee and they didn't know exactly what to expect, but that didn't slow them down at all. Thanks to Paul Rennie I was in much better shape than the Headley therapists expected and was bang up for anything they suggested. Because I wanted to go as fast as possible and bin the more basic exercises they got me straight into the gym where I bench-pressed weights and worked on my abs and glutes again.

There were two forms of physio: remedial

instruction, which took care of core strength, and normal physio, which emphasized stretching and keeping the few joints I had left loose and supple. A lot of effort went into making sure what was left of the tendons in my arms and legs didn't seize up.

One of the physios looking after me was Captain Dale Walker who was in the Army but had been in the Royal Marines Reserve before that. He spoke fluent Bootneck and made sure he gave me a load of grief every day in a language I understood.

Every department had bits and pieces of kit to issue to me and I'd been asked to get myself a bag to store it.

'No dramas, Rammers, I'll get you a bag,' offered Dale.

He came back with what looked like a little six-year-old's daysack, black with yellow lettering on it, something you'd expect to see a kid carrying to primary school.

'Nice bag!' I exclaimed in the most viciously sarcastic tone I could manage.

'For you, Rammers, nothing is too much effort, mate,' replied Captain Dale, laughing his arse off and handing over the daysack.

'This is uber-chad. Carrying this about will get me into a fight.'

'I think it suits you, Rammers. Very fetching.'

I instantly christened it the chad-sack and soon got myself a decent bag to replace it. But that bag was too big and made me uncomfortable in the chair. The chad-sack was actually perfect for the job, and I've still got it. If I'm in the wheelchair, I'll use it. I saw Captain Dale recently and he was like, 'Nice daysack, Rammers, har har.'

At Headley, Dale and another physio, Jenny McMann, put me through my paces and they seemed pleased with the amount I could do.

A few days later I was back in the prosthetics department. The technicians had altered the clear sockets and used these as a master set to mould a hard carbon-fibre pair of sockets for me to walk in. The sockets were attached to two full-sized prosthetic legs with a joint at the knee, but that was only to fold them down when you were sitting in the wheelchair. To walk, you straightened and locked them. They could not bend at the knee or ankle, each leg was a simple steel pylon with a train-ing shoe jammed on a steel foot. They were a basic bit of kit and the target was to stand up in them. I was a bit apprehensive but really wanted to go for it. Standing at my full height again was going to be mega.

With these prosthetics, I used a cotton sock over both stumps instead of the silicone as they didn't work by suction and had to be strapped into place. Each leg had a neoprene harness like a small piece of wetsuit that went around your waist and arse. The sockets were held in place by Velcro straps attached to the harnesses.

Getting both legs on took ages. I was sitting on a chair between the parallel bars. I was pumped up for it and ready to leap out of my seat, sure I could get myself up and standing on my own. The Headley staff were having none of it. They were going to winch me into place using a crane to support my body weight in case I fell.

I was gutted. I didn't think I needed the crane. I wanted badly not to need the crane. But they were worried about me stacking it, so I did as I was told.

A third harness like a vest went on and was fastened over the leg straps. I bent my head forward as they attached me to the crane by a carabiner hook to the harness at the back of my neck.

'All set?'

'Yep, go for it.'

There was an electrical whine as the crane's motor wound in the slack and I felt the harness tighten as it began the lift. In a few seconds I would be standing at my original height and I couldn't wait. The whine increased in pitch and turned into a grinding electrical howl followed by a bang. My arse hadn't got an inch off the seat.

I was about 11 or 12 stone with the legs strapped on, I guess. Whatever the weight, it was too much for the crane. I'd broken it. The winch wasn't used that often in the first place and proved to be badly underpowered. We were all a bit embarrassed and disappointed. I was like, 'Sorry, guys, I didn't think I'd got that fat.'

In typical Headley style they fixed it overnight and the next day the winch cranked me into position between the bars without a hitch. I grabbed the left-hand rail and let the weight settle on to my stumps. It was painful but I could manage it.

Once I'd got my wobbling under control and was standing and stable, I looked up. It felt absolutely fucking brilliant. I was six feet tall again for the first time since the blast. Once again, Mum and Dad were clicking away like two demented paparazzi and I was grinning from ear to ear. Becky gave me a hug as Mum took another picture.

The crane harness wire slotted into a track above the length of the parallel bars so it could follow me as I walked and save me from a fall at any point along the length of the bars. With all the various straps, harnesses and iron legs on I looked like some sort of cyborg still under construction. I didn't care. I leant my weight on to my left arm and leg and managed to lift and swing the right leg forward a few inches, throwing it out to my right to raise it off the floor. Moving my hand along the bar, I leant to the other side and repeated the movement with the left leg. Each step moved the metal feet a few inches forward. My stumps were sore, it was painful, but I could deal with it. Sweat beaded on my forehead and poured out of my body, soaking the harness as I shuffled along between the bars. It was hard going, but there was only one word for what I was doing: walking.

Mum, Dad and Becky were over the moon, and I was thrilled. The effort required was massive and the achievement quite small, maybe six feet, with each pace marking a few inches travelled. I'd moved myself about the same distance that night when I crawled my way across the flat at Selly Oak and pulled myself on to the sofa. But the difference in how I felt about it was huge. The effort required then had made me think life wasn't worth living. This was a ball-ache, but I wasn't shuffling on my arse, I was taller than some of the other guys in the room and walking without anyone helping me. I instinctively knew that I would be able to do much more given time.

They lowered me back down into the chair and started unwrapping me like a big parcel. We went back to my room and the family were all smiles, yapping away about how great it was.

A while later I got a burst of the blues, feeling down because of the crane. I'd only managed to walk because I'd been winched into place, and it was grating on me. 'It's not much of an achievement if you have to be winched on to your feet,' I dripped to myself. 'It doesn't count.'

So I promised myself the crane was history. I was never going to use it again.

I started work on my plan the next day in the gym. The physios had it in mind to push me but soon saw they didn't have to. Where I wanted to be was way ahead of where they needed to get me, so everyone was happy. I saw one guy sitting upright in a bench-press machine with a decent weight selected. 'Right.' I had a glint in my eye. 'From now on his weight is my weight.' Being able to press with one arm what he did with two was going to make a point to myself. I didn't want people making allowances for me, I wanted to do as much as or more than people around me.

I took the strain and shoved forward. The muscles of my chest and forearm sent howls of protest to my brain as I drove the weight forward. Tough shit. Beads of sweat pricked my forehead as I managed about four reps. Not as many as the other guy, but I'd got him in my sights.

Back in the prosthetics department, they got me strapped into the practice legs again. I told the physios there was no way I was getting in the crane. They were happy with my attitude and let me crack on. I sat in the wheelchair with my solid legs sticking straight out in front of me as they pushed me into the space between and beneath the bars. I shuffled my bum forward and lowered the legs at an angle down on to the floor. A physio grabbed my metal ankles to keep my feet in place on the deck. I put my left arm up and grabbed the bar as far forward as I could, then I threw my body weight forward and hoyed myself up. There was no technique to it and it took almost all my strength, but I made it first time.

Now you're talking. The crane could go hang. I didn't need it any more.

For two weeks I stomped up and down between those parallel bars. I learned to turn at the end of each length by rocking my weight back on to the heels of the false feet and kind of swivelling towards the direction I wanted to point in. By the end of that fortnight I'd also worked out the exact force required to get me out of the chair and up using the most efficient grip. At the start I was in a sweat by the time I'd got myself up, and wringing wet with perspiration after I'd stomped a length between the bars. After two weeks I'd practised until I could do it all in about half the time and without getting much out of breath.

I was learning all the time. The physios always introduced a new task with a method that worked for most people. The only problem was, the drills were designed for amputees who'd lost a single limb, or at most a double amputee. With three limbs gone, some of their methods didn't work for me. For a new procedure, like getting into a car for example, I liked to sit and size up the problem for a few minutes before trying it. It helped to visualize moving through each sequence and imagine the strength it was going to take, where my hand should go for maximum leverage, then go for it. In this way we were able to adapt the drills at Headley to make them work for me, and it made me feel good to be contributing something towards my own recovery.

For some of the staff at Headley I was the most seriously injured amputee they had ever worked with. They were learning how best to go about things as much as I was. Between us we had a positive attitude, and I thought that whatever the problem there would always be a way round it. The physios in the department were probably thinking that the fighting in the Afghan and Iraq was going to be sending home more characters like me. The drills we were making up as we went along were going to come in handy in future.

The positive attitude about the place made things better for me and my family. They were suffering massive mood swings, one minute up on a weird high based on the fact I was alive, the next down in a horrible low as the reality of my condition hit home.

The first time I stood up on my sockets, for example. There I was grinning my face off, obviously chuffed to have got myself upright for the first time since my accident. Didn't change the fact that in my mum and dad's eyes the boy they'd raised from a gurgling baby to a 6ft 1in Bootie had just been ripped down to what they were looking at now: a one-armed midget half the size he should be. Of course they were pleased that I was pleased to be standing up again, but on the inside, the state I was in was smashing them to bits.

My attitude to this was a bit harsh. It was like, 'If I can cope with it, then so can you. Now move on.' Like I said, tears weren't much good to me. Mum,

Dad and Becky all picked up on this and it kind of pulled everyone through.

Everyone got a boost from my rate of progress. I was always pushing, and around this time something just clicked. The physios kept telling me, 'We didn't expect you to be at this stage quite so soon.' It was like, 'Give us a minute while we work out what we're going to go for next.' I was always asking them, 'What are we doing next? When would you expect me to make it? End of the week? Let's try end of today.' They responded to that, and we cracked on as hard as possible.

I'd worried about my little girl Kezia's reaction and was really nervous the first time she saw me. She was only just three, but I shouldn't have worried. She came tearing into the room and leapt on to me, squealing with giggles.

When she clocked my legs it was like, 'Daddy, what happened to your legs?'

'Well, when Daddy was away they got poorly so the doctors had to take them away.'

'Oh.' She paused, taking it in. Then, 'How are you going to walk, Daddy?'

'Well, they are going to give me a new pair of legs and I will walk on them.'

'OK. When can I see your new legs?'

'As soon as I get them you can see them.'

'OK. Tell me when you get them, Daddy. I want to see your new legs straight away.'

It was like I'd told her we were getting a new car. Kids are amazing. I was quite relieved. She didn't think I was a freak at all. I was just her dad and I was getting a new pair of legs. That felt beyond good.

Every time she saw me after that she was pestering me, 'Have you got your new legs yet? When are you getting your new legs?' I was almost as excited as her. I wanted to get cracking on these bionic C-Legs and start charging about the place.

After about six weeks I was storming up and down on the practice legs but their basic design was holding me back. I was desperate to get hold of a pair of proper bionic legs like Mick Brennan's and kept pestering the prosthetics team who insisted that a pair had been ordered and was on the way. Once I got into the C-Legs I knew I would be able to walk without a limp. They would change my life.

Then, towards the end of April, one of the nurses was passing the room and asked, 'When's your prosthetics appointment today, Mark?'

'It's twelve o'clock isn't it? Why, what's up?'

'Oh nothing,' she said with a smile.

Hmm. Something was up. I wheeled myself down to the prosthetics department thinking about having a good rant about my practice legs being shite again. I banged through the doors and my jaw dropped. Standing in the middle of the room were the C-Legs. The polished carbon fibre and stainless steel glittered under the bright lights. The

Bionic Man himself would have been impressed.

'There you go, Rammers, your brand new C-Legs, mate. We're just setting them up and then you can try them out.'

I was over the moon. They looked absolutely wicked.

The black of my tailor-made carbon-fibre sockets, already attached to the 'thigh' of the C-Legs, was set off by the stainless steel and polished aluminium below. There were computers and on-board hydraulics encased in the knee. They were made in America and cost £20,000 each. Everything had been paid for by the Marines and the care and kit I was getting couldn't be faulted. Looking at them, I got the same sort of feeling as you do when you see the latest iPod gizmo in the shops. I was thinking, 'How cool is that! How did they make it do all this stuff?'

The physios set them up for me and I got the silicone socks on before they helped me into the new legs. A Bluetooth dongle changed the gait and I used it to lock out the knee for standing still when I first tried them.

When the legs were on I stood in front of the mirror in the physio department. They still looked bionic but what I saw made me choke. The lower leg was a polished metal shaft and only a couple of centimetres in diameter. It's a replacement for your shin bone and doesn't need to be any bigger to cope with the load, but the effect made me look as if I was a great big bloke with two horrible spindly little legs. I was gutted. They'd given me these fantastic prosthetics that could do so much and there I was threaders with the way they looked. I had a word with myself, decided not to act like an ungrateful twat, and got back between the parallel bars.

I changed the gait mode to a walk on level ground and started stomping up and down between the bars. No matter what I did, I couldn't make the knees bend. Despite all the computer wizardry it felt as if I was on a pair of non-articulated practice legs.

The technique was to clench my arse cheek every time I took a pace. The sensors up and down the leg should detect this and bend the knee for me.

I clenched and stomped, clenched and stomped.

Nothing happened.

It was doing my nut in. No matter what I tried, I couldn't get the things to work. I started to feel as if the whole C-Leg system was a big con.

Some extra kit caught up with the legs and was delivered a few days later. It was a pair of shin pads that connected on to the shaft of the lower leg. Putting them on made an immediate difference. They were nothing to do with the mechanism of the leg, they were just there to protect the metalwork, but in the mirror the pads gave the legs a more human outline, like they were pretending to be the calf muscles or something. They made me feel immediately better about myself. It might seem strange to you, but without those shin pads

I thought I looked a freak. With them I thought I looked much more 'normal'.

The physios explained that I wasn't getting enough weight on to the toe of the foot and that if I did the knee would 'give way' and bend for me.

My bottle had gone. I couldn't put the weight on the toe because I was frightened. 'Give way' in my mind meant stacking it and getting my stumps all gashed up.

Imagine you're about to go on a run and you're stretching your thigh muscle by grabbing your ankle and pulling it up towards your backside. Now imagine you're doing that with both legs at the same time and you're suspended a metre off the deck. Someone's going to drop you from there on to a hard surface, your full body weight's going to smash down on to your kneecaps. You can probably cope with the pain involved but it's going to really screw up your knees, maybe do serious damage. All the time I was trying to walk it felt as if I was a second or two from that happening.

Nothing I'd come across in the Afghan had made me scared like this. I hated feeling that way, it made me puke. In the end it got me threaders to the point I decided to go for it and take the consequences.

I leant forward between the bars, loading weight on to the toe, clenched my arse cheek and, 'Wow!', the leg walked. The right knee bent as I moved and threw the foot forward. I staggered to regain my balance and succeeded in staying upright.

Hoofin' effort.

I knew exactly how I'd made it work. I could do it at last and gave myself a new target: to walk a length of the parallel bars with the C-Legs bending every step of the way.

We got a visit at Headley Court from a bloke called Swifty who blasted into the place like a 4ft 6in tall hurricane.

Darren Swift was a Lance Corporal with the Royal Green Jackets on a tour of Belfast in 1991 when the IRA dropped a pipe bomb on him during a patrol. It blew off both his legs and the tops of two of his fingers. He had a through-the-knee and above-the-knee amputation and in the years since had made an astonishing recovery.

He can't get along with prosthetic legs with a knee joint in them, he hates them. Wherever he goes he uses 'short non-articulated prosthetic pylons'. 'Stubbies' is what I call them. They're like two-foot-long hard resin cylinders, one for each stump. Each stubby is like a cross between a prosthetic leg and a giant boot. When you stand on them it looks as if your legs have sunk through the floor up to your knees.

I hated the look at first. 'Swifty, mate, you look like fucking Toulouse-Lautrec in them,' I dripped. 'Can't you get some proper legs?'

'I don't give a shit, mate. Watch this.' And he was off bombing all over the place so fast I couldn't keep track of him. 'Look what you can do,' he went on. 'Anywhere you could go before your injury, you can go on these. Compared to a wheelchair they're brilliant.'

Swifty showed us how the stubbies had transformed his life. He moved around with deceptive speed and independence. Since the explosion he'd become a champion skydiver and was developing a snowboard for double amputees. That got my attention.

The prosthetics team made up a pair of stubbies for me immediately after Swifty's visit. I was a bit ungrateful: 'Yeah, whatever, thanks, lads.' My attitude makes me go red now because once I got into them they changed my life too. There are no joints to bend so they are really stable. Your centre of mass is close to the ground so it's really hard to lose your balance. I was low enough to use my left arm to stop me going over and grabbed things like chairs and tables for support. On the full-size prosthetic legs you're a long way off the deck. If you have a fall it's going to hurt like fuck and do damage that might set back your recovery. From being fearful of going over all the time, suddenly I was charging around the place like a demented midget. I loved it.

I had a good wheelchair with a specially adapted drive wheel that allowed me to turn left, right or move straight forward or back using just my left hand. It was good, but it was slow going. You wheeled up to a door, stopped, applied the brake, turned the handle, pushed the door open, took the brake off and wheeled yourself through. Doesn't sound like much, but people go through doorways dozens of times a day. With the stubbies my hand was free to turn the door handle as I whizzed through. I could pick up – or pinch – stuff as I passed instead of having to stop or risk crashing the wheelchair into someone or something. It saved hours out of every day. You could get into places you couldn't in a wheelchair and make a significantly better getaway. Interesting possibilities started forming a disorderly queue in my head.

Thanks to Swifty, that June I got a trip away from Headley Court with an outfit called the Calvert Trust. They laid on adventure training for disabled people and I had a great time with them. They got me kayaking and sailing on a lake down near Barnstaple. The stubbies really came into their own on that trip.

My pair were pretty slick as they were held on by suction. They were easy to take on and off, with no harnesses or straps to struggle with single-handed. It was barely six months since the explosion, but I was that confident I climbed aboard a quad bike wearing the stubbies and a female instructor took me for a spin.

We discovered their limits of adhesion a few seconds later. She went for it, jamming open the throttle, and as we smashed over a bump both stubbies flew off the ends of my stumps. One landed neatly, digging an edge of the moulded socket into a freshly steaming pile of cowshit.

Nice.

At least I didn't come off the quad.

It was a great week, and I was able to appreciate that I'd travelled light years from my bad night on the sofa. There are plenty of fully able people who've never ridden a quad bike or paddled a kayak or gone sailing. Some people were going to look at me as if I was 100 per cent disabled and assume my life was shit, but that trip made me determined to try every activity I possibly could. Life was going to be tough but I was starting to see that some of it could be real good. I had loads to look forward to, and my attitude to life changed. It wasn't about survival any more. It was like, 'I'm ready for anything. Bring it on.'

16

I was still in the single room for high-dependency casualties next to the nursing station on the ward when they issued me with a prosthetic arm. It wasn't as slick as the C-Legs and needed a shoulder harness to keep it in place. The hand could be detached at the wrist and you had a couple of options: a hook attachment for practical help or a cosmesis, a lifelike fake hand that could pass for the real thing, as long as no one looked too closely. It had fingernails complete with white tips and the plastic 'skin' was etched with lines and pores.

The main nurse looking after me was Pam, and the dedication she brought to the job was unbelievable. At that stage there were no other Bootnecks on the ward and I got quite lonely in the evenings. After my sessions finished at 4.30 p.m. that was me for the night and there wasn't much to do. Pam used to come and chat to me about Kezia and Becky and kept my spirits up. It was like being looked after by a second mum.

I was mucking about with the hand, trying to hold my mobile phone with it, when I had an idea. I took it off and placed it on the side of the bed. It looked for all the world as if I'd fallen out of bed and was trying to climb back in. It made me laugh just looking at it. The phone clenched between its fingers was perfect. Even Pam couldn't help laughing. I went and hid behind the door and pulled the alarm cord. Pam stepped behind the door just as three orderlies came charging in, sized up the situation and leapt to the far side of the room to help me up. They were flapping to the max and couldn't believe their eyes when they saw the arm was on its own. They were checking under the bed and couldn't work out where I'd vanished to. Pam and I burst out laughing, and they saw the funny side in the end. It cheered me up loads.

After they'd gone, it crossed my mind that I'd better not fall out of bed for real from now on. Help might be some time coming.

I worked my arse off at Headley trying to get to grips with the C-Legs and control the gait because an important event was coming up. The men of 40 Commando had returned from their tour of Afghan and were to be awarded the Operational Service Medal on the parade ground of their base at Norton Manor Camp in Taunton. My ten weeks' service in the Afghan meant I'd earned the right to receive the medal alongside them.

I was now walking lengths of the physio department on my C-Legs with a 'quad-pod' walking stick with four rubber-coated feet on the end of it. The knees were bending most of the time and getting out of the bars made a massive difference because I was less worried about getting tangled up and going arse over tit. It was still a struggle but I was getting somewhere. An idea popped into my head. The parade ground at Norton Manor was flat. The whole base was flat. The only thing to stop me walking there would be a couple of steps up to an office or the steep slope behind the front gate.

'That's it,' I promised myself. 'I'm going to walk on to that parade ground. I will stand to have that medal pinned on my chest like any other Bootneck.'

The entire Commando, six hundred fighting men, and two thousand family and friends would be there. The parade would be attended by the Second Sea Lord, Vice Admiral Adrian Johns CBE. Stacking it in front of that lot would be a nightmare for me, the Corps, the Headley staff and my family.

That was the downside. It would be the first time a lot of the guys had seen me since the accident. The parade was in mid-May, four and a half months since I'd had my legs and arm blown off. The looks on the faces of those Booties just back from Afghan when they saw me walking on to the parade ground to get my medal would be priceless.

'C'mon!' I yelled as I loaded weight on to the toe, forced the knee to bend and took another wobbly pace.

A couple of startled physios asked if I was OK. I told them my plan. Smiles lit their faces. It would say something about the care on offer at Headley Court if we could do it, so they were up for it, but that wasn't what made them smile.

I explained that it would be an emotional day for all the lads anyway. There would be a lot of stuff going on in their heads. What I really wanted was to walk out in front of those proud Marines and make them cry like the big girls I knew they really were.

Game on.

I was doing well at Headley Court and lots of people complimented me on my attitude and progress. People seemed surprised that I didn't feel sorry for myself or bitter. What's the use of feeling like that though? We are where we are, all of us. The only thing you can do is keep moving forward. I was surrounded by people who gave me real inspiration. If you can find someone with more personal courage than Ben Parkinson from 7 Para Royal Horse Artillery, then I want to meet that man.

Ben was coping with the worst injuries ever inflicted on a battlefield soldier who survived. He was blown up by a landmine the year before me in Afghanistan. He lost both legs and suffered thirty-seven internal and external injuries. Loads has been written about Ben and his family's fight to get him a proper level of compensation so he can be looked after properly at home. He was one of the first through the system, and that didn't make it easier for him or his family. I have the greatest respect for Ben and his people. I've never seen courage or determination like it. He set a standard that I had to live up to, and you know how hard it is for a Bootneck to say that about any Para.

All the lads at Headley were good blokes with a positive attitude. No one dripped about what had happened to them. Everyone took it on the chin and cracked on.

Ben McBean, the critically injured Marine who shared his flight home with Prince Harry, was hurt ten weeks after me. We shared a room at Headley for a while and it was hoofin' to have another Bootneck in the place. For a start he knew how to speak English properly, unlike all these Pongos, who insisted on calling a 'wet' a 'brew' and their 'scran' their 'scoff'. Ben lost his right leg above the knee and his left arm so we were able to give each other loads of encouragement and abuse.

In late summer a young Para named Tom Neathway came to Headley Court. He'd suffered almost identical injuries to me, the only difference being which arm. He had been searching a compound when he caught it up in a booby-trap IED. He lost his left arm above the elbow and both legs above the knee.

I had been asked if I would travel up to Selly Oak to see Tom and I was more than happy to do so. I remembered all the crap that had brought me down and talked him through it. I tried my hardest to do exactly what Mick Brennan had done for me. Tell him the score with no scrap of bullshit. Tom was a Para so he already knew everything about determination and digging out blind. Life was going to be mega-tough for him but it could still be good. I hoped I'd managed to give him half the encouragement Mick had given me.

The one lad at Headley Court I'll never forget was Sam Cooper. Sam was with 2nd Battalion the Mercian Regiment when he found himself in the thick of a night action that has become an Army legend. For eight hours the Mercians went toe to toe with the Taliban, fighting so close they could hear the enemy's wounded screaming, about 15 metres away. Sam's company lost two of their men, killed, and there were seven wounded, including Sam, who was shot in the head. The Mercians drove the Taliban out of well-prepared defensive positions and the action became the single most highly decorated contact of all the fighting at company level in Afghanistan to date. The men of A Company won a Conspicuous Gallantry Cross, three Military Crosses (one posthumously), two Mentions in Dispatches and three Joint Commander's Commendations for their actions that one night.

The contact happened exactly a month before I

arrived in theatre and a few days before the Mercians were due to rotate back to Bastion and go home. The OC had ordered A Company out of FOB Delhi to attack a Taliban trench system in no-man's land about 1,000 metres south of Darvisham in Garmsir District. They wanted to leave the place in good shape for their replacements and give the Taliban something to remember them by, driving them out of their forward positions.

It was a black night, with visibility down to a few feet. Sam's platoon had achieved their first objective of clearing a ruined compound. They were moving on to attack their second objective and knew that there were Taliban inside. As they tried to sneak around the back of the compound they were ambushed at almost point-blank range by Taliban fighters in defensive positions about 15 metres away. The section had walked into a planned killing zone where the insurgents were able to catch up the Mercians in a crossfire. Private Johan Botha was right in the middle of the zone and was shot and killed immediately. Pte Luke Cole, a Territorial Army reservist, was shot through the right thigh, smashing his femur. Sam was knocked out cold by a round that hit him in the head and smashed off a section of his skull. Another Corporal was hit in the head but his helmet stopped the round and saved him.

Luke Cole could hear the Taliban talking to each other they were so close and he fought them like crazy, refusing to take morphine for his leg so he could protect Sam. Then Luke was shot through the stomach and lost a lot of blood, but he wouldn't lie down and just carried on fighting.

The Mercians refused to leave their dead or wounded to the Taliban and fought with ferocious tenacity and unparalleled courage that night. Their boss, Lt Simon Cupples, crawled forward under enemy fire directing the search for Pte Botha and organizing the evacuation of Sam and Luke while directing the rest of the platoon to put down heavy suppressing fire on the Taliban positions. They knew they were hitting the Taliban hard because they could hear the enemy screaming when they caught it up.

Lt Rupert Bowers got to Sam, put him over his shoulder and sprinted off to the rear with him. How he wasn't hit in the crossfire no one knows. Sgt Craig Brelsford led a team forward to search for Pte Botha. No matter what they tried they couldn't find him, it was so dark. Apparently, if you put your rifle down for a second that night you might not find it again, but there was no way they were leaving anyone behind. As he led this effort Sgt Brelsford was shot and killed; his was the posthumous Military Cross. After dawn broke, the Mercians brought down armoured vehicles and made sure they recovered every single one of their dead and wounded.

The Mercians showed incredible courage

throughout that contact. They'd been put to the test and found to be awesome.

I had massive respect for Sam. His injury had affected the speech centre in his brain and he was partially paralysed but you could tell he was a cracking lad and we got on really well. The problem was, just about the only word he could get out when he started at Headley was 'fuck'. Like I said, he'd been in quite a fight.

Sam and I used to have wheelchair races, charging around the rec room at Headley scaring the crap out of the nursing staff, a danger to clinicians and patients alike. He used to beat me hollow, and he loved it. His eyes twinkled like he was saying, 'Yeah, mate, I might only be able to say one word beginning with "f" but I've got one more hand and two more feet than you and you'll never beat me, sunshine.'

Back in April, Prince William and Prince Harry had come down to Headley Court with a load of press in tow. They were promoting an event they were working on with the City of London called City Salute, due to be held outside St Paul's Cathedral on the evening of 7 May. The Princes wanted to raise as much cash as possible for servicemen and women via the Soldiers, Sailors, Airmen and Families Association (SSAFA) charity and Help for Heroes, who wanted to build the therapy pool at Headley. The Princes' plan was to hold a tribute to be screened live on the BBC that was part concert and part military tattoo. They wanted our help, and we were bang up for it. The Princes were going to invite all of us to come along and we were chuffed up to the max about it.

William and Harry were really chilled when they came to Headley. Harry was over the moon to see Ben McBean standing on his prosthetic leg for the first time. The pair of them had flown home together and Prince Harry had obviously been moved by Ben's condition on the flight. The two Princes spent more than two hours chatting away with us, making sure they spent a good amount of time with every injured serviceman.

We all knew Harry had been to the Afghan and he knew what he was talking about. I'd bumped into him on the OPTAG training and had no idea he was about to deploy. I could never have imagined what would happen to me in the months separating our two meetings. He'd experienced the conditions we'd served under, and that commanded respect. What's more, the Princes were showing they blatantly did give a damn about the lot of us and were prepared to do something about it. It was a hoofin' effort.

When it came for our turn to have a little chat Harry really made me laugh. He gave me a load of grief about being a Bootneck, saying I'd joined the wrong service and if I wanted to be in the infantry how come I'd managed to join the Navy? I didn't take any notice. He was only repeating nonsense the Pongos had put in his head. It was only afterwards I thought about what he'd done there. In about ten seconds he'd put me totally at my ease and raised a smile, saying exactly the right thing.

Prior to the City Salute the BBC came to make a short film about me and Becky that was going to be broadcast as part of the show.

We went up to town on the day with all the wounded servicemen and staff at Headley Court who were invited to join the Princes, Joss Stone, Ross Kemp and the actor Timothy West at the show. The event was hosted by Jeremy Clarkson and it was broadcast live. Clarkson came over and had a chat before the Salute began and Becky and I told him about our plans to get married. Before we knew it, Clarkson had announced our engagement on the steps of St Paul's on national telly in front of millions of viewers.

It was all a bit dazzling to be honest.

The Band of HM Royal Marines did a hoofin' job marching through Temple Bar looking and sounding the business. Ceremonial troops from the Household Cavalry put on a great display, Scimitar tanks charged around at the foot of the steps to St Paul's, and the RAF thundered overhead in a flypast of Typhoon jet fighters and Chinook helos. The Queen's Colour Squadron of the RAF Regiment put on a drill display with fixed bayonets. They didn't put a foot wrong, but the assembled Bootnecks and

Pongos couldn't help coughing a few extremely rude remarks. No one could work out where the Crabs had parked their aeroplanes while they were showing us how to handle a rifle. The display was brought to a thundering close by a broadside fired from the guns of HMS Belfast, the World War Two cruiser moored upstream of Tower Bridge.

Prince William and Prince Harry were a great laugh, relaxed and down to earth, and seemed to be really enjoying themselves. They'd put a lot of effort into the event and were pleased it went so well.

Harry was gobsmacked to see Ben McBean, who turned up for the event in a light grey business suit walking around with hardly a limp in a pair of black leather shoes. You couldn't tell which leg was the prosthetic, he was walking so well. Harry was stunned. He put both hands to his head and stared at Ben open-mouthed before bursting into a whoop of delight. He couldn't believe the change. It was the first time he'd seen him since Headley Court the previous month. Ben had only just learned to stand up on his prosthetic leg then; now, just a few weeks later, he was walking about the place as if he'd been completely rebuilt. William and Harry made a fuss of all of us that night.

There was a party afterwards, and Harry was standing beside my wheelchair when Joss Stone walked past in a slinky black dress. She was looking fabulous and her dress was clinging tightly to her stunning figure as she swished away from us.

'Rammers, do you think Joss is wearing any knickers under that dress?' Harry asked.

I grinned. 'No, sir, I don't.'

A week later, Ben McBean and I got ready for the medal ceremony in the Sergeants' Mess at Norton Manor Camp, home to 40 Commando in Taunton. We had our desert rig uniforms on over our prosthetic legs and were sitting in our wheelchairs. I'd not wanted the prosthetic arm so had my empty sleeve rolled up as far as my stump. It was a formal ceremony but the dress code was desert rig with the sleeves rolled to a certain length above the elbow. Ben had his desert boots on but I was going to use the trainers I'd been practising on with the C-Legs.

The Royal Marines band struck up and the men of 40 Commando marched into their positions and were brought to attention. I was wheeled up in my chair to a position at the edge of the parade ground. It was a sunny May day and thousands of relatives were milling around the edge of the square. All my family were there, including my granddad Fred. They had conflicting emotions swirling around inside them, and Fred in particular had a lump in his throat. They were full of pride that I was being awarded the Operational Service Medal. They knew I was going to try to walk and stand shoulder to shoulder with my colleagues through the whole ceremony and were fretting I would stack it, get hurt and never forgive myself for making a tit of myself. In addition to that they were looking at hundreds of Marines who'd come home without a scratch from the Afghan with hoofin' sun tans and enough war stories to last a lifetime. Looking at them and looking at me gave my family a couple of tough moments, I think.

Against that, everyone on that parade ground knew how lucky Ben and I were to be there at all. We'd been given a second chance and had lives to live thanks to the courage, skill and hard work of so many people. We certainly knew how lucky we were, especially when we remembered the three men from 40 Commando who would never be coming home.

My friend Corporal Damian Mulvihill, who was thirty-two, stepped on an IED during a patrol near Sangin two months after I was blown up. He died instantly. I'd worked with Damian in Air Defence Troop at Stonehouse before the Iraq war and he was a top bloke. In combat he was a natural leader, one of the best section leaders in 40 Commando. He never flapped, no matter what was going on. He won respect up and down the chain of command for the way he looked after the lads in his section. They were devastated to lose him, and so was I.

Equally well liked and respected were Lieutenant John Thornton, who was only twenty-two and a brilliant young boss, and David Marsh, a hoofin' Marine who was just twenty-three. They were both killed when their vehicle hit a roadside bomb up at

Kajaki during a patrol just a few weeks before the end of their tour.

Every single person on the parade ground thought about those three men during the ceremony. That's why I felt lucky to be there, and that's why I was determined to make the best of the chance I'd been given.

There was one more Marine who couldn't be with us for the ceremony: Joe Townsend, who lost both his legs in a roadside bomb blast in the Upper Gereshk Valley. He was in Selly Oak hospital, too unwell to attend. After awarding medals at the camp, the Second Sea Lord, Vice Admiral Johns, was going to fly straight to Joe's bedside to present him with his Operational Service Medal in person.

The Commando was stood to attention and it was time for Ben and me to join them. I launched myself out of the wheelchair and stood up. There was absolute silence on the parade ground, as if everyone was holding their breath.

Ben started moving, and so did I.

I had the quad-pod walking stick and concentrated on taking one step at a time. The weather was good but there was a strong wind blowing across the parade ground and it was the one thing I hadn't thought of. I concentrated like crazy on not getting knocked on my arse by that wind. Following close behind me was Sgt Major Bob Toomey, who'd driven the Supacat to get me back from North Fort to FOB ROB. If he saw me wobbling, I think he was going to try to scoop me up in the chair before I went.

After Ben and I had managed a few steps, I was taken aback. The crowd started to applaud us. It took me a couple of seconds to realize the clapping was for me and Ben. There were no cheers or whistles. Just quiet, polite applause.

Becky noticed lots of people wiping the odd tear away. She said it was the sight of the whole Commando stood to attention in the sun, plus Ben and me walking slowly out to join them, plus the memory of the three men who would not be coming back. It was a powerful sight apparently, and hardly a dry eye watched it.

I walked carefully round to the back row of Echo Company. There was a gap in the line waiting for me. I concentrated on getting myself in the right place and then shifted my weight on to my heel to lock the legs into the standing position. Bob Toomey was giving a discreet running commentary to the rest of the lads who were stood to attention, eyes front, for the arrival of the Second Sea Lord. They weren't allowed to look round or say anything to me so Bob was quietly saying, 'That's Rammers moving into position. He's stood to attention now. That's him squared away. Carry on, lads.'

Bob told me later there were definitely a couple of Bootnecks in the row looking a bit misty-eyed. It was probably the wind. Never mind making them cry like big girls, I was concentrating on not making them laugh their arses off by stacking it in the middle of this lot.

Two Harrier GR9 jump jets thundered low over the parade ground doing about 500mph at 500 feet. Then Vice Admiral Johns stepped up to the podium and told the whole Commando that their professionalism and dedication was what had seen them through a difficult tour and would continue to 'shine brightly'. He told us to remember our successes and that they were not easily won, that three men had paid the highest price for them. He talked about the wounded and singled out Ben, calling him 'Prince Harry's personal hero', and me, calling me a 'legend'.

It's not every day an Admiral pays a compliment like that to a Bootneck like me. To tell you the truth, I didn't feel like a legend at all. I felt like a fucking idiot. All these other hundreds of Marines had managed to come home without stepping on an IED.

The ceremony took forty minutes and I spent every one of them concentrating on not falling over. At last I was presented with my OSM for Afghanistan by the Echo Company commander who'd taken over from Chris Jesson, Major Neil Wraith, and Sgt Major Toomey. They came down the line shaking hands with me. I was willing them to speed up and get the job done.

At last it was over and I'd made it. We fell out and Becky came running up to me. She slid her arms round my waist to give me a kiss. It was one of the first times she'd been able to give me a smooch at my proper height in public, and it felt fantastic for us both.

That moment capped one of the proudest days of my life. I'll never forget it.

17

We had been waiting around for ages in the canteen of the Army Parachute School at Netheravon in Wiltshire. The only weather that could really stop the jump was total cloud cover. If the guys in the plane couldn't see the ground, they wouldn't go. We'd spent a day sitting under 8/8ths of low-level cloud getting threaders for the whole afternoon. A Royal Marines Sea King had flown in on other business and they were itching to take me up to do the parachute jump from the helo, and I was bang up for that. Instead, we sat on the ground talking bollocks and hanging from the 0500 start and long drive up from Plymouth.

I was there to say a thank you to the Soldiers, Sailors, Airmen and Families Association for their help in looking after me. While I was at Headley they had opened some fantastic accommodation around the corner from the rehab centre called Norton House, and I had moved in there. It meant I could get out of the clinical environment of Headley and Becky or the family could come and stay with me. It was a modern mansion that had been completely refurbished. I got a big bedroom and use of a massive kitchen, and a TV room to chill out in. We got a bit of privacy and it gave us a taste of what life would be like after Headley Court. It was a two million pounds project and made such a difference to me I wanted to give something back to SSAFA.

I got talking to the guys at the charity and they told me they regularly organized parachute jumps to raise cash for their projects, getting civvies to raise sponsorship then training them to do the jump. There was a former Pongo officer called Athol Hendry at the charity. He'd served with the Royal Tank Regiment for several years and was a top bloke. He was doing some publicity for the jumps and came up with a hoofin' idea: 'Do you want to have a go at a parachute jump and raise some money for us?'

'Parachute jump? Show me to the plane.'

Netheravon is where the Army's top skydiving teams practise, and the Black Knights were the Royal Artillery's elite display squad. Their chief instructor, Sgt Reg Green, was going to take me up in a tandem freefall jump from over two miles up, and I couldn't wait.

But waiting was all that we got to do at the first attempt. I went home without getting off the ground but was determined to give it a second go.

I was walking quite well on the C-Legs by this time. It was the height of summer and I was getting out and about a bit. I was developing a more natural gait, particularly in short bursts. We'd had some rough times but humour had got me and Becky through a lot of them. Athol Hendry particularly liked the message I had on my mobile back then: 'Hello, you've reached Mark Ormrod, the Bionic Man. I'm not available at the moment as I'm probably having my legs and arm serviced or fixed. Please leave a message after the tone.' It seemed to give people a laugh. We also got one over on Becky's sister with the C-Legs when I went to stay at her mum and dad's house. Becky put a pair of grey tracksuit pants on them with the trainers on the feet and placed them in a sitting position over the toilet. She left them there until her sister went to use the bathroom and screamed the place down.

It was good to get through the bad times because every now and then you'd get a day like this one.

I went back to Netheravon after the aborted first attempt and Reg and the other lads from the team adapted a suit for me. I couldn't jump with the C-Legs on as the impact of the landing could damage them and me. Instead, I wore a cotton sock over each stump. Becky pushed me into the practice hall in my chair and I hopped out on to some mats on the floor and wriggled myself into the suit.

The gunners treated me the same as they would anyone. There was loads of banter. The fact they were giving me such stick felt brilliant. They were like, 'Shall we help him get into the jumpsuit? Nah, he's only a Bootneck, let him do it himself.'

I kept a straight face. 'Thanks, lads, probably be quicker without you interfering to be honest.'

They did give me a load of help getting into the tandem harness and Reg and the lads couldn't have been more patient. Members of the public were allowed into Netheravon to train for parachute jumps so there were quite a few civvies milling about the place while I was getting ready. There was a team lying on their bellies on trolleys like big skateboards practising freefall manoeuvres, spinning round and popping into formations by locking wrists and ankles. Other civvies came walking through in jump gear with parachutes and some of them did a double-take to see me, a triple amputee, sitting on the floor all harnessed up. They took it in, accepted it and carried on. No one gave me a second look after that and it felt good.

I got back in my wheelchair and Becky pushed me outside to where a golf buggy was waiting to take me to the plane. She wasn't worried about me doing the jump in the slightest. Becky had done one herself for charity a couple of years earlier, and to be honest I was green with envy. I'd wanted to jump before my accident but didn't get the time. We were all delighted that the injury wasn't going to stop me ticking that box.

One of the team came over and I asked him, 'Does this ever go wrong then, mate?'

'Well, we do pick up a lot more twisted or broken ankles than we'd like, due to awkward landings.'

'Happy days.' I grinned. 'That can't happen to me, can it?'

That got a good laugh.

There were about eight of us going up and it was a beautiful afternoon, sunny with a few fluffy clouds. There was quite a bit of wind on the deck that was making some teams think twice about jumping, but not Reg. He'd done about 4,500 jumps and was quite happy with the conditions.

The plane was a Cessna Caravan turbo-prop with a sliding side door and no seats; we all just sat around on the floor. Reg shuffled up behind me and clipped up the tandem harness.

The plane thumped across the airfield and we were off, climbing up to 13,000 feet, about two and a half miles off the deck. Lots of the lads had digital altimeters strapped to their wrists like big watches and I could see the figures mounting as the Cessna clambered up into the sky at about 100 knots. I knew we were going at 13,000 feet so when I saw one of the altimeters reading 12,500 I gulped. It was too late to back out now.

The aircraft levelled out and stuck its nose into the wind. They opened the door and the plane filled with hurricane-force winds.

'Ideal,' I thought. 'I must have gone mental,

falling out of a perfectly good aircraft on purpose.'

Reg and I shuffled on our arses towards the doorway. I looked down and couldn't believe how far away the ground looked. The whole airfield was laid out like a kid's toy beneath us. You couldn't see any people, just patches of green fields.

'OK?' Reg yelled in my ear.

I gave him the thumbs up, and we were gone before I knew it.

Adrenalin smashed into my veins as we plunged towards the patchwork a couple of miles below. The acceleration was off the scale: 0 to 130mph in five seconds. The wind roared and ripped at my face, mouth and ears. My brain was tripping out with the sheer buzz. The rush was like being in combat, except it wasn't so dangerous.

Two other lads from the Black Knights came zooming in from the sides while a third took up station in front of us filming video and still pictures.

I stuck my arm out and gave a thumbs up as Reg worked hard to keep us stable. I couldn't balance the forces acting on my left arm by sticking out my right on the other side like other skydivers. Reg was worried we might flip over but there were no problems.

The ground didn't look to be getting much closer as we roared towards it like a rocket heading the wrong way. I was just conscious of thinking, 'What a fantastic ride.'

The harness yanked hard. The other skydivers

shot out of view below us and I started falling upwards. That's what it felt like. I looked up and saw a massive blue canopy opened above us.

It was a different world now. We'd fallen about a mile and a half in forty seconds and Reg had pulled the chute at 5,800 feet – another mile still to go.

We floated around in a series of lazy S turns and I chilled to the max, loving the view as we headed gently over towards the airfield. The other sky-divers got down long before us so I could see roughly where Reg was going to land.

All of a sudden I could see a group of people standing almost underneath us. One of them was Becky, and I waved at her – 'Yeah Becky!' – like some kid on a Ferris wheel. She was waving back and yelling something at me when Reg shouted in my ear, 'Ready?'

'What's he talking about?' I thought. 'We're still way off the deck.'

Just as I finished the thought the ground slammed up at us out of nowhere. 'Whoa!' I just managed to lift my stumps as instructed for the landing as the ground came for us at what seemed like 100mph. Reg flew us across the grass into the wind and set us both gently down on the deck.

It was absolutely brilliant.

Reg was all for me training to do a solo jump after that. There are some parachutes used by the special forces that are designed to be operated with one hand and Reg thought it was entirely feasible for me to have a crack at a solo freefall jump. I'd love to do it. That jump was one of the best days of my life.

Thanks to some generous sponsors, including my family, mates and loads of people in Plymouth, I'd managed to raise almost £3,000 for SSAFA and given them something back for my time at Norton House. It was only seven months since I'd asked Sean to shoot me in the head because my life looked so shit. Now I wasn't just back on my feet, I was sky-diving and raising cash for military people and families who weren't as lucky as me.

That felt beyond good.

The alarm went at 0600.

I reached out with my left hand and grabbed the wheelchair beside the bed, heaving myself across the sheets and into a sitting position at the side of the mattress. I slid into the chair without a board, wheeled into the bathroom a couple of metres away, filled the sink with hot water and massaged shaving foam on to my face. I was right handed originally so it took a while to learn how to shave with the left. I used to make a right mess of my sideys. They looked as if they'd been chewed by a rat until I'd worked out my admin.

I then transferred myself across to the shower seat, put a towel over the wheelchair and pushed it out to an arm's length away. The wheels got a bit wet but no problem.

After the shower, back out to the bedroom to get

dressed. My C-Legs were still plugged into the wall where they had been charging overnight. I'd put my boots and green camouflage trousers, complete with belt, on to the legs the night before and they were standing there ready to go. I dried off properly in the wheelchair and sprayed anti-perspirant on to my stumps. If they started sweating during the day the legs could start slithering around and might fall off. I didn't want that on my first day back at work.

I rolled the silicone socks on to both stumps, slid them into the carbon-fibre sockets and pulled the trousers up to my waist.

Next came a T-shirt, and time to get my arm on. Unlike the C-Legs, the arm is held in place by a harness, a bit like the top of a shoulder holster for a pistol. I threaded my left arm through the loop of the harness then grabbed the prosthetic arm by the metal hook of its 'hand'. I pointed my right stump up to the ceiling and used the hook to drop the socket of the arm on to it. The harness was pre-adjusted to fit neatly across my shoulders and it snapped into place, holding the false arm snug to my stump.

Next I pulled on my Combat 95 camouflage shirt and tucked it in, with a bit of help from Becky.

I was ready.

Placing my boots flat on the floor in front of the wheelchair I pushed off with my left arm and stood up. I walked carefully forward to the lift on the landing and stood as it lowered me down into the dining room.

It was 0645.

'There you go, Mark,' said Becky. 'Loads of people take longer than that to get up, showered and dressed of a morning.'

She was trying to reassure me. I was really nervous about going back to work. I was fussing that I wasn't near smart enough.

'Of course you are, you look great,' Becky said. 'Mark, lots of people spend more time off work with backache than you have. It's only ten months since you were injured. I am so proud of you, you're going to do a great job.'

I gave her a kiss and placed the Green Beret on my head, dressing it carefully to the right. Apart from the metal hook poking out of my right sleeve I looked pretty much as I had before deploying to Afghanistan.

For the first few days settling in at work, 42 Commando in Plymouth had laid on a car to pick me up. The Marine Corps couldn't have done more to look after me since the explosion. They had totally renovated an officer's house, widening doorways for wheelchair access, installing the lift and building ramps in place of steps. The house was mine as long as I chose to stay in the Marines. When I left, it would be available for anyone in my position in the future.

Now I was going back to work for them, not as a

grav unfortunately, but as a clerk. Not in a wheel-chair but on my own two feet, even if they were made of stainless steel and carbon fibre.

Almost all of the 650 Marines of 42 Commando were in Afghanistan for Operation Herrick 9, as part of 3 Commando Brigade. I would be working with a Marine Sergeant and Navy Wren as a movements clerk, part of the rear party at 42's base in Plymouth. The job was to keep tabs on every Marine and make sure their personal admin was all up to date.

I started work at 0825, along with everyone else. I got out of the car and walked towards the office. Through the door on to the polished floor, and my walking stick said 'See ya' as it slipped away from me. I plunged forward out of control and ended up bent double, touching my toes. I didn't fall, and no one had seen me. I straightened myself up slowly and caught my breath. 'Let's not be too cocky,' I thought. This was obviously going to be trickier than I thought, but I wasn't going to let anyone know if I was struggling. I grabbed the stick and walked into the office as if nothing had happened.

Later in the day, another member of the rear party went flying and landed on his arse with a thump. There was nothing wrong with him, he had all his arms and legs. It was just that the floor was polished to a ridiculous shine. It was like an ice rink. That made me feel a lot better. At least my arse hadn't touched the deck when I went over.

The blokes at 42 all knew the score about me as

we'd been introduced before I started, and they got down to training me for the new job. Most of the Commando had been in theatre for just over a month and had qualified for their Operational Service Medals, so one of my first jobs was to order hundreds of them.

It felt odd, sitting in the UK thinking about all the lads in the Afghan fighting their bollocks off while I tapped away at a computer behind a desk. I wanted to be out there with them real bad. If I could get my real legs back, I'd go again in a heartbeat.

I caught the thought as soon as it flashed into my head and refused to let myself think on it any further. It was never going to happen. I had to accept that and move on or I'd never stop dripping about it. The Royal Marines had put a fine roof over my head and given me a good job. I was still part of their family and it felt fantastic.

We started to get invited to all sorts of events, and in late October someone from *The X Factor* rang up saying they wanted me to take part in the show. The finalists were going to release a single, 'Hero', to raise money for Headley Court through the Help for Heroes charity and for the Poppy Appeal. They'd invited loads of staff and patients from Headley Court to go as well, and Becky and me were chuffed up to be invited. We couldn't think of two better causes or a better show to raise money for it.

A camera crew came to Headley Court and filmed

me working out on the parallel bars and climbing off the floor into my wheelchair. They filmed quite a few of the other wounded lads as well. They were also going to use some film taken during the medals parade of me walking out to join the lads. The whole thing would be used to introduce the charity single live on *The X Factor*.

On the day itself they sent a car to pick us up at two p.m. in Plymouth and drove us up to London. It turned out Plymouth was further away than they'd thought and we were in a bit of a panic. We only just made it in time for the show and were whisked straight through the green room without time for a drink or a handful of peanuts. They wheeled me to a spot in the audience and had some difficulty getting my chair up the stairs.

I had my Combat 95 green uniform on with C-Legs and black boots, sitting in the chair. They played the film and I was a bit embarrassed when the studio audience got on its feet to applaud me and the other wounded servicemen there. I smacked the railing next to me with my hand to join in the applause.

The film stopped, and Dermot O'Leary said, 'An incredibly powerful film. We are honoured that Marine Mark Ormrod is with us here tonight. And Mark is joined by other British servicemen and women who've been injured in the line of duty. It is a privilege to have you all here, thank you so much.

'Now, here at *The X Factor* we wanted to help so

for the first time ever the X *Factor* finalists are releasing a single, the proceeds of which will go to both Help for Heroes and the Royal British Legion Poppy Appeal.'

Dermot then walked over to Simon Cowell. 'Simon, I know you're very much behind this, why do you think it's so important?'

He replied, 'Dermot, that film says it all. We're doing it for one simple reason. These are decent people who need a bit of help, a bit of support. The proceeds of this record will go to these guys and we are very honoured to be a part of it.'

I felt a bit awkward being singled out so much, especially when there were so many other injured guys to think about, but if the film helped promote the X *Factor* record and made some money, then I guessed it was a good thing.

During every single ad break Louis Walsh came over to have a chat to make sure we were all right. Dannii Minogue made a big fuss of me, which was fine by me. Dermot O'Leary also came over and said a few words, and Becky thought he was 'absolutely gorgeous' (steady there, Becky). Simon Cowell hoped we were enjoying the show. Afterwards we went to the green room and had a few drinks with the final twelve contestants. It was a great laugh.

They'd laid on a hotel opposite the studio near Wembley. It was a Premier Inn just over the road, and all right, it wasn't on Park Lane, but it suited us perfectly. My wheelchair could go everywhere in it and we had a nice big room.

The single 'Hero' was an instant number one and raised thousands and thousands of pounds for the charities so I was pleased to have played even a little part in its success.

During the film they'd asked me about my future and I'd answered, 'Getting married. Moving into the house with Becky. Getting back to a bit of normality. Leading a happy life.' These were my new ambitions, and I was going for it.

Becky and I were married on 2 May 2009, sixteen months after my accident, at a beautiful eight-hundred-year-old country mansion called Manadon House set in five acres of grounds. The ceremony was conducted by the Plymouth registrar on the porch of this magnificent old building and the sun blazed down all day.

My best man was my dad, Paul, and my unofficial best man was Bob Toomey who was helping to look after me and all my gear.

The owner of Manadon House drove me up to the property in his convertible and I got out of the car a few minutes ahead of the bride. The second I was up, I started having a total nightmare. The shoes I was wearing had heels that I wasn't used to and they were tipping my feet forward, initiating the C-Leg knee bend before I was ready for it. I was almost stacking it every few seconds and struggling to keep myself on my feet. I'd forgotten the strap for my prosthetic arm and Bob and I had wedged it into the sleeve of my dress uniform but it was not secured properly and threatened to drop out.

Unless I sorted myself out, I was going to make a total mess of this. There was no way I was stacking it on my wedding day.

Bob and my dad got me into the house and helped me change my shoes and secured the arm as best they could.

Within a few minutes I was in place on the porch, sweating a bit, but ready. Before I knew it, *The First Time Ever I Saw Your Face* started playing and I knew that Becky had started walking up the open-air 'aisle' leading from the marquee to the porch.

There were a few gasps from our guests as they saw her and I couldn't resist a quick look as Becky walked towards me on her father's arm. She looked totally stunning. She was wearing an ivory silk dress embroidered with diamante and silver thread that dazzled in the sunlight. A tiara and veil completed the headdress.

'Wow,' I thought. I felt smart in my uniform and I'll always be proud and honoured to wear it.

The cap was brand new. A few months earlier I'd been at the premiere of the James Bond movie *Quantum of Solace* with some other injured servicemen and we were all in our best uniforms. Daniel Craig stopped to have a quick chat and say hello. He was a big star and I wanted his autograph. I didn't have a pen or paper handy so he autographed the top of my peaked cap in black felt-tip pen: 'To Mark, All the best, Daniel Craig'. I've got it in the living room next to my Under-16s kick boxing trophy.

The registrar brought us to order and neither of us fluffed our lines. I turned to Becky and kissed her. I couldn't believe how far we'd come and what we'd achieved together.

We turned to face our guests in a blizzard of confetti. My mum was there and had tears streaming down her face.

There was a jazz band playing, and later, like any bride and groom, Becky and I were first on to the dance floor. I'd been practising for months with a nurse at Headley Court who'd been giving me dancing lessons on the C-Legs. I led Becky by the hand and walked on to the dance floor with almost no trace of a limp. We danced carefully to a soppy ballad, 'Amazed' by Lone Star. Becky had chosen it. She said she would never forget the song.

We'd first heard it on the radio before I went to the Afghan. Becky loved it and wanted to buy the single straight away. We'd heard it a few times but hadn't caught the name of the artist so we walked into HMV in Plymouth and asked, but the staff were none the wiser. In the end I sang it to the cashiers. Becky was so embarrassed but the shop staff thought it was hilarious. The bloke behind me in the queue came to my rescue: 'Yeah, mate, that's "Amazed" by Lone Star.' So Becky got her record. Now it was our tune.

We danced in front of all our guests. I wasn't going to give any of the *Strictly Come Dancing* contestants sleepless nights, but I did all right and didn't stack it. As we turned on the floor Becky's eyes were shining, and as the song finished all the guests roared applause. There wasn't a dry eye in the house.

Sixteen months earlier, smashed to bloody bits in the back of the Supacat at FOB ROB, I'd told Dave the medic that my dancing days were over. With my beautiful bride Becky by my side, I'd shown everyone I'd been wrong about that. My dancing days were only just beginning.

Index

ROYAL NAVY

The Royal Marines are the Royal Navy's elite Commandos – a highly trained, specialised force capable of operating anywhere in the world – on land, from the sea or from the air. The Royal Marines have a tradition of bravery that stretches back more than 300 years and are identified by their distinctive green berets, which they wear with great pride. The ethos and the tradition of the Royal Marines is enshrined within their corps crest, known as the Globe and Laurel.

THE LION AND THE CROWN
Distinguishing badge of a Royal Regiment. The Royal Marines Corps was awarded the title "Royal" by King George III in 1802.

THE GLOBE
Incorporated into the crest in 1827, when King George IV decreed that battle honours for the corps were so numerous that the "Great Globe itself" should be its emblem. Also represents the worldwide scope of the corps' activity.

THE FOULED ANCHOR
The Badge of the Lord High Admiral, first worn by the Marines in 1747.

THE LAURELS
Granted for the gallantry displayed by the Marines in the capture of Belle Isle in 1761.

THE CORPS MOTTO
Per Mare Per Terram (By Sea By Land). The Corps Motto is believed to have been used for the first time in 1775 at Bunker Hill.

GIBRALTAR
Commemorates the capture and defence of the famous rock in 1704.

royalnavy.mod.uk